EFFECTIVE THEATRE

EFFECTIVE THEATRE

A study with documentation

JOHN RUSSELL BROWN

Professor of Drama and Theatre Arts
in the University of Birmingham

HEINEMANN · LONDON

Heinemann Educational Books Ltd
LONDON   EDINBURGH   MELBOURNE
TORONTO   SINGAPORE
JOHANNESBURG   AUCKLAND
IBADAN   HONG KONG
NAIROBI

SBN 435 18080 0

Published by
Heinemann Educational Books Ltd
48 Charles Street, London W1X 8AH
Printed in Great Britain by
Morrison & Gibb Ltd., London and Edinburgh

CONTENTS

LIST OF ILLUSTRATIONS

Between pp. 112 and 113

THEATRES

EIGHT HAMLETS

ACKNOWLEDGEMENTS

The author and publisher wish to thank the following for their permission to reproduce copyright material: 'Design Proposals for the National Theatre, London' from *National Theatre, Detailed Design Proposals* Press Statement, 22 November 1967: Denys Lasdum & Partners; 'Elizabethan Theatres' from The Profession of Playwright' in *Stratford-upon-Avon Studies*, 3 pp. 11–27: Edward Arnold Ltd and R. A. Foakes; 'Traders and Artists' from *The Unholy Trade* pp. 31–41: Victor Gollancz Ltd and Richard Findlater; 'The Federal Theatre Project' from *The Living Theatre* pp. 148–57: Heinemann Educational Books and Elmer Rice; *The First Annual Report of the Arts Council of Great Britain: Drama 1945:* The Arts Council of Great Britain; 'The Difficulty of Getting Things Done Properly' from *The Guardian* 16 May 1964: John Arden and Margaret Ramsay Ltd; 'Report on the needs for Drama in England outside London' from *Policy into Practice: 20th Annual Report 1964/5:* The Arts Council of Great Britain; 'West End Managements and the Playwrights' from *Encore* IV. iii (1958) pp. 14–18: Robert Bolt and Margaret Ramsay Ltd; 'Broadway Theatre Myths' from *Tulane Drama Review* Vol. X, No. i (T 29), Fall, 1965: © Copyright 1964 The *Tulane Drama Review* and 1967, *The Drama Review*; 'La Mama Experimental Theatre Club' from *The New York Times Magazine* 9 July 1967: Josh Greenfeld and The New York Times Co; *The Annual Financial Report of the Belgrade Theatre*: The Belgrade Theatre; 'Theatre Staff': Clive Barker; 'Rules of Acting' from *The Theatre of Jean-Louis Barrault*: Barrie and Rockliff Ltd; 'The Hard Job of Being an Actor' from *Stanislavski's Legacy*: Max Reinhardt Ltd; 'Acting as a Controlled Dream' from *Great Acting*, BBC 1967: Sir Ralph Richardson and Derek Hart; 'A Dialogue about acting' from *Brecht on Theatre*: Methuen & Co, Hill and Wang Inc., tr. © John Willett; 'A Setting for Ibsen's Ghosts' from Director's Diary, 1905' in *Tulane Drama Review* Vol. IX, No. 1 (T 25), Fall, 1964: © Copyright 1964 The *Tulane Drama Review* and 1967, *The Drama Review*; 'On the ideas of Adolph Appia' from *The Stage is Set* by Lee Simonson, copyright 1932, by Harcourt, Brace & Co, Copyright Renewed 1960, by Lee Simonson, Copyright © 1963 by Theatre Arts Books, reprinted with the permission of Theatre

Arts Books, New York; 'The Steps' from *Towards a New Theatre*:
The executors of Edward Gordon Craig, Henry Edward Robert
Craig and John Philip Richard Craig; 'Form for the Theatre of
Cruelty' from 'The Theater of Cruelty' in *The Theater and its
Double*: Calder & Boyars Ltd (who will publish *The Theatre and
Its Double* in a collected volume of Artaud's writings) and the
Grove Press Inc.; 'Svoboda: the architect of total theatre' from
'Svoboda: a whole scene shifting' in *The Observer* 2 July 1967: The
Observer; 'Against Falsehood' from *Flourish* No. 5 1965: John
Bury and the Royal Shakespeare Theatre Club; 'Directing the
Classics' from *Stage Directions*: Sir John Gielgud and Heinemann
Educational Books; 'Brecht as Director' from article in *The Drama
Review* Vol. XII No. 1 (T 37), Fall, 1967: © Copyright 1967, The
Drama Review; 'Directing at the Royal Court, London' from
'The Right to Fail' in *The Twentieth Century* Vol. 169 No. 1008
1961: Twentieth Century Ltd; 'Theatre Laboratory 13 Rzedow'
from article in the *Tulane Drama Review* Vol. IX No. 3 (T 27),
Spring, 1965: © Copyright 1965 The *Tulane Drama Review* and
1967, *The Drama Review*.

'The Art of Acting' is reprinted from *The Paradox of Acting* translated by W. H. Pollock, 1883; 'Concerning that Gaiety of Disposition which is Essential to the Comic Actor' is reprinted from
The Actor, ch. XII, 1755; 'Macready's King Lear' is reprinted
from *Our Recent Actors* by Westland Marston, pp. 44–8, 1890;
'Henry Irving's setting for 'Much Ado' is reprinted from *Henry
Irving's Impressions of America*, pp. 369–71, 1884.

The illustrations are reproduced by courtesy of the Governors of
the Royal Shakespeare Theatre and the Shakespeare Birthplace
Library (VII, IX, XIII, XIV, XVI, XVII, XXIII, XXIV); Denys
Lasdum & Partners and Behr Photography (I, VI); the Mermaid
Theatre (II); The Stratford Shakespearean Festival, Stratford,
Ontario, Canada and Douglas Spillane (III); Arena Stage,
Washington, D.C. (IV); the Octagon Theatre, Bolton, and the
photographer, Arthur Winter, Preston (V); the Drottningholm
Theatre Museum and Beata Bergström, Stockholm (VIII); the
National Tourist Organisation of Greece and D. A. Harrissiadis,
Athens (X); the Mansell Collection, London (XI); Sean Kenny
Design Associates, London (XII); the Tate Gallery, London
(XV); Le Théâtre Odéon, Paris (XVIII); L.E.A. (London
Electrotype Agency), London (XIX); Angus McBean, London

(XX, XXIX, XXX, XXXI); the Victoria and Albert Museum (XXI, XXII); the Moscow Art Theatre (XXVI); the Governors of the Royal Shakespeare Theatre and Ernest Daniels, Stratford-upon-Avon (XXVIII); the executors of Edward Gordon Craig, Henry Edward Robert Craig and John Philip Richard Craig (XXXIII, XXXIV, XXXV, XXXVI); Dr Jaromir Svoboda, Prague (XXXVII); Vilém Sochurek, Prague (XXXVII); Reg Wilson, London (XL); *The Drama Review*, New York and Edward Weglowski, Cracow (XLI, XLII); and Dominic, London (XLIII).

PREFACE

This book is in two parts. First, my own view of the theatre, what it is, how it works, and what it achieves; and, in the second half, a collection of illustrations, documents, statements, descriptive articles and notes.

The first part can be read by itself, and it has been published separately in the series called *Concept Books*. This is neither a practical handbook nor a work of scholarship establishing facts and theories. Instead, it is an attempt to think about every element in the complicated process that leads to a play being performed before an audience. It has chapters on training and criticism, as well as on actors. It considers theatre organization, as well as theatre design and stage design. It covers a lot of ground lightly, but I hope responsibly, for it reflects my own encounter with the theatre as a student, teacher and director, and as a member of many audiences. I pay attention to the development of various theatrical forms, and to styles of performance that are now out of date, but the main focus is on today and, while I discuss what happens, now, in our theatres, I have tried to indicate some of the directions in which I believe it should develop in years to come. There is a short, rather packed chapter on 'Future Theatre'.

My aim was not to tell my readers what to think; rather to help them think for themselves. And so, shortly after its first publication, my book reappears in this much fuller version, with a second, larger and entirely new part which provides documentation for further consideration: my choice of facts and ideas that will stimulate and define the reader's own concepts of theatre. Thought *is* free; but to be usefully so, it must be related to minute facts and to the energetic working of many other minds. Here, in as short a compass as practicable, are facts, visual and descriptive, and still more ideas. This second part is a kind of dossier, collected from my library and records. To encourage readers to bring their own theatre experience to bear, I have emphasized in this part the English-speaking theatre and the future. I have avoided aspects of theatre commonly discussed in books on dramatic literature.

Churchill, Worcestershire   John Russell Brown

For Hilary
as all things

PART ONE
A View of the Theatre

THE POWER OF DRAMA

THE NEXT time you go to a theatre arrive in good time and stand in the main foyer for five or ten minutes watching the people come in. They have all paid money and given their time to see the same play, but each one of them brings his own concerns with him which no one else will experience in exactly the same way; no member of the audience will ever know exactly what the other members are thinking as they enter the theatre, nor what sort of men and women they are. Some people talk a lot and others are silent. There is usually a slight impression of relaxation as they pass through the doors, for they have arrived with time to spare and at the right place. But then the bell rings announcing that in five minutes the play will begin, and at once there is a change; then the auditorium lights begin to dim and go out, and there is absolute stillness. Everyone is waiting for the curtain to rise, or for an actor to walk into view. Even when I have seen a production several times and have worked on it for many weeks in rehearsals, this moment never fails to sharpen my attention, and I forget the audience, their concerns and my concerns, in what is about to happen on the stage. And everyone else responds, now, in very much the same way.

The difference between the intermingling individuals in the foyer and the unanimous, concentrated and sometimes excited audience as the play begins is a measure of the hold drama can take on us. It could become a discipline, or a feverish excitement. (Saint Augustine said that drama was like the plague.) At Epidaurus, in grand and solemn landscape some hours' journey by sea and road from Athens, I have sat in the late afternoon among an audience of eighteen thousand, waiting for a performance in the vast open-air theatre. During the day we have been coming through the countryside, by motor-coach, car, cart, bicycle or foot; some have camped on the slopes of the hill within sight of the theatre. And at last we have filed slowly up the steep, dusty paths to reach our seats perhaps a hundred feet above the stage. On such occasions the silence before the play

3

begins is profoundly impressive, and one feels that the performance could well become a great corporate act of initiation or
acclaim. In our own far smaller theatres, the attention which each
member of the audience shares will be more intense, more sharp
or nervous; or it could be more intimate, warm or, even, cosy.
The size of the theatre, its situation, design and furnishings, the
kind of music that has been playing before the curtain rises, the
general expectation of the audience, all control the kind of
corporate response that is given at the first moment of concentration. And the play, of course, will control what happens
afterwards; we are in the author's and the actors' hands.

In some ways going to the theatre is like going to a football
match, or to watch boxing; but then we go to see who will win,
who will play well, score the goals or improve on his earlier form;
and we shall encourage the side we favour by applause or breath-
less attention. In the theatre we do perhaps take sides, and
certainly our response to the actors will modify their performances; but the main issues are never in doubt. The actors know
exactly what is going to happen to the characters they are im-
personating, which one dies, or marries or grows old, and how
soon all this happens. Their movements are all plotted beforehand, and their words all prescribed. If someone on stage upsets
a pile of crockery, or seems to be at a loss for what to say or do,
even that has been planned beforehand. In a good production
of a good play, when the audience's attention is caught at the
beginning it is held right through to the end; and by the end, the
audience will have been conducted through a controlled sequence
of thoughts and feelings. Slowly it can be made to understand
more about a character's motives or the rivalries within a family,
or the meanings of a slogan or proverb, or the importance of
loyalty, or the sources of political unrest. Or it can be shocked
again and again; or it can be kept waiting or guessing, or wishing
for some fortunate occurrence that will never happen; or every
portrayed event on the stage can be happy and lucky. The
audience's sympathy may be drawn towards one character or
towards all of those portrayed; and half-way through the performance its attitudes can be changed from sympathy to abhor-
rence, concern to amusement, almost in a moment. A play can
be continuously exciting, its outcome in balance all the time; or
its final result can be a foregone conclusion and the audience kept
attentive only by the quality of the play.

To realize how all these opportunities arise in a theatre is to gain some idea of the complexity and power of drama as an art form, as a contrivance that will develop, extend and intensify its audience's response. Let us try to enumerate what drama does:

1. *Drama creates a Social Occasion*

When we are watching a theatrical performance, many individuals share the same experience within the same period of time, in close contact with each other. In this drama differs from literature or painting, and is like film or music.

It is not easy to protest aloud against the performance of a play, or to say anything at all in more than a whisper or instinctive ejaculation. When a production is good, no one coughs or fidgets, because everyone shares the joint response, all attention taken from less demanding concerns: the audience is captive and captivated – willingly, surprisingly, revealingly. A communication is established, not merely between stage and audience, but also between individual members of the audience. As music played before a large audience has a greater power of evocation than when it is heard privately, so a play grows in eloquence between its final dress rehearsal and first performance. A single word or cry can be prolonged, or a passage taken at an extremely slow pace, because the audience, assured in its corporate belief, will not withdraw attention. Unreservedly, unashamedly, sometimes for the first time in his life, a member of the audience may weep or laugh at some aspect of human existence to which he would not give more than a passing thought outside the theatre. In all this drama is unlike a novel or poem, for a reader can always disengage his mind and escape from the printed sequence of narrative or description; his response can gather strength from others afterwards, but only at considerable remove from the source of inspiration. Unlike a novel, a play can dare to state the obvious without losing attention and can call upon common, basic responses.

But unlike music and like film, drama can also reflect precisely the world outside the theatre, concert hall or cinema. The ear need not be trained, as for music; if an audience can respond to life it can respond to drama. On the stage the audience may see and hear people like themselves, dressed in the same fashions and speaking the same language and even the same dialect. In this reflection of the audience's life, drama is less thorough than film – the stage cannot show crowds of thousands or the movement of a wild animal, or give the actual impression of being on top of a mountain – but it can be more local and more topical. The production, if not the play itself, is often made in the town from which the audience is drawn, and made all over again at the very time that each particular audience enters the theatre. Instinctively a production will change overnight if some national disaster or celebration has occurred. And intentionally, by representing the person of a politician or even by chalking up a slogan on the walls of the stage, the drama can take sides in local or global struggles for power. When Shakespeare's tragedy, *Coriolanus* was performed in Paris in 1934, the police enforced the closure of the theatre because of the political ferment caused by the production. In Elizabethan and Jacobean England, this kind of interference was common; several playwrights including Jonson and Chapman were put in prison for their part in plays which had already passed the official censor.

Of course, everyone in an audience may not be affected in exactly the same way; in the last analysis only the object of attention is identical. But here, indeed, is another important reason for the strength of drama as a social art: there is a variety as well as unity and immediacy in its appeal. Some elements of a play in performance – visual, musical, verbal, broadly humorous or intellectually subtle – may speak more to one playgoer than another, and some elements may be invisible or incomprehensible to all but a few; but because each element has to be represented by one cast, at one time and place and in one combined – and therefore to some extent unified – production, every element must express in some way or other the basic statement and development of the drama. A play is expressive on so many levels or directions of comprehension that no moment need fail to contact, in some way or other, every single member of its audience. It can draw all members, variously, to one destination.

2. *Drama holds a Mirror up to Nature*

What happens on a stage can look very like what happens outside the theatre, in the ordinary lives of the audience. A play uses the same elements: men, women, children; talk and movement, light and darkness, noise and silence; the actors appear excited, bored, tired, negligent; time passes, slowly, quickly, insensibly. There is nothing that makes up our world – what it is like to be alive – that cannot be represented on a stage and used by the dramatist and actors to impress an audience.

There is no other art-form which can so make use of anything, to which nothing is foreign. Poetry can describe and evoke an imaginary world, where the grass is greener or the sun shines more brightly, or human beings are more beautiful than ordinarily, but it cannot produce them, make them actually present; the poetic world exists only in our mind's eye. It is arguable that the stage world can never be quite so strange or delightful as the world of poetry, but it will always be more tangible – seeable, audible, almost touchable. And it will be more practicable: what happens on the stage may well be brighter or more beautiful than the world outside, but like that world, it must always work; it must be possible. One element cannot be allowed to develop away from all the others – as in a poem we may concentrate attention on a single feature as the brilliance of the sky or the loneliness of the poet – and a kind of reassurance, strength and, even, excitement comes from this.

On stage anything that happens must be seen in relation to what necessarily goes with it in real life: it cannot easily escape from its natural consequences – physical, emotional, mental, and sexual. A dramatist will cheat a little, but he could not, for example, keep someone on stage mentally alert and excited – let us say the invented character knows that he is about to win international renown with a new invention that will surprise and benefit humanity – he could not present such a man without showing his physical and emotional reactions to his thoughts; his need to speak, to move, to express somehow the quickness of his thought, to find someone with whom to share his emotion by telling the secret or by talking of quite another, mundane matter, or by grasping a hand or watching reactions intently. A dramatist cannot avoid all this because he must present his imaginary world through the agency of a living, actual human being – an actor, who cannot simulate one excitement without in some way, with or without the dramatist's help, suggesting some of its consequences. Drama holds a mirror up to the life we live because it communicates through more than words or puppets, or music, or visual design; its expression involves human actors who are as complicated as we are and cannot simplify their performances beyond a certain point, depending on their skill and the dramatist's encouragement.

Usually an actor is seen against a background or within a setting chosen by the dramatist, and in relationship, often visually enforced, with other actors. So drama necessarily reflects more than one human consciousness. In performance actors instinctively respond to each other and to a crowded or empty space, to colour, rhythm, noise and silence. All this is part of drama's reflection of life and a prime reason for its truth and eloquence. A film may be more accurate or complete in reproducing the actual setting of human existence: its action can take place where it naturally takes place; the persons represented can be real, not imitated by actors who simplify and enlarge certain aspects of behaviour; the film-maker can take his audience anywhere in the world and make the weather rain or snow or shine at will. But a film shows nothing that is essentially 'there'. In an obvious sense everything shown on a screen has only two dimensions and not three; but that is not the main difference. The distinguishing mark of film is the use of a camera; it shows nothing but what the camera has seen, and everything in the way the camera has seen it. At one moment a single face can fill the screen and at the next a panorama of the whole earth may be seen from outer space, the face ceasing to have any effect at all. The camera can alter the scale of anything at the film director's will. And it can take its own time: a film is shot over three months or three years, and seldom in the sequence in which the audience views it. More than this, any accident or any reaction from actor, dog or inanimate object that is not to the taste of the director can be 'edited' out of existence in the film-cutting room. Whereas, in the theatre, once a performance starts the audience will see everything; and although it may be led to imagine that the central character has more than ordinary strength, or beauty, or good fortune, the actor who plays him will remain, basically, the same throughout the performance, and his exertions will never be without a full range of effects on himself and on others. Although he may be disguised he will remain identical under the disguise, modified only by what is humanly possible. The figures with whom he is seen will be constant in essentials and inevitably recurring, and his performance will grow only by contact with them – and with the particular audience that is watching the play on each particular night. Although the scene may change many times in the course of the play, the stage-space will be constant, and so the scale of the hero in regard to his world will remain basically the same, despite temporary illusionistic effects. The limitations of the stage, in comparison with the cinema, ensure that in certain basic essentials the mirror of drama is held up to basic facts of living and that what is seen has an inevitable kind of truth.

3. *Drama is a Progressive Experience*

A play usually tells a story, but it need not do so. The essential element here is development. During any performance, changes take place and the audience experiences them in the sequence in which they occur. All this is very obvious and easy to understand, but the consequences of it, upon what drama essentially is, need to be pointed out.

An audience must be held. Its interest has to be caught and its expectation aroused; and, in order to sustain interest for two or three hours, expectation has to be occasionally disappointed. Finally, the audience must know that the drama has ended and to effect this satisfactorily the various interests that have been raised must be satisfied in some way or other. In a word, a dramatist is concerned with what happens with the passing of time. A painter reveals his finished work in a moment and, although it may take a viewer some time to appreciate all that is inherent in the painting, the sequence of understanding and appreciation is not within the artist's control. A novelist or poet can give a progressive experience to his readers, especially when he tells a story, but he cannot so easily control the speed with which this happens nor be so sure that he holds attention without interruption. A dramatist is concerned with development in time and can alter the apparent pace with which time passes for his audience.

Conflict, tension, climax, narrative, development are the very basis of dramatic experience: drama shows what happens, rather than what is. It is an art-form appropriate to a civilization that is aware of change, inevitable change or change brought through the will and activity of man. It is a contemplative art only when the still moment of appreciation is presented as a culmination of active participation in events or as contrast to such activity, or when one state of mind succeeds another. This last possibility has rarely been exploited without some other interest to hold the audience's attention, but it accounts for the acutely sensitive nature of much dramatic experience. (Some kinds of oriental drama remind us that this delicacy need not be 'intellectual' in any narrow sense, for such contemplative drama is expressed more through physical than through verbal means.) Indeed, increased sensitivity of view is an element of almost every considerable play: the audience is progressively involved in what happens on the stage and so views the individual characters with greater sympathy for the inner workings of their minds, or views the whole stage-picture, its presentation of a social group, with an increasingly sharp awareness of the forces that are responsible for its composition.

And – to move from the overall strategy of drama to its moment-by-moment existence – because time is important, so is tempo and rhythm. As in music, the sense of time at any one moment is controlled by varying the time-value of each passing element. Especially strong or precise impressions are made by sustaining and subsequently breaking a regular beat or rhythm, or by repeating certain sequences in new contexts or repeating them in the same context but with slight variations. The various subtleties of musical composition have their counterparts in drama, but the dramatist manipulates not only sound – that would not be effective enough for, even if he is a poet writing verse, he lacks the precise notation used by a musician: he also manipulates the tempo and rhythms of bodily movement. Drama is very like dance; in primitive societies the two arts are sometimes indistinguishable, and in sophisticated societies they continue to interact upon each other. A good dramatist will indicate the speed, size and direction of bodily movement with great care: the slow close of *Othello*, counteracted by the sudden movement of Othello's surprise suicide; the prolonged fights at the end of *Hamlet*, changing from courtly fencing to 'incens'd' fury, and then yielding to the silence of death, the 'warlike volley' of Fortinbras's entry and lastly the 'soldier's music' of the funeral procession; or the still moment when the chorus is suddenly silenced and the naked body of Agamemnon caught in a blood-stained net is revealed at the close of Æschylus's tragedy – the changes of physical tempo and rhythm in each of these great climaxes are as calculated as the words that accompany or prepare for them. The dramatist's means of expression, like his concept or vision, uses everything that happens.

4. *Drama can use Verbal Art*

In silent acting, in mime or dance-like sequences, and in spectacle, drama can exist without words, but many of its most successful forms involve great verbal artifice. Usually a play continues to be known years after its first performance through the evidence of a printed text which is a record of its verbal element only.

But before accounting for the drama's hospitality to verbal art, it is important to recognize the inadequacy of the printed text. Many elements of drama that we have already considered are hardly hinted at in the 'book of the play'; it needs skill and practice to be able to read a text so that the whole drama implicit in the printed record comes faithfully alive in the imagination of the reader. Besides the bare words, there must also be the colour, force and all the variety of the spoken voice. Consider how many different ways the simple words 'Good morning' can be spoken: they can sound confident or tentative; they can imply friendship or subservience; they can be empty or full of meaning, ironic or directly descriptive; they can be quick or slow. Tomorrow morning, listen to the various ways people you meet say these two words to you; and then notice how *you* say them differently depending on your mood, or to whom you are speaking. The dramatist does not simply write down sentences as he hears them half-spoken in the silence of his own mind; he invents them to be coloured by the spoken voice. And more than this, he knows that they will be part of the total performance of the actor who speaks them: physical bearing, gesture, appearance, state of mind, sexuality, position on the stage, will all affect the precise impression made by the words the dramatist writes down; and the tempo and rhythm with which the actor acts and speaks at the moment of utterance. And they will also be affected by spectacle, music, sound, setting, by other actors and by the audience – by everything that happens on stage, *as* it happens. The dramatist cannot make a play with words alone: good poets may well be bad dramatists – they usually are.

But in a play a dramatist may use words brilliantly. (More so than the film-maker, for the verisimilitude of *his* picture does not make it easy for an actor to use many words; and the attention needed to respond to the detailed, ever-changing picture allows the audience little leisure, and gives the wrong frame of mind, for responding to many or complicated words.) All the beauty of

verbal poetry may be exploited by the dramatist, the sharpness
and excitement of verbal wit, the power of rhetoric, fascination of
narrative or description, relentlessness of argument, the slow
impressiveness of the verbal recounting of facts or statistics;
nothing foreign to the printed page is foreign to drama. Moreover,
by manipulating words the dramatist can focus the audience's
attention on exactly that element in his play that he considers
important at any moment. Usually the audience looks at whoever
is speaking, so that if one character dominates the talk he usually
dominates the stage. There are cunning variations of this which
have their own special interest, as when the speaker is waiting
for some action elsewhere on the stage or when his words are
controlled by some silent figure either immediately behind him or
as far away as possible. Normally the speaker dominates, so that
when the lead in stage-talk is constantly passing from one character
to another we can be sure the dramatist wants to focus attention
on contrasting attitudes rather than on the development of a
single point of view; probably he wishes the audience to be
interested in theme rather than individual character. When a
dominant talker pauses and then speaks as if he is not sure what
he wants to say – when his phrases seem only half-formed – interest
can be directed to his unspoken thoughts before speech. If he
suddenly changes the mood or subject of his talk and this is not
caused by any obvious outside influence, or if his speech becomes
agitated beyond the apparent occasion for it, the audience will
again become interested in hidden thoughts and feelings, concerns
not expressed directly in words – the focus is then 'sub-textual'.
Or when a subsidiary character takes the verbal lead away from
the centre of the stage, the dramatist can direct attention to the
implications of the main action and main disquisition.

Speech is also important musically. It is a pervasive influence
on tempo and rhythm merely by being heard; and its operation
in this way is irresistible and unobtrusive because the audience
is influenced while its conscious attention is given to explicit
thought, feeling or action. A verbally skilful dramatist gives his
play a built-in beat and rhythm in the sound that speech makes,
even while speech seems wholly devised to express the thoughts
of the characters.

And speech is economical. A character may step on stage and
say 'I am a villain' or 'I am this man's father', or 'This is London
and this is my house,' or 'I know who killed the vicar' and, if the

delivery of the lines and the visual elements of the drama do not complicate the issue, a lot of time can be saved and the audience left in no doubt. A dramatist has to pay a price for cutting corners in this way, especially in the loss of excitement, tone and realism, but most dramatists are glad to benefit from the economy of words sometimes; many over-indulge the device.

5. *Drama is Fantastic*

We commonly say that there is a magic about the theatre. As well as holding a mirror up to the lives of its audience, developing its understanding, and exploiting language, the drama also shows a world that never was. A dramatist can be a lunatic or a lover, and in his imagination create all sorts of strange fictions and, more than this, within the physical limitation – the essential truth – of the stage, he can make others believe as he does. Performance often compels belief; and many tricks can allow the dramatist to represent on the stage what he – and his audience – wants to believe, or fears to believe, outside the theatre.

There must be a basic truth in any play; but there is also a basic falseness. The events presented in a performance could *not* actually take place there and then, within the actual space and the actual time. This is not a limitation, but a springboard: the concentration of theatrical performance encourages that heightened and confident awareness that is essential for imaginative belief. Seldom does a play show exactly what happens in ordinary life; it is, in essential ways, like life, but it is also more so – more funny, more expert, more beautiful, more heroic, more communicative, more apt. Even in the presentation of boredom, a play can give a more crushing sense of hopelessness, or a more articulate, than we find in life; through the subtle manipulation of tempo and rhythm the weight of boredom can be established more quickly and be more sharply defined. Drama heightens our response because it can heighten any aspect of life that it reflects. It is entertaining.

Drama can also disregard the limitations of ordinary life and present sheer fantasy: wasps can be life-sized and talk; islands can be invented full of wonderful, unheard-of creatures or spirits; a man may live, or sleep, a thousand years. Almost everything that can be thought of by the creative mind of the dramatist can be given the illusion of existence on the stage.

The chief agent in realizing the dramatist's heightening and extending notion of life is the actor. He is skilled at performing prodigious feats of speech and action, controlling his ordinary behaviour until he fulfils, during the two or three hours of performance, the unusual demands of the drama. Other agents are the scene designer and the theatre technician who can realize the imagined settings with appropriate and more than usual clarity, beauty or variability. Everyone working in the theatre collaborates in creating illusionary magic.

6. *Drama responds to its Audience*

In French it is said that an audience 'assists' at a performance, and the phrase is apt. Every actor will tell you that during the run of a production each audience is different from the others, and the play different with each audience. On a simple level, laughs will last longer one night compared with another, and this will alter the timing of a scene. A small matinée audience is less ready to react to comedy or pathos than a Saturday night audience that has entered the theatre in more relaxed mood. But modifications from one performance to another are far more subtle than this, depending on the exact state of mind and body of each member of the cast as well as on the composition and mood of the audience. At moments when a single actor holds attention by a subtle performance, the reaction of the audience is almost unpredictably variable, sensitive to the smallest modification of appeal and reception – mental, emotional, physical, sexual – and sensitive to the way in which the whole play has gone up to that point.

To people engaged in a production the change from night to night is one of the most intriguing aspects of their art; and for the audience, however little its members may understand of their part in a play, the fact that each performance happens only once contributes to the moment-by-moment excitement of drama, to the audience's unique and intensely personal involvement with the illusion of life on the stage.

There is one consequence of this which is crucial in any attempt to understand what drama does: the only drama that is fully dramatic is 'new' drama. Without a performance before an audience, drama does not exist and, since every performance is different from any other, we can never know beforehand exactly what is going to happen in a theatre. We can study the criticisms of past performances, or a play-script, or even a filmed recording of a production; but the full object of our attention disappears when a performance concludes. Depending on each performance and the assistance of each audience, drama can be created and enjoyed; but it can never be studied fully. I do not mean this as a discouragement: we should study and think about past achievements, as best we may, in order to respond better to the drama of the moment – to learn to recognize what are, precisely, the new elements and so appreciate them more fully – and to learn from past experience. But we should also accept with pleasure, energy and intelligence, the thought that we have to create our own drama. Even Shakespeare, Sophocles and Ibsen must be made anew every day of the week. Drama, by its very nature, ensures that, if we try to create or understand it, we are employed in a contemporary art; a social, truthful, completely human, creative activity that relates understanding to change (what is, to what has been and will be), and that must be relevant now.

I. PLAYS

1. *The Variety of Drama*

WRITING 2,300 years ago, Aristotle judged that there were two main kinds of drama: tragedy and comedy. His fragmentary critical work, the *Poetics*, says little about comedy – most importantly, that it presents imitations of 'low' characters, men and women made ludicrous through some defect or ugliness that is not painful or destructive. But for tragedy he enumerated six elements:

> Spectacular Presentment
> Lyrical Song
> Diction
> Plot
> Character
> Thought

He also gave 'rules' for writing tragedy and defined various kinds of plot; for example:

> A perfect tragedy should . . . be arranged not with the simple but the complex plot. It should, moreover, imitate such actions as excite pity and fear (this being the distinctive mark of tragic imitation). It follows plainly, that, in the first place, the change of fortune from prosperity to adversity must not be represented as happening to a virtuous man; for this moves neither pity nor fear; it merely shocks us.

Aristotle was writing about the drama of the Golden Age of Athens from which have survived the works of only four dramatists – Æschylus, Sophocles, Euripides and Aristophanes – writing over a period of a little more than a hundred years. But even for this handful of plays, his words are not wholly satisfactory and now, more than two milleniums later, the confidence with which he divides drama into two parts and lays down the law about how to make a good tragedy, seems extraordinary simple.

Indeed, critics of Greek drama subsequently distinguished three kinds of comedy: Old Comedy, Middle Comedy and New Comedy. And they unearthed the very varied origins of this

16

drama: *dithyramb*, or public poem sung and danced by a chorus
to musical accompaniment; religious rituals of grief, supplication,
purgation and initiation; public ceremonies and processions;
comic and lewd dances; drunken revelry; burlesque and indecent
(or satyric) improvisations.

Since the Greek age many critics have tried to list and limit
the kinds of drama. Tragedy has been defined as:

a play ending in death
a play concerned with noble persons and elevated sentiments
a play presenting the clash between a power outside the hero,
  necessity, and one within, freedom
a narrative of prosperity for a time ending in wretchedness
an exposure of the moral wrongs of man and society
a vindication of divine justice.

Definitions of comedy are as numerous. Even the basic notion that
it involves laughter has been questioned, during the Middle Ages
by the concept of comedy as any narrative with a happy ending
(as opposed to tragedy's unhappy ending) and, at the beginning of
the present century, by the idea (sharply formulated by the poet
and novelist, George Meredith) that the highest kind of comedy
should raise a smile rather than laughter.

Definitions of the many forms of drama have proliferated, as
society has changed and individual talents have been harnessed to
the theatre. Around the year 1600, Shakespeare caused Polonius,
his experienced, pedantic and self-important politician in the play
Hamlet, to tell us that he had been an amateur actor when he was
at the university; this would-be know-all recommends a professional troupe as

> the best actors in the world, either for tragedy, comedy, history,
> pastoral, pastoral-comical, historical-pastoral, tragical-historical,
> tragical-comical-historical-pastoral, scene indivisable, or poem un-
> limited. (II. ii. 392–5)

This elaboration is absurd, but it strives to account for the great
range of plays that were being performed about that time to
courtly and popular audiences. Later ages tried to limit the kinds
of drama by re-establishing rules based, more or less, on Aristotle's,
but the critics' fondness for regularity has always been forced to
retreat before the tide of continual modification and invention. As
Dr Samuel Johnson put it in the eighteenth century:

> The drama's laws the drama's patrons give
> And we that live to please must please to live.

When drama has thrived, it has always been up to date, experimental and impatient of critical decrees.

Here are some of the kinds of drama that have been identified on the wing of change, with brief, one-shot-at-the-target definitions. I give them more to indicate the possible range of dramatic experience than to impress the value of such lists. I have also given the names of one or two plays that could be considered examples of each type.

Classical Tragedy

Great, historical-mythical persons are presented in a crisis of passion and reason, usually ending with a terrible catastrophe that arouses both pity and fear; this central action is often supported by song, dance and speech from a chorus that indicate the events that led up to the crisis and also respond to the play's action so that the audience's response is guided and stimulated.

Sophocles, *Oedipus Rex*
Racine, *Bérénice*

Greek Comedy

Contemporary persons (both individualized and typical), gods and abstract figures, together with one or two singing, dancing and speaking choruses, are involved in a fantastic situation, usually of a combative or ceremonious nature, that illuminates a topical, social or political issue through burlesque, parody, invective, wit, lyricism, obscenity and argument, and ends in revelry.

Aristophanes, *Lysistrata*
Aristophanes, *Birds*

Comedy of Intrigue

Stock characters – as old father, witty servant, shrew, or marriageable widow – are involved ingeniously in a crisis, usually concerned with possession of wealth, a secret or a woman, and always giving occasion for virtuoso displays of dexterity or wit; sometimes the main action is interspersed with song and dance from a chorus; it usually ends with reconciliation and revelry.

Plautus, *Amphitryon*
Ben Jonson, *The Alchemist*
Molière, *The Miser*

Comedy of Manners

Intrigue and romantic narrative provide occasions for showing examples of social behaviour, usually ridiculously exaggerated and verbally inventive.

Ben Jonson, *The Alchemist*
Molière, *The School for Wives*
Oscar Wilde, *The Importance of Being Earnest*

Romantic Comedy

A romantic narrative provides opportunities for lyrical speech, song or dance (in more musical varieties by a chorus as well as individual characters); subsidiary incidents provide topical and burlesque humour or speciality acts; the settings are frequently magical, pastoral or exotic; the principal characters are young, beautiful and, finally, fortunate in love, but there is frequently one or more villanious, old or otherwise unsympathetic characters that must be circumvented.

Shakespeare, *The Merchant of Venice*
Rodgers and Hammerstein, *Oklahoma!*

Farce

A plot (usually of sexual encounter) develops, with growing ingenuity, misunderstanding and improbability, towards complex, violent and grossly exaggerated activity; verbally the drama is often repetitive and mundane; physically it is invariably dextrous; and in both these respects it is frequently lewd: all is obviously calculated to raise the audience's laughter and temporary belief in irrational and fantastic behaviour.

Labiche, *The Italian Straw Hat*
Feydeau, *A Flea in her Ear*

Tragi-comedy

A narrative drama (often with both romantic and intrigue interests) that arouses both pity and fear but yet ends happily or has considerable comic, lyric or happy episodes; its plot usually allows intense alternations of mood and marvellous incidents.

Corneille, *The Cid*
Beaumont and Fletcher, *A King and No King*

Melodrama

A narrative drama of frightening, passionate and, frequently, supernatural or exotic adventure; extreme conflicts of passion and morality are common between characters and within them; large opportunities are given for temperamental performances.

Tourneur, *The Revenger's Tragedy*
Schiller, *The Robbers* (an English adaption is *The Castle Sceptre*)
Charles Reade, *The Lyons Mail*

Narrative (or History) Play

Numerous episodes from the story of a nation or hero are used to present a general theme or panorama rather than a single crisis; often individual episodes are linked by a narrator or presenter, and usually the large cast represents many classes and functions in society.

Medieval Miracle Plays
Shakespeare, *Henry IV, Parts I and II*
Ibsen, *The Pretenders*
Brecht, *Galileo*

Expressionist Play

Dramas that avoid the direct representation of the ordinary life of individuals to show the general and inner life of humanity; the settings are frequently abstract, the characters (including choruses) typical, or abstracted from psychological, moral or social forces; the language is frequently versified or rhythmic arrangements of current catch-phrases and ordinary talk.

Everyman (medieval Dutch in origin)
Strindberg, *The Dream Play*
O'Neill, *Dynamo*

Noh Play

Short plays, performed only in Japan and on a bare stage; one masked actor and one unmasked, together with a chorus, perform the main action in chant, dance, song, mime and dialogue; two sections are separated by a prose narrative recounted by a third, unmasked actor; the characters are mythical-historical and the plot usually consists of a meeting; the conclusion is a dance.

Seami, *Atsumori*

The list of kinds is practically endless and very bewildering. What faith can we have in definitions which permit Shakespearian comedy and the musicals of 1930s or 1950s to share the same label? Many of the plays that have won lasting renown require double-barrelled definitions as odd as those invented by Polonius: Marlowe's *Jew of Malta* is a tragic farce (or farcical tragedy); John Webster's *White Devil* is a satrical tragedy, or revenge tragedy, or tragedy of blood, and partly a narrative play; Shakespeare's *King Lear* is both narrative play and (non-classical) tragedy, and in some scenes it is comic and possibly expressionist. Dramatists have more trouble with labels than anyone else. Chekhov called his *Cherry Orchard* a 'comedy', and *Three Sisters* a 'drama', but *Uncle Vanya* was simply *'Scenes from Country Life'*. Ibsen used 'A Dramatic Poem' for *Peer Gynt*, 'A Domestic Drama' for *Ghosts*, 'A play' for *An Enemy of the People*.

From the end of the nineteenth century onwards, with the growing technical ability of the theatre to imitate actual life, a fuller knowledge of the wide variety of drama and, perhaps, a stronger scepticism that questioned labels with most other aspects of organized life, the definition of kinds became less and less regarded. The non-committal and unhelpful 'A Play' is probably the most usual description for a piece of dramatic writing today. Some contemporary authors, like the French playwright, Ionesco, enjoy mocking the terminology: he uses 'A Comic Drama' (for the murder-narrative of *The Lesson*), 'An Anti-Play' (for *The Bald Prima Donna*), 'A naturalistic Comedy' (for the bizarre *Jacques or Obedience*), a 'Pseudo-Drama' (for *Victims of Duty*).

Besides such comparatively 'regular' plays – they all have fixed verbal texts and named characters – there are many dramas that use non-textual means, and sometimes dispense with named characters. Primitive societies have ceremonial dance-dramas enacting the changing of the seasons, fertility rites or historical events; and more highly developed dance-dramas often borrow from such models. Improvisational comic dramas have a long professional tradition and enjoy a new vogue today in the 'Happenings 'of experimental theatres, and in educational drama. Between the two World Wars, 'Living Newspapers' and other documentary dramas employed photographs, news-films, real-life recordings and placards, together with live actors and some ordinary stage-dialogue, to create thought-provoking entertainments; and this kind is being rediscovered today. Moreover, there are many dramatic elements in the public life of almost every age: ceremonies of initiation, remembrance, judgement, sorrow, thanksgiving. And drama is present in most ordinary private lives: we act parts as host or dutiful son; we set scenes for home-comings or departures; we become aware that others are putting on acts, and we delight in becoming an audience for children's make-believe. Drama is as ubiquitous as it is varied.

2. The Quality of a Play

Most of the customarily accepted kinds of drama are definied by reference to action or plot, character, setting, theme and utterance (whether prose, verse, song, activity, mime, or dance), which are more or less the very elements observed in tragedy by Aristotle. These may be called the outward dimensions of a play; and taken together they give some account of its substance. But if we continue to look only at these separate elements we will continue to list new kinds and find that they overlap each other, and we shall fail to account for differences which are immediately apparent in performance.

To gain an idea of what a particular play is like we must do more than measure these dimensions. There are three further questions to ask: what is its dramatic style? what does it do to an audience? and thirdly – remembering that every single performance of a play is different from another – where and how is it performed?

Dramatic Style

To consider style is, on the one hand, to look at all the outward dimensions of a play in order to observe how they affect each other, to ask: 'How does this play work?' But this is a difficult approach to the problem and it is often better to start with a very close examination of that part of the play which can be most minutely described: its utterance, the moment-by-moment life of its dialogue and stage activity. Treat the play like a cake, and cut one slice or, better, several small slices from different parts. Then take each sample in turn and separate each crumb, examine it carefully and discover of what it is composed and then ask how these minute elements fit together and react on each other. In this small scale, it is easier to ask 'How does this play work?' If the samples are chosen well – from the introduction and the end, for example – a good indication of a play's quality can be gained.

It is worth asking literary and linguistic questions first, because they are more familiar:

What sort of vocabulary? What sort of things do nouns represent and how precisely do they do this?

Are there many adjectives, adverbs, personal pronouns, demonstratives?

Are the verbs simple or complicated?

What tenses are common?

and so on. Then we should proceed to ask:

How long, simple or complicated are the sentences?

Are there many repetitions?

What figures of speech?

Less familiar questions follow, such as:

Is there a basic rhythm? and, since there usually is in a good piece of stage dialogue, how can this rhythm be described?

Does one character dominate the dialogue? Or is the lead shared between several?

Do all the characters speak in the same way, with the same vocabulary, sentence-structure, rhythms, etc?

How much surprise is in the interchange of talk, and how much sustained development, and of what kinds?

Are speeches long or short?

If the dialogue is in verse, the effects of metre must be considered, how regular, how far from ordinary speech rhythm, how musically subtle. Then there are questions that could only be asked about a play. The first of these are:

Is the actor offered opportunity for suggesting subtextual

thoughts and feelings, or are his reactions wholly and explicitly expressed in words?

Does physical performance or gesture, or the colour and rhythm of the dialogue, allow the actor to express reactions not explicit in the words he speaks?

How much, with the words or against them, is expressed by specified gesture or physical bearing?

When these questions have been asked about samples of the play's text, the other, larger questions should be asked again with reference to these small sections. First, about visual presentation:

What are the visual effects of groupings, stage-movement, or stage-setting?

Here it is important to ask where and how the audience will be led to look – what is the 'focus' of the scene. Sometimes the audience is encouraged to sit back and take everything in, to see the whole stage-picture; at another extreme it is made to concentrate on a single point in expectation of some movement or in search of an explanation of a hitherto strange impression. A usefully precise question about visual presentation is:

How much detail about physical things is given by stage-directions or the implications of dialogue, and what kind of things are these?

Some plays emphasize dress, others furniture or properties held in the hand (as swords or telephones), or the quality of light on the stage, signs of rank, race or family.

Character will already have come to attention in observing the details of what is said and done by individual figures on the stage, but there are further questions under this head of a more general sort:

How many and how varied are the characters? Are they old or young, male or female, intelligent or sensitive? Stupid, brutal, ordinary, fantastic, unchanging or mad?

How much is known about them, and what are the limitations of that knowledge compared with our knowledge of intimates, or of strangers, in real life?

Theme, too, will have been considered in asking about the vocabulary of the dialogue, for where the words come from, the choice of this one rather than that, can show the bent of the author's mind – what magnet operates in the great field of millions of words, drawing these specific words out and not others. But at the end of the detailed analysis of small sections of the play, these general questions should be asked again to make sure that we know what is happening at these moments. We should also ask:

How like life is what happens on the stage?

– not because a play is good or bad in so far as it is close in every detail to the life it mirrors, but because the ways in which it departs from life are a good indication of how it works upon an audience.

Such analysis of style is fundamental to the task of judging a play. It will quickly account for the obvious differences between Tourneur's *Revenger's Tragedy* and *The Castle Sceptre,* both of which may be grouped under the same kind of play by an assessment of outward dimensions alone; or between *The Merchant of Venice* and *Oklahoma!,* which are both romantic comedies.

As an example of the value of this kind of detailed stylistic analysis, consider briefly a passage from Dryden's *All for Love,* based on Shakespeare's *Antony and Cleopatra.* The plot, characters, setting, action and some parts of the speech are close to Shakespeare's; and there is a closeness, though not identity, in theme. But the styles of the two plays are quite different. Here is Dryden's version of the end of Cleopatra:

Why, now, 'tis as it should be. Quick, my friends,
Despatch; ere this, the town's in Caesar's hands:
My lord looks down concerned, and fears my stay,
Lest I should be surprised;
Keep him not waiting for his love too long.
You, Charmion, bring my crown and richest jewels;
With them, the wreath of victory I made
(Vain augury!) for him, who now lies dead:
You, Iras, bring the cure of all our ills.
IRAS: The aspics, madam?
CLEOPATRA: Must I bid you twice?
                                        [*Exit* CHARMION *and* IRAS
'Tis sweet to die, when they would force life on me,
To rush into the dark abode of death,
And seize him first; if he be like my love,

He is not frightful, sure.
We're now alone, in secrecy and silence;
And is not this like lovers? I may kiss
These pale, cold lips; Octavia does not see me:
And, oh! 'tis better far to have him thus,
Than see him in her arms – Oh, welcome, welcome!

Enter CHARMION *and* IRAS

The nouns are in three groups:

domestic: friend, town, hand, stay, jewel, cure, abode, death, lips, arms
heroic: lord, crown, jewel, wreath, victory, augury, death
temperamental: friend, love (*twice*), secrecy, silence, lover

None of them is especially rich in sound or allusiveness; considering the complexity of the situation, they are all remarkably simple and direct. They give a clean, rather repetitive effect. The passage has numerous personal pronouns especially the first person singular: *my, me* and *I.* But the first person plural also features and the third person singular; there is again a domestic note in all this, a limited view. Adverbs and adjectives are fairly numerous, again domestic and simple: *long, richest, now, all, twice, sweet, dark, now, alone, pale, cold, better, far,* and *thus.* There are two exceptions here, relating to temperament and personal response: *vain* and *frightful.* The verbs for the most part follow suit, with the verb *to be* frequently used; only death (not love) raises a short sequence of verbs with an exceptional (in this passage) physical impact: *force, rush* and *seize.* (Notice, also, that Antony's dead lips alone raise a double epithet, 'pale, cold'.) The verbs are predominantly in the present tense, with some inclination to the future and only one use of the past for a subordinate phrase concerned with Cleopatra's own activity ('the wreath of victory I *made*'). The mood is frequently imperative, and in keeping with this the sentences are often short and ejaculatory; but there is also a neatness in parenthesis and subsidiary phrase that gives precision to the utterance, as in:

With them, the wreath of victory I made
(Vain augury!) for him, who now lies dead.

The phrasing is generally short, giving a brisk, almost nimble rhythm, frequently pausing several times within a single verse-line. The most sustained passage is in the address to death, spoken before Antony's dead body:

'Tis sweet to die, when they would force life on me,
To rush into the dark abode of death,
And seize him first;

but even this has a careful adverbial and antithetical phrase, and
it leads back to shorter phrases with ejaculations; see, especially,
the 'And, oh!' at the beginning of the last line but one, and the
concluding 'Oh, welcome, welcome!' Metrically, the iambic
pentametres run smoothly, the chief irregularities being the two
half-completed lines, both at moments of thinking about the
dead Antony. The personal pronouns do not attract particular
stress from the metre until '*I* may kiss', which introduces
Cleopatra's thought of Octavia. The handling of Charmion and
Iras has a double effect, first, by contrasting 'The aspics' with 'the
cure of all our ills', to underline one of Cleopatra's rare figures
of speech, and secondly by removing the attendants from the
stage to accentuate Cleopatra's climactic embrace with Antony's
corpse. This action is carefully emphasized: the metrical stress
on '*all* our ills', followed by Iras's pedestrian reply and Cleopatra's
impatience; the physical verbs; the reassuring 'sure'; the metrical
pause and slight though exceptional irregularity of metre on
'secrecy and silence'; and the demonstrative 'this', demanding
some precise gesture from the actress. Then there is a sudden
movement of thought and feeling, only half-prepared for by the
words: 'Octavia does not see me'. The end of the passage is
activated by physical sensation expressed in the ejaculations, the
continued sharpness of jealousy and the half domestic, half
possessive, 'welcome, welcome!' The re-entry of Charmion and
Iras at this precise moment, marks the pressure of events, the need
for haste, and also adds to the sense of neatness – of efficiency,
almost – that is expressed also by the vocabulary, sentence structure and rhythms of the passage as a whole.

The style of the passage is consistent, and so is the visual focus
that remains upon Cleopatra, except when she requires some
action from her attendants or when they return. The animation of
the scene comes from the heroine, who also is responsible for
awakening interest in what may at first be the spirit of Antony
('my lord looks down concerned'), but which later is clearly his
dead body that in a previous episode had been seated on a chair.
Later Cleopatra herself will die alongside Antony: 'Now seat me
by my lord. I claim this place'. So the dramatic focus in this
passage is upon Cleopatra and the dead body and the thought of

Octavia (that Cleopatra alone re-awakens). It is a tidy, domestic, intellectual, feminine play in which passion and sensuality are the slaves of thought; it is clear in both action and thought, sharp, swift yet unflustered, a study in line rather than depth, in brightness rather than light and shade.

All for Love is very different in quality from Shakespeare's *Antony and Cleopatra*, as the same tests applied to the similar moment in that play will show in detail.

What a play does to an audience

A necessary way to consider a piece of dramatic writing as a whole is to think of it as a mechanism for catching and controlling an audience's attention. Aristotle wrote about the awakening of pity and fear during a tragedy, and Ionesco, introducing his play *The Chairs*, has said that it

> progresses not through a predetermined subject and plot, but through an increasingly intense and revealing series of emotional states.
>
> (*International Theatre Annual*, 1957)

But the process is not only emotional. An increased understanding may come, as in Chekhov's *Three Sisters*; by the end of this play the audience sees and hears the characters knowing that many of their reactions are habits of useless optimism or, in the sisters themselves, evidence of a newly accepted instinct for survival and mutual help. Sometimes the audience is continually tantalized and puzzled: obviously this is a risky procedure, but in Samuel Beckett's *Waiting for Godot* it is largely successful in awakening and never satisfying a desire in the audience to know who 'Godot' is, and what is the meaning of the repetitive and casual-seeming episodes that make up the action; here, perhaps, the only continuously developing reaction in the audience is an appreciation of the stoicism of the characters, who move repeatedly from hardly-won hope to despair, and then to renewed hope and renewed despair; and from perception to blindness, and then to a further search for perception. In Shakespeare's plays, which are justly famed for their characterization, one of the most consistent effects on the audience is an increased sensitivity to inner thoughts and feelings; this is brought about as much by the impression of moving progressively closer to the main characters as by the characters' tendency to drop various disguises of appearance or speech and become both more direct and more sensitive. Cleopatra dies expressing several contradictory feelings, but this is the last flare of her complex personality after the necessarily simple encounter with the clown. Lear dies enigmatically, but only after the affecting clarity with which he acknowledges 'I am a very foolish fond old man'. Malvolio is silent when he is baffled by his enemies, but then his last response is hard, direct and unambiguous: 'I'll be revenged on the whole pack of you'. In the movement from episode to episode in Brecht's *Mother Courage,* the audience is provoked to question and make comparisons, as the heroine moves from activity to defeat, and back again. Perhaps in this play the most developing impressions made upon the audience are a growing realization of the forcefulness of the soldier's singing and marching, and the sudden knowledge that Kattrin, Mother Courage's dumb (and only surviving) child, can fearfully and defiantly give her life to try to save a city.

Important too, is the harmony and rhythm of a play as a whole, as the audience responds to it. The narrative development of *Waiting for Godot* is unsustained, with a continuous series of anti-climaxes; but a firm, visual, thematic and temperamental unity derives from the continuous presence of the same two characters on stage, always dressed the same and never accompanied by more than two others. At the end of each of the play's two Acts, immediately after the boy who appears to be Godot's messenger has left the stage, the sun sets and the moon rises. This takes little space in the stage-direction of the printed text, but is another impressive unifying element for the audience, relating the events of the play to the common alternation of light and darkness; and it also involves the audience in the closer scrutiny that is needed to observe the last minutes of both Acts, with their suicidal words and dumbly consoling movements, through what Beckett calls the pale 'light on the scene'. The final sight in each Act of Estragon and Vladimir silent and still on the stage, despite their spoken agreement that they ought to move, will by this repetition gain emphasis, force a second look, challenge the audience's comprehension. We may describe such a play in Aristotle's terms of plot, action, themes, character, utterance, scenery, but we must also ask what impression these elements, together and in the sequence of performance, make upon the audience. What does the play do?

The judgement of performance

Increase the tempo of a production and cut half an hour off the playing-time or, more simply, change the basic colour-scheme of setting and costumes from dark colours to light, or stage it in a theatre double the size of that used at first, and the quality of the play will alter at once. Recast one main role, introduce a great deal of movement among the crowd, have an audience of war veterans or of schoolchildren, and again the play changes radically. That it will be more or less satisfactory, according to the aptness of the change, everyone who has taken part in rehearsals where some such modification has been made will know from experience.

We cannot simply say that a play will be good when it is given its appropriate performance, in its appropriate theatre, before its appropriate audience, for what is 'appropriate'? What the author envisaged – but do we know what that was, nor was he always in the best position to realize the effects which his chosen production would have given. We will be much more sure of our ground, and more in tune with the nature of drama, if we insist that every play-text (or scheme for silent or improvised performance) can be judged only as if through the filters of individual performances, each one modifying the play's achievement, some more effective, or sensational, or intelligent or baffling than others. A proper assessment of any play should say that the demands of its style are these, and that with such and such conditions of performance this will happen to the audience, and with these other conditions *this* will happen.

Anyone who wishes to go beyond an immediate assessment and enjoyment of a play to learn something of how it works and so gain more enlightenment and more enjoyment, must, besides studying the text, know about theatres and audiences, actors and production methods.

II. THEATRES AND AUDIENCES

1. *Three Elements*

A THEATRE, for the performance of drama, is composed of two or three basic parts: a place for the audience, a place in which the actors perform and, optionally, a setting for the dramatic action. If these essentials are kept in mind, we can clearly describe every kind of theatre and gain some idea of their usefulness.

Most theatres we visit today are of the same kind, one considered very advanced and 'modern' some fifty years ago (see Fig. 1, p. 33). The audience sits within a squarish building, in straight or slightly curved rows on one, two or three levels, facing a large hole in one of four walls; this opening is usually surrounded with lavish decorations. Within this opening, as in a frame, the actors perform on a level platform extending a considerable distance away from the audience. Then, surrounding this acting area, there is space above, at the sides and a little to the rear which is fitted out to support painted canvas and other kinds of scenery, to store and hide further pieces of scenery which can rapidly take the place of that which is in view, and to hide the various sources of artificial light and other items of stage-equipment. This sort of theatre is called a picture-frame or, less accurately, proscenium theatre.

The form came into prominence with the development of artificial lighting, first gas and then electricity. While a play is in performance the audience usually sits in the dark so that the brightly or subtly lit stage holds attention from behind its dividing arch or frame. This theatre is capable of precise imitation of real-life conditions with particular tones and lights, and when tricks of perspective are employed it can give an impression of great spaciousness. Because every member of the audience sits facing much the same way, groups of actors on stage can be deployed in complicated formations without obscuring anyone's view of them; and one grouping may be held for some time with only slight variations – rather like an old-fashioned photograph of a family group set in a lavish frame. Lighting and complicated scenery can also represent conditions of life quite surpassing in brightness, gaiety, splendour or mystery anything outside the

31

theatre. It is a theatre in which the audience watches another carefully and secretly organized world set up before them, for their pleasure, precise scrutiny, or wonder.

In the years since the Second World War, the notion that a picture-frame theatre was obviously the right one to build in a technological age – so that stage-lighting might become more and more realistic or wonderful and the actors controlled ever more precisely – has been challenged from many sides. Actors want more freedom to move around and some want to be able to 'get at' their audiences, 'to break out' of their 'frame', to experiment rather than assume studied postures. Dramatists do not want to compete with the cinema in providing an illusion of actual life, or in panoply and brightness; some want to simplify the background for dramatic action so that only the most significant details are shown – as in a cartoon or medieval icon – and others want no setting at all so that they can gain undeflected and excessively intimate attention for one or two characters. Some directors want to keep the action moving incessantly, or to challenge their audience and elicit their co-operation in ways not possible from within a picture-frame. So the clock has been put back and old theatre forms have been rediscovered, or re-invented, and then modified to make the best use of technical devices that have become available since they were last built.

Theatres today are being built with an open stage, thrust stage, arena stage or traverse stage; and auditorium and setting are reshaped to fit. The open stage is the simplest (see Fig. 2): here the auditorium remains almost unchanged, but the frame has gone and the setting is only at the back or actually *on* the acting area. The Mermaid Theatre at Blackfriars in the City of London and the Phoenix at Leicester are post-war examples of this form that had earlier been in common use for temporary theatres in banqueting and assembly halls of various sizes throughout Europe during the Renaissance and later. Both the Mermaid and Phoenix have turntables in their acting areas to effect changes of the three-dimensional scenery that is often erected in front of the backcloth. In this way some measure of scenic illusion can be achieved, but less than completely realized, and never self-contained. The division between stage and auditorium is no longer a fixed line, for the frame has gone and light spills from the stage on to the audience; the actors can address the audience easily, for they do not exist in another 'world'. Moreover, the audience feels closer to them because the front of the stage is wider and hence the rows of seats for the audience are wider and more people can sit within a few yards of the performers.

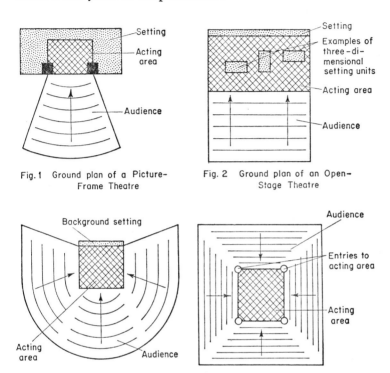

Fig. 1   Ground plan of a Picture-
           Frame Theatre

Fig. 2   Ground plan of an Open-
           Stage Theatre

Fig. 3   Ground plan of a Thrust-
           Stage Theatre

Fig. 4   Ground plan of an Arena-
           Stage Theatre

A thrust stage brings the audience still closer, on three sides of the acting area, not one (see Fig. 3). In Spain and England at the end of the sixteenth century, this was the usual form in which to build theatres. In the Spanish coralles or Elizabethan public play-houses, the audiences stood or sat around the stage, both below its level and in galleries or small rooms above it. In our newly-built thrust-stage theatres, as the Festival Theatre at Stratford, Ontario, or the Tyrone Guthrie Theatre in Minneapolis, the spectators are seated in rows raised one above the other, and in one higher balcony. The Elizabethan playhouse could accommodate two to three thousand, all within forty or fifty feet of the stage, and the Stratford, Ontario, theatre seats nearly two thousand so that the farthest are only thirteen rows from the front. In a picture-frame theatre of similar capacity, many of the audience would be twice as far from the stage.

With a thrust stage, contact between actors and audience is still closer than with an open stage, but if the actors wish to address the whole audience they must either move to the back and centre of the acting area (and thus remove themselves from everyone by some twenty to forty feet), or move around the stage so that they project some part of their speech to each of the three sides. It is a theatre for processions, choregraphic movement, spirited comedy and pageantry. The setting is confined to the fourth side of the stage (in Spain and Elizabethan England this background was almost unchanging from play to play) and some pieces of scenery or large objects (like thrones or tombstones) on the acting area that are not big enough to obscure the view of the audience across the stage. For many of the audience the background setting on the fourth side of the stage would be within their line of vison only when an actor stood back close to it, or was making his entry from the changing-rooms situated behind it; for most of the play's action the main background would be the audience some forty feet away on the other side of the stage. So this form isolates the actors more from their setting; they become moving statues, viewed from almost all sides. Group activity easily holds attention and the individual actor will dominate only when he is able to command the audience by the dynamic qualities of his performance, either with expressive movement and speech, or with highly-charged emotional excitement.

The arena stage completely eliminates full-scale settings (see Fig. 4). The audience sits (or in early times stood) on four sides of the acting-area, as around a circus ring. The most carefully developed theatre in this form today is the Arena Theatre in Washington, D.C. But, because it is the cheapest in both building and running costs, there have been many experimental or temporary theatres of this kind: the Library Theatre at Scarborough, run for several years by Stephen Joseph, is an example. Entry to the acting area is usually from its four corners and, occasionally, through a trap-door; and the actors' grouping and movement is viewed from all four sides. The form accentuates the characteristics of the thrust stage, but loses the scenic support of the fourth-side background. This has two very important consequences. First, there is only one basic place for the dramatic action at any one time; it is difficult to suggest that some characters are within a house or a prison while others are without, for any structure on stage has to be very small so as not to obscure the audience's view across the stage. Secondly, the back-stage, central position from which an actor can dominate the whole theatre on a thrust stage, has disappeared; even the protagonist at the end of a tragedy must move around to address himself to all parts of the theatre. In effect, this theatre cuts every performer down to the same potential effectiveness, and makes any one place on the stage equal in importance to any other; and it requires movement almost incessantly.

At the Sant' Erasmo Theatre in Milan and the Traverse in Edinburgh, a further theatre form has been used (see Fig. 5). Both are small buildings and in each the stage runs side to side across the middle, with the audience ranged on two sides. Here two scenic backgrounds and fixed points of reference are obtained, but both are seen at acute angles and therefore have little importance in the audience's view of the stage unless the dramatic action is purposefully concentrated near them. Direct address to the audience has to be delivered on two opposing sides, but duologues can be played across the stage so that the audience has a fixed and equally accentuated view of both individuals or groups taking part. The traverse-stage theatre is pre-eminently suited for intense psychological encounter.

Besides these forms of theatre now being used, there are many other possible variations of the three basic elements. Some were once common, but appropriate only to particular conditions that no longer exist. In the seventeenth and eighteenth centuries a platform stage was used in conjunction with a deep background that accommodated changeable scenery (see Fig. 6). The English Restoration theatres were good examples of this form. Stage-settings could not be so brightly illuminated as the platform stage set before them, so in the plays of this period you will come across stage-directions like this from Farquhar's *Recruiting Officer* (1706): '*A Court of Justice*. Balance, Scale, Scruple *upon the bench*. . . . Kite *and* Constable *advance to the front of the stage*.' Often the characters did not enter from within the setting, but from one of two 'proscenium' doors that opened directly on to the platform on the audience side of the picture-frame. This theatre was suitable for a very verbal kind of drama, where the action was forwarded by talk between two, three or four characters standing as close as possible to the audience and in relation to a background picture of an actual location. Scenes of chase, procession and over-hearing were also well accommodated, and asides, disguises and revelations, dance and song interludes, and long complicated monologues are all well adapted to its conditions of performance.

The simplest theatres are some planks raised above a standing audience, or a space cleared in the centre of a hall, while the audience sits around after a feast. In medieval times and for popular performances from the early Renaissance to much later (and even in a few fair-grounds today), theatres have been con-trived almost anywhere, in the streets or market-squares. Some-times a platform-stage was fixed on a cart so that it could be moved around: episodes from miracle plays were often performed on this kind of 'pageant wagon'. Sometimes a curtain screened off a small back-stage area in which the actors could prepare, so that the improvised theatre had a thrust-type stage with its audience on three sides. Often several small stages were used in conjunction with each other for a single play that could thus show a compli-cated narrative moving from one location to another: by using several of these stages, several locations could be represented simultaneously and a multiple setting provided for panoramic dramas. Most of these various forms were very suitable for popular drama because they were both cheap and readily accessible, and could have no fixed or reserved seats for specially privileged members of the audience. In single units the simple, open stages were suited to small bands of itinerant actors; in multiple units, or with large and complicated pageant-wagons, they could accommodate huge amateur casts.

In no case did these simple theatres attempt to give an illusion of a real or a complete 'world', and because of the small-sized acting areas, the usually standing audience and the open-air or informal surroundings, the dramatic action had to be lively and arresting. On the other hand, contact with the audience was easy and direct: indeed, improvised talk with the audience and audience-participation in the drama were common; and charac-ters in the plays frequently entered the acting-area from among the audience.

In medieval times especially, churches and churchyards have also been used for religious drama. Here the actors might perform at several places within the building, according to the nature of the dramatic action: at the font, crypt, choir entry, or high altar.

Each location for the drama had its appropriate setting in the architecture, decoration and iconography of the church, and so gave a liturgical reality to its action: death was represented where the devout customarily meditated on death, and a mechanical dove descended to represent the coming of the Holy Spirit at the place (and indeed at the time of year) appropriate to the liturgical plan of the church-theatre. The choir, vestments, music, visual symbolism and holy writ of the church services became part of the drama.

In many ways, medieval stage-conditions were comparable to those of experimental theatres today. For with the increased cost of providing special theatre buildings, improvised stages are gaining currency; and with new sophistication in dramatic writing there has sprung up a counter search for a more popular theatre and one directly involved with the streets and public places of our cities. But another form of popular theatre is not so rapidly copied: the classical. This existed with various modifications in Greek and Roman times, and as a coterie theatre, it was revived during the Renaissance. The Theatre of Dionysius in Athens is a prototype. It was constructed on the hillside beneath the Acropolis, and its ruins may be seen today. It was an open-air theatre accommodating many thousands in a raked semicircle around two acting areas, one circular (called the orchestra) in which the chorus chiefly performed, and one long and narrow at the back of the other and raised slightly above it. Behind this second area was the setting, at first the distant prospect of hills and sky, but soon provided with a variable architectural frieze, with a large central and two subsidiary openings and a practicable upper level. In later theatres, directly descendant from this model, the orchestra was lessened in size to become first a semicircle and then, in neo-classical Renaissance theatres, a mere gap between audience and stage.

With a full-sized orchestra this theatre form emphasized the contribution of a visually expressive chorus for they performed at the centre of the circled audience; and, since every member looked down upon the orchestra, patterned group movement was unusually impressive. The raised rear stage allowed the protagonists to dominate the orchestra when the drama required this; in this position the actors were not related directly to the audience as the chorus was, but to the setting, each other and, when appropriate movement or verbal response was introduced

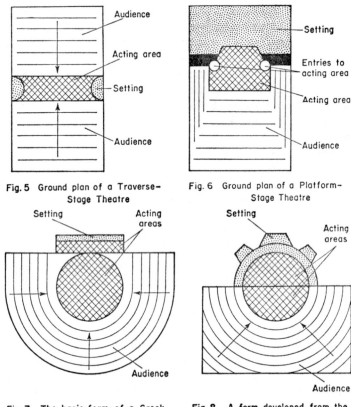

Fig. 5   Ground plan of a Traverse-
Stage Theatre

Fig. 6   Ground plan of a Platform-
Stage Theatre

Fig. 7   The basic form of a Greek
Theatre

Fig. 8   A form developed from the
Greek Theatre

in the orchestra, to the surrounding chorus. In the earlier theatres
the narrowness of this acting-area was more suitable for orations
than for group action or interchanges of dialogue. The Greek
and Roman theatres were open to the sky and this, together with
the large size of the Greek auditoriums, could give an immense
scale to the dramatic action when the protagonists or chorus led
the audience to be conscious of this vast, natural canopy.

Obviously a theatre is not created by juggling the three elements into a new combination but is dependent on inherited conditions and theatrical purpose. We must consider any theatre
building in conjunction with its technical resources, its place in
society and history, and the type of play which is to be performed.
The best way of understanding how a theatre works is to study

one actual example of any one form and inquire where it was sited, how planned and decorated, how managed and what audience attended; then two or three specific plays should be visualized in production there, and the reactions of an audience imagined. This will not be easy to think through, but the difficulties encountered will lead to the right kind of questions. Certainly this exercise should give some impression of the size and complexity of the concept of a theatre and that, for a start, can be surprising and stimulating.

2. *Theatre Equipment and Planning*

To reduce any theatre to three elements is a sweeping simplification. Several other factors that influence its characteristics we have already mentioned by the way. First size: as a large political rally is different in feeling and style from a small one of a hundred or so committed members, so a large theatre differs from a small. They can never have the same effect: should the same people that filled the small one be the entire audience of the large, the same production would give them a quite different experience. A play is not the same on a large stage as on a small: an impression of isolation is not easy within a small acting-area and, while individual dignity is harder to obtain on a large stage, once achieved it is far more impressive. Proportions as well as size are significant: how wide, deep, high the stage? How straight or curved the lines of seats in the auditorium? How lofty the whole building?

Technical equipment will also help to fix a theatre's characteristics. Will the audience be in the dark or within range of the stage light, or will the whole theatre be open to the daylight? Will the play finish with the fall of a curtain or the emptying of the stage? How subtle, how powerful, how flexible, in control will the stage light be? What trap-doors, lifts, movable (turntable or truck) stages are provided, and what sound equipment, stereo or mono? Is there provision for an orchestra? Is the stage surface well sprung, quiet or noisy? What facilities are there for flying (that is raising out of sight) pieces of scenery, and how quickly can these operate? Obviously such technical aids will govern the extent to which an illusion of real life can be achieved, but also the speed, neatness, magical surprise, extensiveness of the changes that can be effected in staging that has no illusionistic pretensions. They will also govern how much assistance can be given the actors in creating atmosphere or tone – and sometimes, of course, it is most exciting for the actors to do all this work for themselves.

The decorations and fittings of an auditorium and entrance foyer are also significant; and the services provided for an audience by the theatre management such as bars, cloakrooms, art exhibitions, bookstalls, chocolate stalls, ice-cream vendors within the auditorium or outside; whether smoking is forbidden, and so on. The audience can be warned that the play is about to commence by the usual bell, or by the recorded voice of Sir Laurence Olivier (as at the opening seasons of the Chichester Festival Theatre), or by a six-man brass band playing a fanfare in the foyer (as at Stratford, Ontario). Such details are important because the expectation, including the sense of comfort or familiarity, corporate good spirits or polite decorum, which is induced by its surroundings, governs the audience's response. For example, compare the effect on an audience of the usual gilt and sham opulence of a Broadway or London theatre with that of the bare restraint of the Moscow Arts Theatre during its early days when it was decorated wholly with white walls and seasoned, unpainted wood.

Detailed planning of back-stage accommodation is just as important – arguably more so. Will each important actor have an individual dressing-room, or share with one, two, three or more? How comfortable is the green room (or common, waiting-room for the actors), how spacious the rehearsal-room – if either of these is provided; how ample the properties store; how convenient the workshop, wardrobe, paintframe, stage-manager's office, and so on? These will affect the quality and nature of the dramas presented. And organizational details must also be considered. Is a drama school attached to the theatre (this is a common practice in some countries)? Is the theatre capable of running plays in repertoire (that is several different plays within a week) or must one play succeed the demise of its predecessor because of limited storage and company facilities? Is the theatre designed to be run by a manager or by an artistic director? Does one office control Front of House operations (that is relationships with the public) and the back-stage and directly artistic activities, and if so, where is this situated?

Finally, where is the theatre located and – a question that is closely allied to this – what audience can it expect?

3. *Theatre and Society*

A theatre's audience is an indication of its function in society. The relationship between the cost of seats and the cost of productions is obviously a basic problem. Some theatres have always insisted on free seats, others on all seats costing the same amount so that the audience is not stratified (this is particularly likely to happen in theatres with two or more levels in the auditorium placed progressively farther away from the stage). Other theatres price a few, private and very favourably placed seats far above any others – court theatres and Shakespeare's Globe are obvious examples. Some companies spread an inadequate budget more or less equally over all productions confining all artistic endeavour, and others spend as much as is called for on each performance as it goes into rehearsal, and shut the theatre when the money is gone.

A theatre's location and times of performance also affect the nature of the drama presented there. In Elizabethan days theatres were not allowed in the City of London, so they were built in the suburbs on the south side of the Thames outside the jurisdiction of the City Fathers: and across the river came almost all kinds of Londoners to see performances. It was an afternoon expedition and merchants complained that their young apprentices skived off from work to waste their time in the theatre; preachers complained that theatres were resorts for the idle and irresponsible. But still the public went in large numbers; on holidays audiences were especially lively. During the early years of the seventeenth century, a small, indoor theatre became established as a second house for the King's Men actually within the City boundaries but on a specially protected piece of ground exempt from the City's control. This was the Blackfriars Theatre and here the players encountered different trouble: now it was the neighbours who were likely to complain of the great number of coaches that fashionable people brought to the theatre so that they could not get to their own front doors. And whether they owned one theatre or two, the King's Men were also invited to play at court or in the great houses of the nobility; and sometimes they went on tour playing in halls and inn-yards up and down the country.

The restriction of one company to one theatre in one town, which is often the pattern for today's theatre enterprise, is, in fact, a comparatively new arrangement. Even when a company goes on tour today, it usually performs only in theatres as like its own as possible. This is because we now value a 'production' more than a company, dramatist or star actors; and each production is tied to the physical conditions for which it was originally designed. Or perhaps we should put this the other way round: because a director knows how to exploit the characteristics of a particular theatre building and audience, and rely upon its technical equipment, the work he does in and for that theatre is no longer portable. Probably these are two ways of looking at a single process: the progressive specialization of theatrical art.

Audiences for theatre productions today are also composed of special sections of the community. In London there is a fashionable audience for 'challenging' plays and productions, a faithful and often educationally oriented audience for Shakespeare and other English classics, and a far larger audience, coming in motor-coaches from the suburbs or visiting London on business or pleasure, that goes to long-running, star-studded, extravagant, television-promoted productions of musicals, comedies, farces, who-dunnits and other pieces of so-called light entertainment. These audiences seldom mix with each other, and they are much the same on any day of the week or year. In New York, there seem to be two audiences: one patronizing Broadway and spending about twelve dollars on a seat, and another going chiefly to the cheaper, much smaller, less well-equipped and more experimental theatres of 'off-Broadway' in Greenwich Village, or off-off-Broadway in East Village. These two do mix a little, when notorious success draws the wealthy to a small theatre or makes the other audience think that Broadway prices might be worth while. In the provinces of England, there are large audiences for light entertainment on the London pattern, and small audiences of 'regulars' and some young people for repertory theatres giving more or less challenging productions. In the United States, new prestige repertory theatres are being founded, often with little artistic preparation, outside New York City; and there are some touring companies with replicas of Broadway productions. That is about all the professional theatre outside New York: in addition there are numerous universities and community (or amateur) companies with well-equipped theatres and their own academic or loyal followings.

We are so used to these kinds of audiences and companies that we scarcely expect any others. But consider what has happened at other times and in other countries:

A permanent, self-sufficient group of virtuoso actors travelling great distances, carrying all their equipment with them and coming to town for very limited engagements, like a circus: a familiar example is the company that comes to Elsinore in *Hamlet*.

A company, professional and amateur, presenting a large-scale work once a year – or once every ten years – on a special holiday and usually in a special place: the ancient Greek theatres were run in this way (and they are being used again in a somewhat similar fashion today), or the miracle plays in many towns in Europe during the later Middle Ages.

A company touring with a large range of productions suited to performance in three or four especially designed and equipped theatres.

A company sharing a building with some other activity (in Elizabethan days, cockfighting or bear baiting; today ballroom dancing or bingo), and performing plays on a limited number of occasions depending on demand, to much the same public.

A small group sharing a common artistic method, or vision, or training, who work in isolation to prepare one or two plays at a time, primarily for a small local audience: examples are the group of semi-amateurs in which Stanislavski first worked, the Polish laboratory theatre run by Jerzy Grotowski, or theatre workshops run by Herbert Blau in San Francisco in the 1950s and early 60s and by Joan Littlewood in the North of England from 1945 to 1953.

A company subsidized or otherwise supported by a limited social group for their own entertainment and presenting plays during a short season and on special occasions: the court theatres of Louis XIV in France, or of Charles II in England, are examples.

A company organized to serve academic interests by historically informed or experimentally useful productions: examples are the professional company at Stanford University in California and the productions in the late fifteenth century at the Teatro Olimpico in Vicenza.

A company organized to provide entertainment that en-courages, if not promulgates, specific social ideas: the Group

Theatre in New York in the 1930s and Centre 42 in England in the 60s are organizations of this sort.

A company specializing in performance before children in schools or in theatres for matinées at the week-ends, or during school holidays.

A company working mainly on the plays of one dramatist and seeking the best style for him and for themselves: examples operating today are mostly dedicated to Shakespeare, but the Berliner Ensemble has special concern for Brecht, and some eastern European theatres have resident dramatists, as Topol and Havel in Prague.

These and other possibilities for theatre organization would make their own demands on finance if they were followed today, but those would be small difficulties compared with the potential effect of such experimentation on every aspect of a play in performance, every stage in the preparation of a production. Today we frequently hear talk about the need for new theatre buildings to experiment with audience-stage relationships, but we do not hear enough about new theatre organizations. Why should we tackle the most difficult and expensive problem first?

Of course different theatres have different capabilities, show new aspects of plays and develop new acting styles; but different organizations, costing far less to introduce and continuing to be infinitely adaptable, could effect quite as much. Some plays absolutely require vast, exceptional, festival audiences; others will reveal depths of feeling or subtleties of thought only by means of the intense and precise acting that is the prerogative of a small, permanent and single-minded group of actors. Some authors will write more readily and better if they can work closely with their actors over a long period, and others are stimulated by knowing the particular audience for which they write. Some actors need constant association with only a few fellows; others need stable conditions, long runs or short runs, or scope for improvised performances; some like a great deal of scenery and others none at all. Some audiences can be collected only once in ten years, others need constant and intimate association. For such reasons, variation and experiment in theatre organization are necessary for dramatic enterprise.

III. ACTORS

VERY OCCASIONALLY an actor on stage appears to be exactly the same as he is off stage, in ordinary life. But he never is: he is acting before an audience in a prepared drama. At other times, an actor does things which we have never seen before, or never imagined humanly possible – his heart seems to break, he dies and then recovers; he gives a great cry, or a sudden, ludicrous leap – and yet he does the same feat, night after night, for a year or more. Sometimes acting looks very easy and wholly delightful, so that we imagine ourselves as actors, perhaps improving on the most gifted performance: this is one of the reasons for the large band of amateur actors, students and part-timers, who all seek the enjoyment of acting. Indeed it is an instinctive art: but it is also one of the most demanding. Constant training is necessary, for unless voice and body are kept in the fullest possible control, the actor will not be able to realize his conception of a role. There is no part of an actor's life or being that is not drawn into this art, no boundary on which to hold back: this artist's material is himself, every part of himself and used in every possible way.

But acting is a profession as well as an art, and it is so complicated a business to manage that relatively few are able to live by it: it is a career only for the highly gifted, lucky and tenacious. Yet success in the profession is absolutely necessary for full artistic achievement: the right role must be found for each stage of development; too long in one role, or one company, can hinder growth, and so can the wrong colleagues or wrong play, or inadequate and unsuitable conditions. This is why there are so many ex-actors.

Acting is a full-time occupation: it is collaborative and highly individual; unpredictable and highly technical; instinctive and imaginative, and yet professional.

Perhaps all this can be summed up by saying that an actor is a man who needs, finds and keeps an audience. He needs one to support him, to work for and to work with. To get this audience, the actor has to be remarkable; he, himself, must be worth attention and capable of holding attention throughout a performance and for a lifetime of performances.

45

1. *The Actor as Instrument*

Anyone trying to work well as an actor must be high-powered; he must have many natural gifts and they must be controlled and developed.

He must train his voice so that it is worth listening to. That is not so easy as it sounds. The actor has not, simply, to make the right noises at the right times, for what are the right noises? Speech mechanically recorded is not the same as when it was first spoken, because sound is only one part of the total impression of a human being in some kind of involvement, with himself, with others, with a complex set of physical conditions, with the passing of time.

In his early training, the actor is often encouraged to consider voice as a separate organ. He learns how to control his breathing, and explores the various consonants and vowels so that he can make any one of them at will. He needs a good ear for this and plenty of intelligent practice. Then the student proceeds to control volume, pitch, tone and texture. He learns to sustain speech for long periods and to project his voice so that it carries a great distance without strain. One part of his training is most surprisingly effective to someone unfamiliar with it: that is the timing of speech. The actor should be able to control tempo, rhythm and phrase so that his utterance has a musical quality: he can then give a beauty to logical statement and a kind of meaning to random sequences of words or even mere sounds. Like a musician he can, by the noise he makes, compel attention, caress or excite his audience as he chooses. This is why an actor will pride himself on his 'voice', and why acting schools have 'Voice Teachers'.

But in a theatre, speech never exists alone, and it is dangerous for an actor to concentrate on developing his voice as a separate element in performance. In so far as he speaks intelligible words on the stage, meaning must be communicated; that is to say, his speech must be attuned to the inherent values of the dramatic text. This is a primary requirement: it is quite possible for an actor by speaking well to destroy the musical qualities of the words themselves, or to obscure their meaning, allusiveness, point or ambiguity. The actor must be able to find the appropriate musical speech.

But still we are considering the matter far too simply. Voice must be properly related to the demands of verbal language and to every other element of the drama: a sound recording of a stage performance should be inadequate in the same way as a recording of real-life speech, only more so.

If a character says 'I love you very much', the actor must consider the speaking of these words so that:

1. *The audience will listen.* The sounds should be interesting: they may be beautiful or, to use a less difficult phrase, musically arresting. They must certainly be audible.

2. *The audience will understand and appreciate them in their context.* The sounds should communicate something that is helpful to the progress of the drama. This may be the words' 'dictionary' meaning but, possibly, the very opposite; for example these words could mean what is usually comprehended by the words 'I hate you a little'. The actor has to know what the person or figure he represents wants to communicate (this is variously called his 'inner action', 'objective' or 'subtext'); and he must know what this character is capable of communicating: for example, the actor may represent a young man who, by saying 'I love you very much', *wants* to say 'You have been very unfair to me', and who seems to say 'I am not very interested in you'. It is a great presumption in drama – as in life – to think that a speaker's words are an accurate account of his thoughts or of his feelings. Further examples of the use of the words 'I love you very much' readily suggest themselves. They may be a secret message given by one spy to another, meaning 'I have the poison'; perhaps the speaker is a little unsure of the code, or he may be sure of the code but also mean what the words mean in the dictionary. Or the words may be said as a prescribed response in a marriage rite and imply a formal committal of one person to another for life.

Words, in drama as in life, can have double implications: 'I love you very much' can mean both 'I love you' *and* 'I hate you'; or 'I love you a little' *and* 'You don't believe me', *and* 'Here we go again'. The actor must know the range of meanings for anything he says, and must choose which to stress and which to underplay; and he must know how to do this.

3. *The audience will accept them as part of the drama.* The words must fit in with everything else. The actor must not learn to control his voice and breathing in such a way that he has to

hold a fixed posture or use facial contortions; always his voice and physical bearing must be appropriate to the style of the production as a whole and to the dramatic situation at the time of utterance. Nor should the actor so emphasize the secret, private meaning of his words that the other characters on stage seem to hear too much to tally with the limited knowledge indicated by *their* words and actions; that is the actor must not give too much away when the play requires the other characters to remain in ignorance of his inner thoughts and feelings.

Above all, the actor's voice must seem appropriate to his own total involvement in the drama: this means that speech is convincing as a *part* of his whole physical, emotional, and intellectual response. An arresting way to say a line that involves so much breath that the actor cannot maintain the calm demeanour and still bearing appropriate to the situation, must be rejected. Occasionally a vocal performance should contrast with the physical performance, but it must do so convincingly: a character could say 'I love you very much' very slowly while physically he is alert and quick, if at the same time he suggests that it is an act of will to speak steadily and soberly when all the time he wants to jump for joy.

Any aspect of an actor's performance may be considered under these three headings: interest; communication; acceptability, or truth, to the whole impression.

Clearly he must train his body, like his voice, to fulfil the demands of his roles. This needs more than physical fitness in the usual sense of that phrase. Considerable physical feats must be performed, but cleanly and efficiently, without contortion or any unwanted sign of stress; this is necessary both for dramatic illusion and to minimize the demands made on the actor who must go on to the end of his performance without pause. Especially important is the actor's ability to take up a neutral, co-ordinated position so that he is capable of making very small physical responses clearly and without fuss, and so that he can economize on physical and nervous energy during a long and arduous role. And, as with the voice, the actor must seek beauty of expression. Movement has dance-like qualities that can be perpetually at the command of an actor, like the musical qualities of his voice. Timing is again of great effectiveness, so that some actors become conscious of a regular inner pulse, or beat, every moment they are on stage; slight variations from a regular tempo and variously sustained phrasing of movement, can then make huge impressions. A basic rhythm may be established for a characterization and subtly varied for each phase of the drama. All this affects the audience without recourse to words and, therefore, without the great majority of the audience having any clue as to why they sense a change of dramatic intensity, or why they look at one small gesture at a crucial moment, or why they laugh more and more freely, or why they are suddenly arrested by doubt or insecurity.

But the full control of an actor's movement gives more than aptness and the ability to catch attention: it is an opportunity for imagination and inventiveness, for the actor's creative instinct. Movement is another language, powerfully expressive in its own right. An actor in full control of his body and of his timing can give to gesture, movement and posture the freshness of original creation; there is a traditional language of gesture to claim as his own but, more importantly, he can make new and beautiful statements as if he were a poet inventing words or a musician inventing tunes. This is why a great actor can walk on to a stage and astonish thousands before he says a word: this can look so simple that the actor is said to be a 'star' and have an inexplicable appeal.

Body control also serves the actor's need to imitate. First of all, someone whose body is well trained is able to observe another man objectively and recognize the points of tension within his body; and secondly, he can reproduce those stresses within himself, and so seem to take on the very form and being of the man impersonated. There is an analogy in voice here, too; for the ability to recognize all vowel sounds and consonants is a great aid to the conscious assumption of a dialect pronunciation. In both, an innate gift for mimicry is helpful, but impersonators are made as much as born.

Vocal and physical training and the knowledge that training brings are the sources of power in an actor. This comes not only through efficiency, but also through natural growth, the strengthening of the natural instincts to act that comes through the efficient use of them. So we can talk of the training of an actor's imagination and temperament. By increasing the effectiveness of his physical and verbal utterance, the actor grows more accustomed to expressing his imaginary involvement in a situation, clarifying and simplifying his reactions, changing suddenly, and yet wholly, from grief to pride or, even, to joy. His emotional resources are strengthened and his mind sharpened and quickened. With fuller means of expression, he himself becomes more resourceful and remarkable; what is usually called his 'personality' is more assured, and he seems more open to the audience's appreciation. Quite naturally, every actor is impatient with his training which must concentrate first on this technicality and then on that, and can do comparatively little in a direct way for his co-ordinating ability and for the all-important growth of his imagination. The actor needs technical training as much as any other kind of artist – more, for example, than a writer – and, like the others, he needs to find, and trust, himself in his work.

If an actor is impatient so are his teachers. When Gordon Craig, one of the very few English theatre theoreticians, considered what he wanted an actor to be, he concluded that he should not rely on any man but use a super-efficient marionette; the technical challenge is so complicated and huge, that an inhuman second-best seemed preferable to the third-rate and all too human actors Craig was accustomed to see and hear.

2. *Different Kinds of Actors*

The basic resources of an actor are constant, but the uses to which they are put are infinitely varied. This is right and proper: for not only should drama hold the mirror up to life and therefore its characters be as varied as human beings, but drama should be capable of showing those individuals from differing viewpoints. Sometimes an actor must present only outward behaviour, without any sign of the hesitation or confusion that obscure issues in ordinary life. Sometimes he must accentuate the inner tensions of a character, prolonging moments of irresolution and giving explicit clarity to thoughts which usually drift, half-formed through human consciousness. Sometimes he must emphasize one emotional (and usually, in ordinary life, imprecise) response to the neglect of all others, and so become a representative of all the hate or grief that his audience has ever felt or has ever imagined possible. In farces, an actor must simplify his reactions and at the same time speed them up, so that they become almost incredible in their animation and oddity. In a documentary play, an actor may have to become an impersonal official 'voice', or thirty-six different characters in turn of varying ages, sexes and opinions. In some comedies, an actor must appear to be himself but more secure in response, warmer in affection and more open in approach to others (including his audience) than he as a person (or as an actor) could ever be; in other comedies, he must leave many details to improvisation during each performance.

Some theoreticians say that what an actor does with his resources is one of two things: either he presents himself in various thin disguises, or hides himself in a number of impenetrable disguises; he is a personality or an impersonator. But this is too simple. Frederick Schyberg, in his *Art of Acting* first published in Sweden in 1949, lists four kinds of actor:

showman-artist (or virtuoso)
penetrative-artist (or psychological actor)
versatility specialist (or character actor)
personality actor

But try to fit these four hats on actors you have seen and at once you will find some wearing three hats and others whom you feel bound to keep uncovered. The truth is – to repeat myself – that actors are even more various (and more variable) than human beings: perhaps that might serve as a definition.

Rather than try like another Adam, to find names, I shall turn historian and, in very broad terms, consider three recurrent phases in the story of acting. In this way we may conceive something of the range of this art.

Classical Acting

The plays of Æschylus, Sophocles, Molière, Racine and Schiller, the Greek and Roman theatres and the neo-classical theatres throughout Europe in the seventeenth and eighteenth centuries, encouraged a 'classical' style of acting. This kind of actor seeks above all the exploitation of himself as an instrument and a clear, unified impression. His aim is not to imitate nature in its variety, nor to distort it. Without violence to what is natural, he seeks to transfigure it. He observes himself and others, in history and contemporary life, and then, while imitating this behaviour on the stage, will simplify it, or generalize, purify or universalize it – all these words have been used by the classicists – and so be able to strengthen, enlarge and intensify it.

In ancient Greece, the actor wore special shoes and head-dresses to exaggerate his height and dignity, and masks to help fix a single impression of character. Later the classical actor dispensed with the mask and stilts, but continued to simplify and strengthen his appearance by make-up and costume. He is always highly conscious of voice, bearing and movement, priding himself on clarity, economy and decorum. He prefers to act in plays with only a few major roles – often only one – many long speeches, careful balance and co-ordination between the separate Acts, generalized or 'universal' themes, and a progressive build-up towards intense emotion or a crisis in the opposition of differing wills. He prepares each role for a long time – in Greece performances were at annual festivals – and, whenever he is able, he continues to perfect his interpretation for many years. (Thomas Betterton, the English classical actor of the late seventeenth century, continued to play his version of Hamlet until he was seventy years of age.) Everything is thoroughly worked out, leaving as little as possible to improvisation during performance.

The dangers of this kind of playing is that the actor becomes too selfishly the star, so that he cannot gain from interaction with the rest of the cast; or his performance becomes too stiff, too settled in technical accomplishment and too remote from observed behaviour. The great excitements of classical acting are amazing range and power, made possible by finely developed voice and physique, and emotional intensity made possible by technical control which can hold back reserves of power for an overwhelming climax.

Colley Cibber, theatre-manager, actor and playwright, wrote in praise of Betterton, as of a super-human hero; his descriptions, especially in *An Apology for the Life of Colley Cibber,* are probably the best English introduction to classical acting. Here are some selections:

> Betterton never wanted fire and force . . . yet where it was not demanded, he never prostituted his power to the low ambition of a false applause. . . .
> In all his soliloquies of moment, the strong intelligence of his attitude and aspect, drew you into such an impatient gaze and eager expectation that you almost imbibed the sentiment with your eye, before the ear could reach it.
> In the just delivery of poetical numbers, particularly where the sentiments are pathetic, it is scarce credible upon how minute an

article of sound depends their greatest beauty or inaffection. The voice of a singer is not more strictly tied to time and tune than that of an actor in theatrical elocution: the least syllable too long, or too slightly dwelt upon, in a period depreciates it to nothing: which every syllable if rightly touched, shall, like the heightening stroke of light from a master's pencil, give life and spirit to the whole.

In the classical tradition the finest acting I have seen is that of Aspassia Papathanassiou, in the *Electra* of Sophocles as directed by Dimitrios Rondiris for the Pireaus Theatre Company. Such exact control has been attained by this actress that Rondiris can stop a rehearsal at the height of an emotional climax and then start the scene again at exactly the same point without needing to 'work up' to the climax all over again. The whole company is like an orchestra of instrumentalists who can be conducted by their director, as Toscanini would control his musicians. And yet Aspassia Papathanassiou has a very distinct and powerful personality; her own individual imagination seems freed, not restrained, by so much technical control. The rank and file of actors give an individual impression through easily recognizable traits, mannerisms of speech or movement, or even a certain affectation in dress; but if an actor eradicates such obvious idiosyncrasies as imperfections and heightens the impression of great emotional involvement, he can expose, release and develop the deeper secrets of personality, those indelible marks of individuality, experience and environment which are basic to our natures.

There are few English-speaking actors today in the classical tradition. Sir John Gielgud is probably the best known, although his technical accomplishment is more evident in voice than in physical action. His greatest roles, Hamlet and Richard II, are ones which obviously make large vocal demands, and his various recordings of them give some impression of the intensity and shapeliness of his impersonations. Sir John's account of Richard II, in his book *Stage Directions*, emphasizes pattern, symmetry, line, grace, beauty and the 'musical intention' of the text. He says that the inner character of the king is developed in a 'series of exquisite cadenzas and variations', and that the overall aim of a production should be to present the dramatic action and verbal music so that they 'create a complete harmony of effect'.

Perhaps the classical tradition is most alive today in opera singers, the stars of musical comedies and some of the most accomplished and consistent in style of our comedians. These are all performers who can hold a huge theatre attentive by an out-sized impression of temperament and personality. They exercise their technical skill in a comparatively narrow range of parts, and they are also highly calculating artists who know the value of simplicity.

Primitive or Epic Acting

During the later centuries of the Roman Empire, theatre activity was largely confined to farces, spectacles and light entertainments. Barbarian invaders and church fathers were able, in their different ways, to suppress drama for about five hundred years. But suppression was not destruction, and in the Middle Ages drama emerged again, largely as a folk activity, in both pagan and Christian forms. In churches the actors could get trained clerical help with playwriting, music and, to some extent, costumes, but in general it was an amateur movement. It was also a drama for festival days: the actors lived ordinary lives but on annual occasions took upon themselves the role of Jesus or Herod, the King of May or the King of Fools. We know that a basically new style of acting was developed, because there were no star actors, no acting companies, little training and little criticism; the actors also performed a new kind of play that presented, not a crisis or climax, but a narrative or panorama. The actor did not have to draw all attention to himself, but mark sharply and forcefully a certain part of an emblematic picture, or stand for one figure in a narrative, so that the audience observed what happened rather than felt sympathetically with the persons involved. The directly affective language used for moments of great feeling in many of the medieval miracle plays shows that these actors were capable of emotional performances; but the brevity of these incidents and the simplicity of expression for individual thought and feeling, also show that these potentially intense moments were not dwelt upon, not built up to provide overwhelming sensations of individual involvement.

In a new sense the actor created his part: he assumed a few clear indications of his role and its relation to other characters in the drama and allowed these signs to speak for his 'character'. Herod had a loud voice and raged; devils were black and often had tails and carried pitch-forks; the souls of the blessed had white, skin-tight coverings, and so on. Characters presented themselves clearly and were able to address explanatory comments to the audience in pauses of dramatic action; indeed such explanation was part of the dramatic experience.

When, during the fifteenth and sixteenth centuries, professional troupes of actors began to perform, they at first kept the same style of acting. We can observe a highly developed vehicle for such performances in the plays of Christopher Marlowe. Now speeches are elaborate, but still not subtle or intriguing like Shakespeare's: the colours of speech are primary, and elaboration derives from the arrangement of different responses one after another, each in itself simple, hard, direct. Marlowe's visual elaboration has an emblematic clarity rather than Shakespearian atmosphere: Tamburlaine dressed in black, standing with drawn sword beside the golden hearse of Zenocrate, rather than the alert darkness (with owl-hoots and thunder) of Macbeth's castle, or the light, wayward freedom of Arden, or the formal manners of *The Merchant of Venice*. Marlowe has heroes, but sequence of events and plan of the action are always more significant in his plays than any of their characters can realize; the audience must witness and consider a process or picture, rather than share with the principal character in a progressively intense, emotional and intellectual experience. (Only at the end of *Faustus* does Marlowe use a more expressive, 'Shakespearian' style.)

In the present century, important elements of this epic style have been rediscovered, almost single-handed, by Bertolt Brecht. For his own company in Berlin, he took actors before they had completed their studies at conventional acting schools; they trained by working on productions. He distinguished his own style partly by opposition to Aristotle and partly by insisting that the audience must be encouraged to observe a picture of the world, to 'face something', rather than be drawn into the exceptional experience of an exceptional man. Brecht did not want his actors to 'cook up' emotional sensations that would 'carry away' the imagination of the audience, but to represent or retell events accurately, and from the juxtaposition of almost independent episodes to create a subtle, challenging imitation of life. He did not want to mix laughter and tears, or to hide a character's basic reaction until the end of a play. He wanted full, bright, even stage lighting, no half-lights. In rehearsal, Brecht sought economical 'gestures' that would express the characters' response unambiguously and he pared down responses until at each moment they were as simple as possible. With clarity, he gained a strong story-line, sudden changes of fortune, an elaborate and provocative succession of different views, and what he called *Spass* – which might be translated as sport, fun, energy, vitality.

With Brecht and with early Renaissance and medieval drama to help us, we can define the primitive or epic actor. He is clear, vigorous, emblematic. He 'stands for' a character, instantly recognizable and yet efficient as one part of a wide picture or narrative. He works for each episode as it occurs, and neither lays subtle traps for the audience nor leads them by the ears and eyes towards a long-prepared emotional climax. He is much less 'special' as a human individual than the classical or virtuoso actor; but he is efficient and keen; he is observant of human behaviour and able to choose and reproduce salient elements from what he has seen, one after another. (He is not unlike a cartoonist.)

Psychologically Expressive Acting

Euripides and Shakespeare made new demands on actors by asking for prolonged manifestation of conflicting emotions. For their plays, neither truth to observed behaviour nor emotional power is sufficient. Possibly their writings were in advance of their actors' powers of expression; certainly no criticism of plays or performances that was written before the eighteenth century gives any indication of the subtle psychological interest that during the last two centuries has been – and continues to be – discovered in them. In England, Macklin, Garrick, Kean, Macready and Irving were the principal agents for exploring in their rehearsals and performances the opportunities for establishing an astonishing depth of psychological reality. Shakespeare's tragedies were the established basis for this new kind of acting, but melodramas and plays with classical pretensions also provided these actors with vehicles especially conceived to show off their powers.

The new actors were highly individual, lacking the polish and all-round accomplishment that were the classical ideals; and each of them discovered his own, challenging interpretation of well-worn roles: Garrick's Hamlet was active, Irving's thoughtful; Kean's Macbeth fiery, Macready's agonized, Irving's fearful. According to Macready, the chief part of acting was to

> fathom the depths of character, to trace its latent motives, to feel its finest quiverings of emotion, to comprehend the thoughts that

are hidden under words, and thus possess one's self of the actual
mind of the individual man.

Both Garrick and Irving were criticized for faulty verse-speaking,
but their defenders argued that they alone among their contemporaries spoke as if they had felt the need to speak the words they
uttered. They were concerned above all with motivation, and
moments of emotion and physical tension – known for a time as
'points' – became more important then the slow building up of
climactic sensations:

> Where Hamlet says to his interposing friends: 'I say, away,' – then
> turning to the Ghost, 'Go on, I'll follow,' Garrick's variation from
> extreme passion to reverential awe is so forcibly expressed in eyes,
> features, attitude, and voice, that every heart must feel. Where the
> Queen says the Ghost is but the 'coinage of your brain,' his turning
> short from looking after the apparition with wildness of terror, and
> viewing his mother with pathetic concern, is most happily executed.

Actors began to look for occasions to 'play against the text', to
suggest an 'inner action' or 'subtext' that could not be expressed
through words or even through physical actions. Irving's scene
with Ophelia was a notorious example of this, for he played it as
a love-scene with a tenderness that Hamlet dared not make
explicit in words.

As a consequence of such psychological expressiveness, actors
became more interested in apparently unconsidered actions, small
details of behaviour that might betray otherwise hidden concerns.
Records of Garrick's performances provide examples as, once
more, in his Hamlet when the Ghost re-appears in his mother's
closet:

> Hamlet immediately rises from his seat affrighted; at the same time
> he contrives to kick down his chair, which, by making a sudden
> noise, it was imagined would contribute to the perturbation and
> terror of the incident.

In fact it was soon found that small details of this sort could help
the general impression of the scene. At the end of the nineteenth
century, the actor's concern with expression of complex motivation became part of a new 'realistic' movement in drama.
Throughout Europe, theatres vied with each other in giving an
impression of real-life on the stage, and about the same time
Constantin Stanislavski, familiar, as a Russian actor and director,

with a debased classical tradition, began to describe the various ways an actor could train himself to present an 'inner truth' and varying degrees of outward realism.

Stanislavski's influence has been so widespread that any attempt to understand contemporary acting should begin with a study of his works. He was concerned, like the classicists, with voice, movement, tempo, physical efficiency and so forth and recommended the actor to practise dancing, fencing, acrobatics and other physical skills. But he was an innovator in that he wanted the actor to be trained in feeling as much as in the means to express it: mind, will and emotions had to come under the same sort of control as the actor's voice and body. He devised exercises to strengthen the actor's power of imagination – his ability to imagine in rehearsal that what is meant to be happening on stage is happening and so to realize all its implications: what are the effects of thinking, for instance, 'I have failed to place that ladder against the wall six times, and do not know why', or 'I have just escaped death at the hands of my brother'? He taught actors to consider the 'Magic If' – to imagine and react to a dramatic situation by considering a close analogy of it: few actors have escaped death at the hands of their brothers but many might get close to the appropriate reactions by considering the situation *as if* it were made up of one or more of less extraordinary events, *as if* the character had escaped with his life in a road accident, or, because imagination can change the scale and colour of an event, *as if* he had nearly been pushed, or had nearly walked, off a precipice or *as if* his brother, as a child, had stolen a cherished toy. In framing his exercises, Stanislavski was influenced by the psychological thought of Pavlov; this is especially apparent in his use of mental associations to train emotional memory. When an actor had to feel in a certain way, Stanislavski encouraged him to remember an incident from his past that had aroused analogous responses. His task was not to recreate feeling, but to remember the circumstances that gave rise to it. He was told to become quiet and relaxed, and then rethink where he was at the time of the incident, what he was wearing, who else was there, the time of year and of day, the colours of the objects involved, their shape and size; and so, by consciously becoming aware of the context for feeling, the feeling might again be released. After repeating this exercise many times, the actor became able to simplify the process so that remembering only one apparently trivial item might do the trick – perhaps the appearance of a specific tree-trunk with the sun striking it at a certain angle could recreate a highly-charged feeling of desperation, because the perception and feeling were at one time accidentally co-existent.

Stanislavski also devised exercises for concentrating an actor's attention at will and for strengthening his belief in stage fictions – for giving the impression that cold tea is whisky or deadly poison, or that the stage is the top of a mountain. He taught actors to become more conscious of their own temperamental equipment, how to retain a hidden conscious control in emotional crises, how to 'act with others' on stage, how to maintain the expression of contrary emotions – in this instance to effect, what Brecht was soon to despise, the mingling of tears and laughter.

With Stanislavski a long line of psychological actors reached a new consciousness of ends and means. His kind of actor was working to reveal the usually hidden battleground of human consciousness – in its subtleties and simplicities, power and helplessness, blindness and momentary clarity, isolation and openness, and even in its boredom and stunning irrationality – and, in order to reveal all this, the actor had first to discover and, then, master his own inward nature. Instead of classic strength and shapeliness, he sometimes had to appear weak and imprecise; instead of epic objectivity and firmness, he often relied on subjectivity, sensitivity, or imprecision.

IV.   STAGE DESIGN

IN A THEATRE we are sometimes conscious only of the actor, his eyes or tone of voice, and sometimes we lose all distinction between stage and reality, and are aware only of a projection of our own imaginings. On these occasions, we react so intensely that we ourselves seem to create what we see and hear, shape it to satisfy our own desires; or else we think and feel for the character, there, on the stage as if he had no separate existence. It is tempting to believe that at such moments nothing counts but the dramatist, the actor and us, and that the theatre provides a direct and unimpeded interplay of consciousness between all three. But this is too simple a view: the strength of the drama is that, even at its most private or impersonal, the theatrical experience is established through all the senses; it takes command of our imagination by controlling every possible response. Even if the actor stands upon bare boards, dressed as one of us, at a level with our own eyes and in the same daylight, we are affected by more than him: the shape of the boards, the exact cut of his clothes, the direction of the sun or the rain. There is always a complicated situation and, at some point in the performance, a multiple response. Everything counts in the theatre: nothing is wholly neutral. Our ability to focus entirely on the eyes or words of a single actor comes after we have been aware of a much wider context and of conflicting reactions. And this complex preparation controls the way we respond at the moment of greatest simplicity.

So it is necessary to talk about stage design. By this I mean much more than what is usually called 'a stage design', that is a small illustration of a stage set, without actors, lighting or third dimension, and incapable of modification. Neither do I mean a model stage with puppet figures and mechanical devices, nor choice of style, period and colour-scheme. Stage design is more than a background for performance or a machine for acting on. It includes the use that is made of individual actors in a comprehensive theatrical performance, and how it speaks to an audience by shape, weight, scale, light, line, rhythm, texture, colour, sound, smell, and by changes and interactions of all these elements.

A stage designer has an enormous and crucial task. Change the dress of the hero, or give him a dead white face, and *Hamlet* is a different play. And a single costume will help one actor, hinder another. Keep Hamlet close to his fellow characters whenever possible by restricting the effective floor area, and the emotional pressures suggested by the play in action will be different from those on a spacious stage. Alter the lighting, and a scene played, word for word and move by move, in exactly the same way as when the audience was helpless with laughter, can cease to be funny.

The first task of a stage designer is to know his play, actors, theatre and audience, and the second to get some idea of what he wants to happen in general and, as yet, impractical terms. He does not always attempt this basic conceptual work, but where he neglects his task others take over from him – actors, theatre architect, stage manager, business manager, or, more usually in the theatre today, the play's director. Somehow every production gets a design, an over-all physical composition, whether it comes about through compromise, collaboration, luck, the survival of the strongest, or the judgement of a single mind.

In the seventeenth, eighteenth and nineteenth centuries, the stage designer shared his task with the principal actors. This was partly dictated by the form and lighting arrangements of the theatres then in use. The platform stage on which the actors performed was so far separated from the stage-space used for displaying scenery, so much closer to the audience and so much better lit, that the 'scene painter', as he was then called, worked for his own ends and was chiefly responsible for providing an informative and sometimes noble, sumptuous or fanciful background for the play's acting. The principal actors frequently chose their own costumes and ordered their own movements, so that much of the stage design was in their hands. The audience was impressed by an unpeopled picture or made at home by a familiar background, but then it was caught up in the actors' exhibition of dominating personalities. At times these two kinds of entertainment were varied by elaborate group spectacles of dance, procession, combat or ceremony, or by trick-effects like moving scenery or trap-door entries.

In the Middle Ages and early Renaissance, before elaborate, indoor theatres were built, stage design was similarly dominated by the actors, but within traditional settings. Plays were performed 'within', rather than 'in front of', their settings, for those elements that changed from production to production were mostly three-dimensional – large, practicable objects, or 'properties', rather than painted cloths giving a complete picture. They had general significance and could be used, variably, time and again: tomb, arbour, tree, fountain, throne, bed, table, 'study', city or prison gates, 'hell mouth'. Sometimes they were not practicable but representative (or iconographic), such as sun, moon, mountain, 'city of Jerusalem', 'the Red Sea'. Hand properties and costumes were especially prominent against the unchanging background of the stage: spears, swords, armour, liveries, surplices, boots, nightgowns, chains of office, even rings – the plays of the period are full of specific references to such items. Often simple and large physical gestures were of crucial importance for the design of a scene, such as embracing, kneeling, disrobing, fighting with fist or weapon, rites of wedding, funeral or homage. Some theatres at this time had two or more stages, set one above the other, and then the actors' ascent and descent added to the general shape of a production. In this age the dramatist probably had almost as much hand in designing a production as the actors, for his words and the action they implied controlled the use of traditional equipment and costume, and of the dominant movement and activity of each play.

In the theatre of Æschylus, Sophocles and Euripides, the dramatists had unrivalled control. We know that he could design costumes and perhaps scenery; he might direct the acting, choreograph the movements of his chorus, compose the music and also be chief actor in his own play. Crucial in the design of a play were the masks worn by the actors – of which many illustrations have survived – and the movements of the chorus on the vast circular orchestra which presented, as a circus ring, an unchanging background for group patterns, individual movements and attitudes, and eloquent empty space.

But it is our own theatres, with their sophisticated lighting, stage machinery and acoustic equipment, that have made actors, dramatists, managers and audiences more conscious than ever before of the problems and opportunities of stage design. With improved gas lights, 'lime light' and then electrical switchboards controlling hundreds of infinitely variable circuits with computerised exactitude, the actor has become part of a three-dimensional picture than can change colour, perspective or form every minute; a single face or hand, can be given a 'high' light; the sun or moon may appear to rise or set; the whole stage can seem to be under water. With the invention of electric lifts and hoists, electrically propelled trucks and radio-controlled, free-moving pieces of scenery, every object placed on the stage by the designer has become plastic, obedient to his will at any point in a drama. Stereophonic equipment reproduces the impression of sound coming from a great distance and from various sides of the stage, so than an actor can appear to be surrounded by crowds, a carnival, wildlife, or approaching footsteps through tall grass or over hard stone.

At first the new opportunities were greedily exploited to bring sensational realism to the theatre. At the end of the nineteenth century there were many productions with waterfalls, express trains, shipwrecks, snowstorms and macabre hauntings that compelled belief as if the events were real. An example of this comes from the last Act of Ibsen's *When We Dead Awaken* (1897-8):

> *A wild, broken mountain-top, with a sheer precipice behind. To the right tower snowy peaks, losing themselves high up in drifting mist. To the left, on a scree, stands an old tumbledown hut. It is early morning. Dawn is breaking; the sun has not yet risen . . . The mist closes tightly over the scene.* RUBEK *and* IRENE, *hand in hand, climb upwards over the snowfield to the right, and soon disappear into the low clouds.*
>
> *Sharp gusts of wind hunt and whine through the air. . . .*
>
> *Suddenly a roar like thunder is heard from high up on the snowfield, which rushes down, whirling, at a fearful pace.* RUBEK *and* IRENE *are glimpsed momentarily as they are whirled round in the snow and buried beneath it.*

At other times an historical occasion or notable piece of architecture would be meticulously re-created, so that the audience had the sensation of 'being there'. The world outside the theatre could also be brought inside, often a part that was unfamiliar to the majority of the audience; here, for example, is part of the first stage-direction in Gorki's *The Lower Depths*, first performed at the Moscow Art Theatre in 1902:

> *A cellar resembling a cave. The ceiling is heavy with smoky stone vaulting and falling plaster. The light falls from the audience's side and down from above – from a square window on the right side. The right-hand corner is occupied by* PEPEL'S *room, fenced off with thin partitions; near the door into this room is* BUBNOV'S *plank bed. . . . Near the wall between the stone and the door is a wide bed covered with a dirty chintz canopy. . . . In the foreground near the left wall there is a block of wood with clamps on it and a little anvil fastened to it, and another block, shorter than the first. . . .*

And so on: the dramatist expects the stage-world to be precisely habitable by precisely realized characters; and everything must work and must be seen to have worked on previous occasions.

Most of the devices used at the close of the nineteenth century would seem ludicrously inefficient in our theatres. Occasionally we see a production reproducing, for example, the Blitz on London during the Second World War, but generally such transportation of an audience to a specific and complete reality has been left to the film-makers. The wonders of stage equipment are now put to other uses. Already in the eighteen-nineties, Adolphe Appia, a Swiss publishing in Paris and Munich, called for a new, plastic use of stage lighting to add expressiveness to stage design. He wanted light used like music, continuously, positively, and 'vividly'. Its task should not be confined to illuminating the acting area or reproducing the light effects of the real world, but it must also accentuate or transfigure chosen aspects of the stage-picture, evoke emotional responses directly, by colour, intensity, shift or focus; it can express an 'inner reality' and create its own world. Darkness so becomes a positive instrument as well as light, and the audience's attention can be held and developed without the actors moving or speaking, without an actor on the stage.

In his book, *Towards a New Theatre* (1913), Gordon Craig argued for a similar use of light by reproducing four drawings of a flight of steps: the steps do not change from one picture to another, but the light playing on them does and the disposition of a few figures. The emotional effect of each design is distinct and strong: light and gay; substantial; mysterious; weighty and tragic. Each is unmistakably theatrical, with the minimum of reference to real conditions of life.

As the structures set upon the stage became more plastic – more variable and controllable – so they were freed from the rules of perspective and normal proportion mattered less and the practicability of doors, windows and properties. Several locations could be shown on the stage simultaneously, each illuminated when needed for the action. Or, by the use of gauzes that could appear solid or transparent according to the light playing on them, one scene could 'dissolve' into another, transporting the action as far as China from Peru, palace from hovel, Settings were suggested by a single structure that was moved silently on to the stage, or given new prominence by a change of lighting. Bold simplifications were used, as a plain gold cloth brilliantly illuminated for a royal scene, or rigging and masts moving continuously from side to side for a ship at sea. Even costumes were made that were neither contemporarily nor historically 'correct'. For a production of *Hamlet* in Moscow, Craig designed Claudius the King in a vast gold robe that covered the full width of the stage, so that his courtiers looked out through holes in its glittering surface. More recently, in Brussels, the Czech designer, Svoboda, constructed a set for *Hamlet* with a great mirror hung across the stage at forty-five degrees to the perpendicular. He made the rectangular units which comprised the set capable of moving backwards and forwards to provide stairways, rooms, platforms, and even a bed, and all could be reflected in the giant mirror. So Elsinore, the world of the play, could be a compact level rectangular structure at the back of the stage above which the isolated figure of Hamlet was reflected as an accompanying ghost; or, with the various elements sent forward silently, it was a complex, geometric jigsaw, sometimes made oppressive by a further perspective in the suspended mirror. For a production of *King Lear* at Stratford-upon-Avon in 1956, Isamu Noguchi, a Japanese designer working usually in the United States, brought a succession of sharply coloured shapes on to the stage as a mobile support for the action: red diamonds, three times man-height, coming forward together for conflict, or a huge, black belly-shaped cut-out dropping downwards for the storm and so oppressing the stage.

Supernumaries – actors with no character names and little or no individual speech – that had served in the nineteenth century to fill out realistic or ceremonial crowd scenes, were now used to contribute to the plasticity and expressiveness of stage design. The German director, Max Reinhardt, was a master of this and combined a well-drilled crowd with lights, formally expressive settings and music in lavish productions of plays such as Sophocles' *Oedipus Rex* (1910), *Everyman* (1920) and, most notoriously, a new religious mime-drama, *The Miracle* (1911). His actors could sing, dance and speak in unison, and he set up special schools where they learnt the Eurythmic method of Jacques Dalcroze. Mass movements with contrasting gestures of single figures made bold visual effects, the whole sustained by a compelling rhythmic structure: often without words and with the total submergence of his actors' individualities, Reinhardt's stage-design evoked a sense of wonder and emotional intensity. Similar use of crowds and orchestrated sound and movement sustained the expressionist plays of the first decades of the nineteenth century in Germany, and elsewhere. The last scene of George Kaiser's *From Morn to Midnight* (1912) with its Salvation Army songs and anonymous responses will not respond to a realistic enactment but depends on rhythmic climaxes and a full, surging and controlled crowd design. Among the most memorable plays written in English in this manner are Eugene O'Neill's *Hairy Ape* and *The Emperor Jones* and the second Act of Sean O'Casey's *Silver Tassie*.

In Germany between the two World Wars, Erwin Piscator experimented further in the use of film in stage design. He discovered that he could enlarge the reference of the action by film shots of actual events and also speed narrative and exposition by the ease with which film cuts from one picture to another: he also gained a new kind of irony by counterstating the dramatic moment created by the actors with that of the film in the background. Again the designer had become directly and solely responsible for elements of the drama. His methods are now widely used, as in the projected still pictures and the captions and statistics recorded in flashing light bulbs at the back of Joan Littlewood's production of *O, What a Lovely War* (London, 1963): as the actors dressed as Pierrot-clowns perform sketches about the First World War, the reality of the situation is presented visually and silently in the stage setting. For Alfred Radok's production of Gorki's *The Last One* in Prague in 1965, Svoboda designed a setting far from the realistic one envisioned by the author. The interior of a house was transformed into a large sloping platform on which significant pieces of furniture were given a more than life-size representation – a huge dining-table, a monumental grandfather clock, a washtub and wide-spread chandelier. The acting had to become broad, or operatic, to fill the space, but subtlety came from two kinds of counterstatement: from military and romantic music played by a uniformed band in a balcony at the back of the stage surrounded by bright red theatrical curtains and from film shots projected on to the back wall of the stage-set showing incidents referred to in the text but supposed to happen off-stage – such as military business, pursuit, flagellation, rifle-shooting. The films also showed news-reel items of crowned heads in social gatherings and stills of family groups. The domestic and melodramatic play had been given social, political and emotional depth by stage design.

The new effectiveness of stage design has not always worked by main force. Stage designers have, however, a new confidence and ambition. They choose, now, from many possible styles and recognize the ramifications of their decisions in all parts of a production. Often they will simulate an old style of setting, especially for revivals of Molière, Shakespeare or other 'classics', but they add a fluid lighting scheme or crowd movements that give a changing 'atmosphere' or emotional support unknown to the original productions of these plays. If they wish to give a realistic impression to match subtle, psychologically expressive acting, they may restrict realism to hand properties, costume and make-up, and then set them and the actors within dead white, undecorated walls with intense unchanging lighting that throws the minutiae into sharp relief. Or they may restrict the colours used, as in John Bury's set for Harold Pinter's *Homecoming* (1965), where the living-room of a house in London was represented entirely in a dark bluey-grey: the setting was square, uniform, timeworn, solid and, yet, because of the diffused light and the spacious proportions, menacing, grand and empty, like a cold underground mausoleum.

The multiplicity of effects at the command of a stage designer has encouraged radical rethinking about the utility of each of them; and now dramatists and designers have also learnt to rely on simple but perfectly calculated means. Samuel Beckett's *Waiting for Godot* is an example of a play requiring the barest setting; the author asks simply for '*A country road. A tree. Evening*', and for his second and concluding Act: '*Next Day. Same Time. Same Place.*' The single tree is used repeatedly in the play and gains an iconographic importance like the large properties of the medieval stage; only here its significance is never limited by complete statement and varies from moment to moment; it is always, at least in part, simply 'A tree'. Still more recent playwriting and production techniques suggest that stage design can work primarily with actors alone, not in a crowd but as highly controlled, dancer-like individuals. In this kind of work, the designer, author and actors must work in closest accord; often they attend rehearsals together and the production evolves, in all its aspects, in the theatre where it will be performed, in a single process of design. The Living Theatre of New York, Jerzy Grotowski's Laboratory Theatre in Wroclaw, Poland, the plays of Ann Jellicoe, David Cregan and David Selbourne in England,

and the *Plays for Dancers* by the poet, W. B. Yeats in Dublin as early as 1916 and 1917, are various recent attempts at actor-dominated design; but troupes of itinerant actors of the Italian Commedia dell'Arte and other small sixteenth- and seventeenth-century troupes enjoyed, without making the conscious choice and without elaborate stage equipment, much the same conditions of work.

If the complex art of the theatre is to be fully responsible to creative idea and means of production, an intimate collaboration extending to all elements in the process of creation and production is the ideal situation in which even the most complicated theatrical work should be undertaken. In a few notable instances, as in Athens during the Golden Age, perhaps in Shakespeare's London and Molière's Paris, in Meyerhold's studio in Moscow before the First World War and in Brecht's productions of his own plays for the Berliner Ensemble after the Second World War, the theatre has sometimes come close to this unification of vision and effort. But economically it is difficult or impossible on a large scale today. Usually a co-ordinator, called a director, is brought in to impose unity and ensure fair play between the various artists.

V. PRODUCTION

THE PREPARATION of a dramatic entertainment demands co-
operation, freely given or enforced. The best and longest way is
through a combination of many talents in a common, original
enterprise: a free yet concerted interplay of individuals. But someone usually takes charge. Different ages have submitted to
different guidance: in the Greek theatre, to the author; in the
eighteenth century in England to the chief actor of a company, or
to a theatre manager; today, in commercial theatres, to the producer (sometimes known as 'impresario') and the director (in
some theatres confusedly called the 'producer').

Basic Decisions

In London or New York the first decisions are made now by the
producer, the man who controls theatre buildings, organizations
and, at first or second hand, finance. A production may start with
a theatre building that is available at a certain time, for a certain
period, or with an actor who wants a certain kind of part, or an
author who has written a new play. As these basic steps are taken
the nature of the ensuing production is already taking form. An
intimate or large theatre will influence acting style and choice of
play. A small cast can be given longer rehearsal period, but their
production will look and feel slight in a large theatre. If a play
is new in conception or manner, its producer will probably arrange
for a long out-of-town trial run, and undertake it only when he is
sure that he could bring another play in quickly to his main
theatre: the financial gamble of his enterprise will affect the
actors' attitudes to their roles, the amount of cash used for the
setting, the choice of director. Some productions are so safe –
currently popular stars, modish setting and clothes, an admired
contemporary author or a 'classic' that is both respectable and
the subject of fashionable talk, a new theatre building, a reliable
publicity campaign – that the play in performance has a gloss and
assurance that can defeat an author's attempt to surprise his
audience, or an actor's ability to exhilarate it.

Beside choosing directors, actors and theatre, the producer is
also responsible for hiring the designer, composer, musicians,

69

choreographer, lighting or special-effects consultants, front-of-house and publicity personnel, and so forth. He may consult both actors and director, but the responsibility is his, and involves far more than business talents: his ability to relate everything to a basic concept will affect the play in performance and is therefore an artistic talent. If he wishes to provide gay, light-hearted, fashionable, expensive entertainment, he must always be conscious of this; he must permit no deflection from this aim without careful consideration. Nowhere, in the most technical or commercial details of a production plan, can a producer afford to forget his imaginative involvement.

In today's commercial theatres most productions are unique enterprises, each mounted for its own sake, with no thought of a sequel. But the basic decisions are so many and difficult that producers tend to favour their own group of associates, technical and artistic, to give some continuity to their work and make choices easier. Non-commercial theatres, with permanent companies of actors and technical and business staff, have less ability to respond uniquely to each production, but gain in having established ways of working and, most important, of working together. It is a question whether the strength which comes from established associations is preferable to the excitement of unique productions. Most critics prefer permanent companies, despite the obvious dangers of mere routine and unsatisfactory adaption from the demands of one play to another. Large audiences, on the other hand, often prefer highly charged, 'special' productions, although these may well strive for immediate and sure-fire effect without deep consideration or the full possession of a common style of acting such as needs years of preparation.

Practical Work

Once the organization is complete, the director usually takes charge. There are various ways of starting. He may insist, first, on telling his assembled company about the play and about his own intentions in staging it: he will talk about themes, dramatic structure, plot, relevance to contemporary life or thought, acting style, excitement, emotion, interest; he may indicate where and how he hopes to make the major impact on the audience. Most directors will take a very early opportunity to show the company his designers' model of the set and sketches of their costumes. Or the director may sit the whole company around a table and have them read the play together, once, twice, many times. Some start by reading the play themselves, single-handed. Jean Vilar, when he was in charge of the Théâtre National Populaire in Paris, wrote in his book *de la Tradition Théâtrale* of the necessity for many reading rehearsals, about a third of the total number:

> Manuscript in hand, seat firmly planted on a chair, body in repose: thus the deepest sensibilities will gradually pitch themselves to the desired note, as the actor comes to understand, or feel, the new character that is to become himself.

Other directors start by 'getting the play moving', or 'blocking' it. This means that their conception is primarily pictorial and dynamic, and that they can gain co-operation best by moving their actors around like pawns, leaving the verbal and inward qualities of performance to grow slowly in response to the larger, visual effects, as much as to the text of the play.

There are probably as many ways of working as there are directors; and some vary from play to play, from one set of conditions to another. When there is a single star actor in the cast, who has long experience, perhaps in the very role which he is about to recreate, the director may well play a waiting game, keeping his company engaged in textual investigations or technicalities of movement while the central performance is established. On the other hand, the star might insist on a director revealing his hand first, as a stimulus to his own innovation. If a director has been given a play that requires specialized activities on stage with every appearance of actual life, such as army drill or the provision of food on a large scale for a restaurant (to take examples from Arnold Wesker's recent plays, *Chips with Everything* and *The Kitchen*), he may well start his actors with special physical training and visits to real-life barracks or kitchens; and he will probably follow this up with improvisations in which the actors explore the situations from which the play-text has selected only moments for exhibition. Sometimes a designer or composer may make such a large contribution to a production, that the director will begin by familiarizing his cast with their actual costumes or, perhaps, masks, or by making them listen time and again to the music, and then improvise to it with gesture and movement. When philosophical or political ideas must be clearly presented in a production, the director may initiate unscripted arguments between cast members, or improvised scenes in which they can take differing sides in a dispute, or move a single situation in turn to opposite conclusions. When authenticity to historical facts is required, work may begin with study of period costume, illustrations, furniture and buildings with little regard to the text of the play: for a production of Tolstoy's *Tsar Feodor,* Stanislavski took his principal actors on a protracted visit to museums and ancient cities, far from Moscow where the production was to be given. Such productions start by getting behaviour and appearance right.

Perhaps three main considerations govern all directors. First the need to co-ordinate and give unity. This may be ensured by pedantic attention to detail, as by William Poel's careful annotation of stress and pitch for each word in his controversial productions of Shakespeare and other classics at the beginning of this century. Or unity may come from a continuous insistence on a certain mood, tempo or range of gestures, as in Franco Zeffirelli's production of *Much Ado About Nothing* for the British National Theatre, which was predominantly buoyant, burlesque and operatic. Unity may be applied externally, by details unrelated to the actors' individual involvement with their roles or the implications of the author's text; but it is most secure when it is deeply rooted.

Secondly, a director must be able to help his actors, designer, composer, lighting consultant and every member of his team. He must evoke the best work they can give for the production in hand. He may bully or cajole, excite or suggest; and he may use one technique for one actor and the opposite for another in the same company and same production. Some directors accommodate their own view of individual roles (or even of the play itself) to the views and talents of the actors; some may appear to do so in order to awaken lively responses. Other directors work with military firmness, requiring exact and constant response to precise instructions to achieve a required sharpness or intensity. But whichever tactic is used, the overall strategy is the same: to use the assembled artists with appropriate fullness.

Thirdly a director must be responsible to his author, dead or alive. There are innumerable ways in which the author, through the play-text, can help in production. For example, Harold Pinter writes dialogue that is most carefully punctuated, not only with commas, full stops and so on, but with stage-directions reading '*Pause*' or '*A Silence*', and with division of speeches into paragraphs, the use of capital letters, italics and so forth. The actor will have these in his text and they should govern his reading of the lines, but the director can also use them as indications of stage-business and rhythms appropriate for the progress of a whole scene. Dramatists who write in verse have also given minute directions about the form of whole scenes at the same time as directing particular points of utterance, for the music of speech controls rhythm of action. Words repeated from scene to scene, often by different characters and in different situations or tempi, should also be heeded by the director if he wishes to co-ordinate the various performances along the lines of his author's imagination; even if he is engaged on an eccentric production that crosses his author's intentions, the director should be on the look out for such repetitions that might tend to pull the play back on to another course. In deciding on his principal aims for the production, the director must quarry carefully into the author's text, and also in discovering appropriate business, settings, acting styles.

Today the director is the most important man in many theatres: the governing idea behind each production is his, much of its stimulus, almost all its cohesion. The audience may not know him by sight, but it comes to know his style and often holds him responsible for success or failure. But, as we have already noticed the director's rise to power is comparatively recent, and it is open to abuse. He has too many tasks, for he is seldom a specialist in all branches of theatre work, and when he is, he seldom has the time to exercise his control on every detail. His shortcomings are most noticeable when he has not had the opportunity (or interest) to learn the techniques of acting at first hand; so he either leaves the more experienced actors on their own or else, if he has sufficient prestige, tries to impose performances on actors without giving sufficient consideration to their individual talents and the secret workings of their art. Very few directors are wholly pleased with their own work; but the exciting task of orchestrating such diverse resources has attracted dynamic personalities to the profession, and a few who seem endlessly sensitive, patient and demanding.

Final Preparations

After the basic decisions of interpretation and intention, of casting, design, music and acting-style have all been made, and everyone set upon his task, a play begins to develop in rehearsal. It is like a suit of clothes being given life by being worn, or a tree being clothed with leaves, or a person, who is formerly known only from correspondence, gradually becoming known through repeated meetings. Or we may consider the play-text as a painter's first outline, and the rehearsal period as the process of working up to the finished painting which will follow the original sketch but add colour, light and texture, obscure some details and heighten others; add figures and lines, or indicate perspectives and establish backgrounds that were not represented before.

Each of these comparisons omits the gathering excitement of last rehearsals, the cohesive life and assurance that come through realizing the inherent truth in the intellectual, emotional and physical co-operation within the time and space of the play's enactment. A production stands or falls by the last week or so of preparation; only then can everyone engaged in the enterprise begin to judge what they have achieved by their unique, corporate effort. In earlier rehearsals details have been worked out without regard to tempo, or size of performance, so that several 'run-throughs' are now required to adjust balance from scene to scene and ensure continuity of interest and interpretation. There will be dress rehearsals to add many practical problems which would have been daunting in earlier rehearsals when the actors were still discovering what, precisely, they wished to do at each moment. During the last few days, when the physical tasks grow ever more complex, many directors call simple 'text rehearsals' in which the cast moves easily through the play, simply reproducing its words and movements, with gestures and business only lightly indicated; so the actors refresh their knowledge of the play as a whole by limiting their particular concerns. During such relaxed rehearsals, surprising and eloquent new business, new relationships between characters, or new verbal interpretations are often discovered. Then, when conditions permit, there will be several 'preview' performances before invited audiences in which actors can gauge the effectiveness of every detail of their performances and the director can make yet again readjustments of tempo, balance and co-ordination.

So a production reaches its first night. Thereafter it will 'settle down' by small, often unconsidered adaptions until it 'works' efficiently and, if all goes well, with an immediate response to the audience of each successive night.

VI. TELEVISION DRAMA

CAN DRAMA as an art take place only in direct contact with an audience in some kind of theatre?

Film and theatre are easily identifiable as two different art-forms. The one reproduces what the camera has seen on a two-dimensional screen, adding some aural accompaniment, the other allows an audience to see, hear and, to some extent, share what actually takes place before it. Moreover, a film is assembled out of many small elements in the cutting-room, whereas a theatrical entertainment is witnessed as a continuous performance in which occasional mistakes, inventions or happy accidents all have a part as they arise, without intervention. No one could mistake even a second of film, for a second from a theatrical performance. But for television the distinctions have been obscured. What should we think of a medium that can reproduce a continuous series of pictures of a theatrical performance taken by cameras in a theatre during an actual performance?

Some commentators claim that television is a close relative to the theatre, much nearer tied than film. But this may well be wishful thinking: television is rich and popular, while theatre is in financial difficulties, due to rising labour costs, insufficient advertisement, difficulty of centralizing effort and organization, and lack of a popular, let alone mass, audience. If television could be claimed as a relation, the poorer cousin might benefit.

Certainly in the early days of television there were remarkable family likenesses. The actors were nearly all theatre-trained – film actors were then too expensive. Moreover, before the introduction of videotape recordings, which allow scenes to be edited as if they were on film and whole programmes to be assembled in the cutting-room, dramas were often transmitted live, giving one continuous and unedited performance taking place in one studio, as if it were a stage. But now those conditions are fast disappearing as far as major productions are concerned, and telerecordings are more the rule than the exception. Further means for cheap, and therefore extensive, editing are being developed. With camera and editor dominant, television's family ties seem much closer to film, than to theatre.

It has been argued that since a television screen is small and the sound which accompanies the pictures can be life-size, it is a less visual medium than film and one whose reliance on the spoken word is much closer to theatre. But even this resemblance may soon be developed out of existence with new forms of projection television for domestic use that could enlarge the picture to a size that would dominate any ordinary living-room. Already the Ediphor projection unit will allow television on a cinema-size screen in any large hall or cinema.

Assuredly television has to make its own distinct way. The intimacy and familiarity, in which it is usually viewed, make different demands from cinemas and their large audiences sitting in rows in the dark. The disturbances to which its reception is subjected (as the ordinary routines and little surprises of domestic life take place in the same room) force those who work in television to relate all they do to ordinary family life: the length of each programme must be limited; fantasy must be curtailed or else disbelief will follow quickly by comparison with the domestic competition; tension must build up quickly and sharply; complicated exposition must be avoided, so that a programme can make an immediate impact whenever it is switched on. Any one programme has to stand in sequence with others, so that an invented drama is viewed immediately after news-reels of disasters in India or poverty on the other side of town. These have sometimes been viewed as disadvantages, as it was once considered regrettable that film was not three-dimensional. Rather they are opportunities for television to discover its own forms and unique achievements.

time
of switching-on

VII. CRITICISM AND STUDY

Writing and thinking about what happens in a theatre cannot be easy. Words do not easily cover the subject. Imagine a critic of painting trying to write a book about Giorgione or Giotto without being able to reproduce a sheaf of photographs of the paintings to which he refers, whole reproductions and enlargements of important details. Imagine the same critic being unable to refer his reader to a single picture by his artist: the theatre critic is almost in that position, because the performance he saw is almost certainly not that which his reader has seen. Moreover, the theatre critic is faced with more than a visual problem: he must also write about the passing of time, about tempi and rhythms, simple and complex: and he must respond to the complicated, intimate and always changing art of individual actors.

The basis for much writing about theatre is textual. On the printed page one element of theatrical experience is held steady for our attention. A huge library of books about dramatic texts has accumulated, at an every-increasing rate. There are analytical studies, taking words, images, themes, narrative structure, argument and character, and the actions and settings as described in dialogue and stage-directions, and subjecting some or all of these elements to count, description, comparison, division into smallest particles. Mostly these studies are directed to old plays; examples of Shakespearian analytical criticism are A. C. Bradley, *Shakespearian Tragedy* (1905), R. B. Heilman's *This Great Stage: Image and Structure in 'King Lear'* (1948) and L. C. Knights, *Some Shakespearean Themes* (1959).

Texts can also be studied historically, looking for meanings now lost through the passage of time and seeking to place each play in its own age and in the development of its author and of drama and literature generally. Shakespearian examples are Lily B. Campbell, *Shakespeare's 'Histories': Mirrors of Elizabethan Policy* (1947), and Muriel Bradbrook, *Shakespeare and Elizabethan Poetry: a study of his earlier work in relation to the Poetry of the Time* (1951).

Thirdly, and most prolific, is the study of texts for what they awaken in the mind of the reader. Often the fact that they are texts of plays is forgotten, but sometimes, in the mind's eye of the critic, the words have awakened a three-dimensional, imaginary life. When practised by a poet like Coleridge, or a man of widest culture like Samuel Johnson, this criticism has value long out-lasting its own age, for what it tells us concerning the critic as much as for its dramatic enlightenment.

Many scholars, apprehensive about considering only verbal texts, have tried to study theatrical conditions in general and in particular. There have been antiquarian reconstructions, such as W. Beare's *The Roman Stage* (1964) or Allardyce Nicoll's *Masks, Mimes and Miracles* (1931). Enid Welsford's *The Fool* (1935) tries to reconstruct the impact of one dramatic character-type in a wide setting of time and space. A full-scale modern study of particular theatrical conditions is John Willett's *The Theatre of Bertolt Brecht* (1959) which has chapters on 'Theatrical Practice', 'Music' and 'Theatrical Influences', as well on the ideas and sub-ject matter of individual plays. Perhaps the detailed nature of this reconstructional approach makes particular study the most fruitful, but there have also been general works on the conditions of theatrical art, such as Harley Granville-Barker's *On Dramatic Method* (1931), Stark Young's *The Theatre* (1927) and, more recently, Eric Bentley's *The Life of the Drama* (1964).

No firm division can be made between scholarly study of theatre conditions and memoirs, personal views and manifestos. Gordon Craig's *On the art of the theatre* (1911) and his life of *Henry Irving* (1930) both represent most strongly the author's developing understanding of the theatre and his hopes for it. Stanislavski's *My Life in Art* (1924) is both autobiography and a kind of running argument with himself; it is the most accessible of his works.

In all these ways, the critic uses a single mode of inquiry or establishes a single point of view. But the complexity of theatrical art necessitates such self-denial in critic and student, and good books on theatre are usually limited books.

The most obvious limitation is to write about single performances, which is the way in which the dramatic critics of newspapers work. Journalists are, of course, concerned with news and have to make rapid judgements in order to provide copy in time for the printers but, among the most readable books about theatre which give some impression of the excitement and overall effects of plays in performance, collected reviews are often the most rewarding. James Agate's *The English Dramatic Critics* (1933) or A. C. Ward's *Specimens of English Dramatic Criticism* (1945) will give a taste of their quality. George Bernard Shaw's *Our theatre in the 90's* is especially alive with a dramatist's instinct. More recent collections worth study are Harold Hobson's *Theatre* and *Theatre 2* (1948 and 1950), Kenneth Tynan's *Curtains* (1961), John Mason Brown's *Dramatis Personae* (1963) and, with unusual carefulness, Stark Young's *Immortal Shadows* (1947).

If there is any form of writing about theatre that needs to be encouraged, I think it is extended, considered reviewing. Occasionally a critic can write about a single production twice or even three times, as it moves from one theatre to another. But if he could see it many times, keeping touch with first impressions, and so compare one night's performance with another, and relate every detail of the production to every detail of the published text and, perhaps, to records of other productions; if he could assess an actor's performance in the light of his career as a whole, and compare the director's achievement with the designer's or the chief actor's; and if this critic had time to consider what the journalistic reviewers have said and what explanations of intention the artists have published, and time to consider what the production has achieved in his own consciousness and to relate this to his personal views about man, society and life and to the views of others – then the critic might have found a full and careful way to study and criticize one theatrical experience. (As far as I know, this recipe has never been followed.)

VIII. TRAINING FOR DRAMA

ANYONE WHO wishes to start work in the theatre will need help. In the past the young actor learnt his art from a formal or informal apprenticeship, by close and prolonged association with an established performer or by keeping his eyes and ears open while in a very junior or menial position in a theatre company. Today specialized schools and colleges offer courses in acting, design, stage management, direction, and administration. Universities have drama departments and the Arts Council of Great Britain and private foundations, like the Rockefeller or Gulbenkian, provide opportunities for apprentice directors, designers and managers.

There are many ways of training an actor, but all have to take into account certain facts: the complexity of the art, the need for learning by practice, individually and in a group, the importance of individual imagination and initiative, the advantage of starting basic training in voice, music and, especially, movement at a very early age so that regular and continuous development is comparatively easy.

Then there are practical difficulties, the chief of which is that teachers of acting are very scarce. Someone is needed who is an actor: French can only be taught by someone who can speak the language, or swimming by someone who can float. There are all kinds of physical and psychological difficulties in the path of a student of acting – fears to be overcome, unexpected reactions to recognize, a considerable number of difficult feats to do at one moment, with precision and confidence. Unless the teacher has experience of these tasks, which often present themselves as intense crises with emotional and physical side-effects, he will be unable to help. Of course, he cannot do the job for his student; but he must understand the lonely predicament.

In Elizabethan days some of the chief actors of a company were responsible for one or two apprentices. But this seems impracticable today: the necessary permanence for such an arrangement is missing from our commercial theatres and few actors have time or interest for such work. Some schools use part-time staffs, so that the teachers can continue to be active in their profession;

but such arrangements often lead to divided loyalties because actors cannot afford to remain faithful to their students if a new and attractive theatre engagement offers itself. There are advantages in learning from a succession of teachers – the student can choose for himself from a great variety of methods – but these cannot replace the long-recognized need for a 'master', one whose knowledge of the student is as complete and intimate as possible and, more important, whose interest continues throughout his development.

Then there is the question – 'What kind of acting should be taught?' It is not easy, perhaps not possible, for a young student to become proficient in every style of acting that directors look for. Some theatre managers, such as Peter Hall of the Royal Shakespeare Company, have said that it hardly matters which school a young actor has been to, because on joining his company everything has to be learnt afresh; and if the schools taught his way, the students would be unfitted for engagements in other companies, and in productions by other directors. The best solution would seem to be a school that introduced students to all kinds of acting and then allowed them to specialize in one: the difficulties here would be that the student might easily choose wrongly, being attracted by a teacher rather than recognizing the method that suited himself best, and that he might choose a style that was in little demand.

Everyone who works in a theatre should know about acting, the centre of every production, and that is why it is best to start by learning to act, whatever the student's ultimate ambition. Unfortunately, this is not always possible. Many schools of stage design, for instance, are quite separate from schools of acting, and there are courses in management and direction which have little or no opportunity for learning anything else. A course in administration which does not give an introduction to the nature of the machine that is being operated must be incomplete and dangerously out of touch with the realities of theatre work. That stage design should be taught in studios and workshops, with only drawing-boards, models, tailor's dummies and never-used stage sets on which to practise, encourages an unreal, improper attitude to the play-texts, to which all design must be responsible, and to ways of working in a theatre; such schools will not teach a young designer to help actors and directors.

E.T.—4

The best training for the theatre may seem to be in association with a permanent company, so that students can relate what they learn to actual, full-scale productions. This is the pattern in many European countries, where each State Theatre has its own school. But it is open to abuse, noticeably in a tendency to waste students' time in 'spear-carrying' – that is filling out crowd scenes – in long-running productions. Every actor must be able to 'stand on the stage' as an inconspicuous part of a large picture, but students also need to develop their imaginations by attempting large roles, and their confidence and control by holding the stage alone. Too much work as a supernumerary can retard growth at the most important levels. In my view, the best solution is the provision of a theatre for each school, full-scale and in a prominent position in the town. During a student's final year, he could then take parts of various sizes and kinds in a continuous repertoire, and so relate what he knows, and what he has become, to nearly normal conditions while still attempting larger roles than he will get in his first professional engagements and still being in touch with his teachers should he need them. The productions in such a theatre should not be directed by those who have trained the student, so that a proper self-reliance is developed. Acting is the most individual of arts, for its instrument is an individual human being, and therefore the student must be encouraged to create the actor that only he can be. His training should help him to understand both the responsibilities and scope of his art; he then needs large opportunities and he must face them by himself.

Universities also provide a useful setting for training. One of the limitations of the stage as a profession at the present time is the self-absorption of many who work in it: they seem to have interest in nothing but the theatre and become 'stagey' or, in a derogatory sense, 'theatrical'. In a school devoted solely to the theatre arts, a student may become specialized too soon, whereas in a university his contemporaries will be reading literature, sociology, law, medicine, mathematical physics, and the whole range of undergraduate courses. A university student of theatre will gain a view of himself in the world at large and be prompted to ask why he wants to be an actor and what use he will be compared with fellow students who are preparing for life in quite different ways.

Most teachers of theatre arts will ask themselves whether they are providing too many entrants for an over-supplied profession. Far more young people want to train than can be accepted in the existing schools and university departments, and unemployment in the profession is notoriously high. Should only a few pupils be admitted each year?

My own opinion is that more, not fewer, should be trained, or at least start as student actors. Only after a year or two can talent be measured adequately and often gifted actors have not shown their power until a final term or in the year after they have left their school. That is one reason for not applying the axe at the beginning. But a still more persuasive reason should be that training for drama can provide a fully humane education, especially if work centres on acting and is undertaken in a context, like a university or group of schools, where students mix with others with different interests. Training for theatre is physical as well as intellectual, involving doing as well as reading and thinking. It is visual as well as verbal; co-operative as well as individual. Theatre students live very much in the present, for the sake of each production as it is rehearsed and played before actual audiences, and they are also in contact with the past as they seek to recreate the finest plays of earlier ages. They make the words of great poets in some sense their own, so that their thoughts seem to borrow the vigour and colour of Shakespeare's or Sophocles': in this way they learn by collaboration and imitation, and so are influenced in the deepest parts of their beings. Best of all, the theatre student cannot be over-reliant on his teachers: he is repeatedly and responsibly alone, in rehearsal and performance, having to make what he says and does effectively his own; his teachers cannot be content with mere repetition of words and actions learnt in class – that, unmistakably, is not good acting.

I sometimes think that all education should be a little like training for the theatre. Pupils should know and control their minds and bodies, be able to work with others and to develop their individual imaginations; their minds should be open to a great variety of ideas and their sympathies to the wide range of human life: all this the student of acting must attempt.

IX. FUTURE THEATRE

THIS MUST be a short chapter. But it is essential in a book about drama, the art that must always be made anew; and especially pertinent at a time when, according to some assessors, there may be no future for the theatre.

In 1959 the Arts Council published a report on *Housing the Arts in Great Britain* which showed how many theatres were being closed or demolished. In 1936 there were nearly sixty full-sized theatres in London; between then and 1958, eighteen went out of use, and four small, private theatres. A further report on the English provinces, published in 1961, showed the same trend and a growing reluctance of managements to send out the touring companies that had been an important source of theatrical entertainment until just before the Second World War. In the 1960s a few new theatres have been built and companies established but almost daily, in the national and provincial press, there are pleas for financial help, news of resignations, articles on the plight of writers, and new and old companies and of the growing estrangement from the theatre of all but 5 to 10 per cent of the population. The same story is true, with local variations, in other countries, except that where television is not widely available the downward trend is less marked.

Obvious questions must be asked. Can television and film replace theatre? Are these new media the right ones for our new electronic age? Can new buildings, new organizations, new plays, new staging and production techniques, new acting styles make theatre boom again? Should theatre be content to satisfy minority taste and think in small scale, or should all-out effort and large subsidies be used to mount vast productions and build up-to-date palaces for the patrons of drama? Should we support permanent companies, or encourage expensive, individual, long-running productions, or create small, experimental theatre groups?

In earlier ages whole towns have stopped work so that the populace could attend a theatrical entertainment: could this happen again? How would you persuade someone who had not been inside a theatre since his schooldays – and there are many of these, probably your next-door neighbour – to try again? An if he did take your advice, do you think that what he saw would make him want to return on his own account?

My answer to that last question – would a visit to the theatre win a new theatre-goer? – is that ten to one, perhaps a hundred to one, it would not. That is a guess: statistics are not available. But it is a guess based on an appreciation of the innate conservatism of the theatre.

The theatre cannot easily change in response to new social, economic and ideological conditions. It nearly always wants to, but its mechanism is so complicated, involving so many different functionaries, that the basic reorganization and necessary redeployment can only be brought about slowly.

I believe that the theatre has a future because its art is so instinctive, so completely humane, so powerful and direct in impact that theatre is irreplaceable. But it must be truly effective. I think that continued support for organizations and techniques that were evolved in the pre-electronic age is folly: the horse-drawn carriage could not compete with the internal combustion engine. Society, finance, mass communication, work, thought, feeling and imagination have all changed basically in the first half of the twentieth century. Effort and public money should now be spent, in the sixties and seventies, largely on experiment: this is not a time for defending bastions, but for exploration and experimental application. We need new theatre companies, new plays, new design and equipment, new buildings and production methods, new ways of presenting old plays, and as always, new actors who can hold a mirror up to contemporary consciousness in its uncertainties and certainties.

How can these necessary experiments be made?

1. Small studio theatres are a prime requirement. Each should be given to a group of artists – director, designer, actors and, probably, author – to work consistently for one or two years with no obligation to show any production to the public for the first half of their tenure.

2. Established repertory companies and commercial managements should be given special grants for one or two productions each year, on which the director, designer and principal actors could spend three or four months, instead of the usual three or four weeks.

3. A technical, design and organizational team should be set up to investigate ways of making productions more transportable, using sound, lights, projected images and films to replace cumbersome three-dimensional sets; and then a company should be established to serve a group of theatres or other buildings, such as cinemas, that could receive these portable productions.

4. More acting schools and university departments of drama should be equipped and financed to offer a year's work to their graduates in theatres run for that purpose and for service of the public; see Chapter Eight, p. 82, above.

5. Research must be undertaken on many fronts. First, using techniques developed by sociologists, into audience habits and reactions, and the effects of various means of advertisement. Secondly into theatre practice in all aspects. In Great Britain, the study of acting, production, design, equipment and administration needs a specialized research institute, with its own journal and series of publications. Its practical work would need a small, simple theatre, with a permanent company freed from the task of serving the general public. Funds would also be needed to initiate theatrical productions in different social environments and various kinds of buildings. The Arts Council of Great Britain supports theatrical enterprise and establishes committees to discover how theatre operates in Britain today; but it cannot (or does not) initiate experiment, without which discovery, growth and new development are impossible.

SUGGESTIONS FOR FURTHER READING

STUDIES OF individual dramatists or plays are readily found in libraries, bibliographies and bookshops. But 'theatre books' are more difficult to trace: in libraries they are usually placed in a small section to themselves (often with a 'PN' reference, rather than the 'PR' used for dramatic and other literature); in bookshops they are often shelved alongside, or even among, 'Hobbies', 'Fine Arts', 'Professional' or 'Miscellaneous'. The lists that follow here give my own choice of books for following up the interests of each chapter in this book; they exclude studies of individual dramatists, plays and other more literary subjects.

Introduction

A brief, sensible, elegant and provoking general study is Stark Young's *The Theatre*, first published in New York in 1937 and reissued in paperback in 1954 by Hill and Wang; this is not an introduction, but a book that opens up wide views and attempts to clear the reader's mind.

Evidently one-sided and personal are the following theoretical and practical writings: C. Stanislavski, *My Life in Art* (1924), Gordon Craig, *On the Art of the Theatre* (1911), Bertolt Brecht, *Brecht on Theatre*, edited by John Willett (1964), and the fervent *The Theatre and its Double* by Antonin Artaud that was published in paperback by Grove Press in 1958.

There are many short histories of theatre. Hugh Hunt's *The Live Theatre* (1962) is readable and more than usually sensible; its author is both theatre director and teacher. Allardyce Nicoll's *The Development of the Theatre* first appeared in 1927 and is now in its fifth edition (1966): widely accepted as a standard work, it is fully illustrated and comprehensive. A. M. Nagler's *A Source Book in Theatrical History* (1952) reproduces extracts from numerous documents to give first-hand accounts of theatre practice from the Greeks until the present day.

A general reference book is *The Oxford Companion to the Theatre*, edited by Phyllis Hartnoll (1951) and now in its third edition

(1967); recently a smaller, *Penguin Dictionary of the Theatre* (1966), edited by John Russell Taylor, has become available.

David Cheshire's *Theatre: History, Criticism and Reference* (1967) in The Readers Guide Series, offers a detailed and experienced commentary on the many theatre books now generally available in bookshops.

Chapter One: Plays

Aristotle's *Poetics*, which continues to influence most attempts to describe plays, is available in paperback in a translation by S. H. Butcher and with a helpful introduction by Francis Fergusson (1961).

Eric Bentley's *The Life of the Drama* (1964) and Harley Granville-Barker's *On Dramatic Method* (1931) offer accounts of how dramatic texts work in a theatre; Bentley's book is especially useful in providing a full range of critical terms.

A critic, a director and a journalist have written useful books of advice on writing plays. William Archer, the critic and translator of Ibsen, wrote *Play-Making: A Manual of Craftmanship* in 1912; it has been republished in paperback by Dover Publications, in 1960. Kenneth Macgowan's *A Primer of Playwriting*, first published in 1951, appeared in Dolphin Books paperback series in 1962. Walter Kerr's *How Not to Write a Play* (1955) is witty and forthright.

Granville-Barker's *Prefaces to Shakespeare*, first published between 1927 and 1947, were issued in a collected paperback edition in 1963; these are among the best accounts of theatrical qualities in individual plays. My own *Shakespeare's Plays in Performance* (1966: paperback Penguin edition, 1969) tries to consider more generally 'what makes Shakespeare's plays so actable and stageworthy?'

Historical surveys of British drama include Allardyce Nicoll, *British Drama* (1925), W. Bridges-Adams, *The British Theatre* (1944) and B. Ifor Evans, *A Short History of English Drama* (1948, paperback).

For accounts of British and American plays in recent years, John Russell Taylor's *Anger and After: A Guide to the New British Drama* (1962) and the Stratford-upon-Avon Studies volume on *American Theatre* (1966) can be recommended. *Playwrights on Playwriting*, edited by Toby Cole (1960), collects statements on their art by dramatists from Ibsen to Ionesco.

Chapter Two: Theatres and Audiences

A general introduction to theatre buildings and their influence on dramatic experience is Richard Southern's *The Seven Ages of Theatre* (1961). Two books edited by Stephen Joseph collect various studies of the problems of designing theatres today: *Adaptable Theatres*, for the Association of British Theatre Technicians (1962), and *Actor and Architect*, being papers given at a conference at Manchester Univerity (1964).

A superbly illustrated, multi-lingual book by Roberto Aloi, *Architetture per lo Spettacolo* (Milan, 1958), is well worth consulting in large public libraries.

Mordecai Gorelik's *New Theatres for Old* (1940) is both history with documentation and a plea for radical rethinking about the design and use of theatres.

There are few books that deal with organizational and sociological aspects of theatre, but for Great Britain in the twentieth century, Richard Findlater has written a book, *The Unholy Trade* (1952), and a pamphlet, *The Future of Theatre* (1959), that present facts, opinions and arguments. William Gibson's *The Seesaw Log* (1959) is a frank and unusually complete account of how one play reached production on Broadway. Numerous issues of *Tulane Drama Review* in the 1960s consider administrative problems in the United States: see especially number 29 (1965), on 'Dollars and Drama'.

Chapter Three: Actors

Two long-established and still-provocative studies, *The Paradox of Acting* by Denis Diderot (written in the 1770s and published in 1830) and William Archer's *Masks or Faces?* (1888) have been reissued in one paperback volume by Hill and Wang (1957). Frederik Schyberg's lectures on 'The Art of Acting', are, in my opinion, the most balanced general account available; the English translation appeared in successive issues of *Tulane Drama Review* starting with number 12 (1961).

Toby Cole and Helen Krich have collected accounts of their art by various actors in a volume called *Actors on Acting* (1950). Collections of interviews by living actors are *Actors Talk About Acting* (1961), edited by Lewis Funke and John E. Booth, and *Great Acting*, edited by Hal Burton (1967).

For a recent account of acting in the classical tradition, see the first three chapters of *The Theatre of Jean-Louis Barrault,* translated by Joseph Chiari (1961): here are eminently practical sections on 'Gesture', 'Emotion'; 'Diction', and so forth, as well as 'Rules of Acting'. John Gielgud's *Stage Directions* (1963; Mercury Paperback, 1966) considers the growth of his powers as an actor especially in classical roles.

Stanislavski's writings are both thorough and suggestive. The English translations are: *An Actor Prepares* (1936), *Building a Character* (1949) and *Creating a Role* (1961). It is far from easy to draw a coherent, basic account of this influential teaching: Sonia Moore has published one summary, intended for student actors who wish to work along his lines, called *The Stanislavski System* (1965); and Robert Lewis a more descriptive account of his own experience of working as a director influenced by Stanislavski, called *Method – or Madness?* (1958). Michael Redgrave has written two books that relate his own discovery and use of Stanislavski's writings: these are *The Actor's Ways and Means* (1953; Mercury Paperback, 1966) and *Mask or Face* (1958).

Brecht's views on acting are found in *Brecht on Theatre,* edited by John Willett (1964).

Studies and biographies of individual actors are very numerous. Two books on David Garrick complement each other: Carola Oman's comprehensive *David Garrick* (1958) and Kalman Burnim's *David Garrick: Director* (1961). Other English actors are studied in Yvonne ffrench, *Mrs Siddons* (1954), Herschel Baker, *John Philip Kemble* (1942), Giles Playfair, *Edmund Kean* (1939), J. C. Trewin, *Mr Macready* (1955), Laurence Irving, *Henry Irving* (1951). Gordon Craig's *Henry Irving* (1930) is far shorter than any of these comprehensive surveys, but is one of the rare books on actors that are both impressionistic and technical.

For the United States, one's reading may well begin with Daniel Blum's *Great Stars of the American Stage* (1952) or Garff Wilson's *A History of American Acting* (1966), which is more dictionary than descriptive history; and George C. D. Odell's *Annals of the New York Stage* (1927–49) which is in fifteen volumes and frequently to be found in public libraries.

Comic actors are less often (and less easily) studied: in my opinion, the best account is Richard Findlater's *Grimaldi* (1955). Findlater's *Six Great Actors* (1957) is an expert introduction to reading about actors; his examples are Garrick, Kemble, Kean,

Macready, Irving and Forbes-Robertson. Bertram Joseph's *The Tragic Actor* (1959) is a survey of tragic acting in England.

Chapter Four: Stage Design

Lee Simonson's two books, *The Art of Scenic Design* (1950) and *The Stage is Set* (1932; third, paperback edition, 1960), provide a historical survey, theoretical discussion, criticism and illustrations of sets by the author as well as many other designers. Photographs of many stage sets are provided in René Hainaux's comprehensive and necessarily expensive books: *Stage Design Throughout the World since 1935* (1957) and *Stage Design Throughout the World since 1950* (1963).

James Laver's *Drama* (1951) is concerned with costume and décor; he followed this with *Costume in the Theatre* (1965) which is notably generous and sensible in its illustrations.

Two practical handbooks are Michael Warre's *Designing and Making Stage Scenery* (1966) and Motley's *Designing and Making Stage Costumes* (1964).

Chapter Five: Production

Unfortunately, and surprisingly, there is not a general and comprehensive history of stage production. Stanislavski and Brecht, and many other directors, have written on their own methods and views, but only briefly. *Directors on Directing* (1963), compiled by Toby Cole and Helen Chinoy, collects many statements of aims and descriptions of method, and is prefaced by a short history. Norman Marshall's *The Producer and the Play* (second, enlarged edition, 1962) is an introductory guide with some account of the development of the director's part in a production.

Chapter Six: Television Drama

Among introductions and handbooks are Arthur Swinson's *Writing for Television* (1955), *Television in the Making,* edited by Paul Rotha (1956) and Roger Manvell's *The Living Screen* (1961).

John Russell Taylor's *Anatomy of a Television Play* (1962) is an account of a single production, together with the text of the play, Alun Owen's *The Rose Affair.*

Chapter Seven: Criticism and Study

The books named in this chapter will provide examples of critical and scholarly method but I do not know any book that studies the whole subject, the important problem of how to be intellectually responsible to the whole range of theatrical experiences.

Chapter Eight: Training

Every school, college and university department of drama will have a printed syllabus, brochure or information pamphlet: write for a dozen or so of these and the variety and range of teaching methods will at once become apparent.

The last section of Michel Saint-Denis's *Theatre: The Rediscovery of Style* (1960) gives a lucid account of the three 'non-conforming' schools that the author has founded and directed. Stanislavski's works are as much concerned with training as with practice.

Chapter Nine: Future Theatre

Every book on theatre is relevant to thought about the future theatre; a surprising number of them are specifically concerned with it. Because most productions fail in one respect or other, writers on theatre are more than usually concerned with the creation of better conditions for work and new achievements. It is an art that encourages idealism, projects and prophecies: you will find them in current journalism, administrative reports, advertisements, criticism and scholarship.

Perhaps some cautionary reading should be advised here. I happened to find in a secondhand bookshop John Palmer's *The Future of the Theatre*, published in 1913; I recommend such a book, more than fifty years old, as a means of comparing and evaluating our contemporary enthusiasms.

PART TWO

Documents on the Theatre

I. THEATRES

(i) *Design Proposals for the National Theatre, London* by Denys Lasdun & Partners

THE PROPOSALS for re-housing the National Theatre on the South Bank aim to provide it with a setting where it can be seen to best advantage by the largest possible number of people.

Early in the development of the proposals it was decided that two auditoria were absolutely essential to this purpose. It was clear that at least 2,000 seats would be needed and that a single auditorium with this number could not give the public value for money since visibility and audibility suffer when even an open stage theatre has more than about 1,200 seats. A single auditorium, in any case, would have to be physically adaptable in order to house everything from Greek tragedy to the plays of Coward and Osborne and a theatre that can be adapted to house everything is never properly suited to anything. A vast single auditorium, in fact, would be a hopeless artistic compromise.

Two auditoria, which can easily provide the necessary number of seats, enable twice as many productions to be mounted so that a large and properly balanced repertoire can be maintained giving a far wider choice to the public without a proportionate increase in the size of the company.

The National Theatre will inevitably be expected to play host, from time to time, to major companies from overseas and while some need a proscenium theatre others, like the Shakespearean Company from Stratford, Ontario, can only operate on an open stage.

The two auditoria proposed for the new building are designed, therefore, to accommodate the two great traditional styles which constitute the main stream of European drama. On the one hand the open stage, for which the Greeks and Elizabethans wrote and to which many modern playwrights are attracted; on the other hand the proscenium stage, for which most dramatists in the past three centuries have written. Great works have been (and will continue to be) written for both forms of theatre and it is the duty of a National Theatre to present both to the best advantage.

The upper open stage theatre is designed to seat 1,165 people with an unobstructed view of the stage and excellent audibility for all. The seating is arranged into two main stepped tiers linked visually by intermediate tiers on each side to form a bowl. It is disposed so that the attention of the audience is focussed on to the acting area of the stage, giving the actor command of the whole auditorium. The configuration of the stage in relation to the seating avoids the possibility of members of the audience looking at each other across the stage and is such that the excessive movement sometimes associated with open staging will be completely unnecessary. The stage itself allows great flexibility of use providing the advantage inherent in the open stage form of increased audience/actor intimacy without the usual disadvantage of having to sacrifice all but a minimal scenic environment.

The stage is equipped with a fly tower for which it is intended to develop a new system of unit hoists for flying three-dimensional scenery. A revolve with integral lifts is proposed for the stage floor and this, together with the three rear stages, equipped with wagons, will enable the change-over from production to production to be handled efficiently.

The lower (proscenium) theatre has its seating disposed in two stepped tiers confronting an end stage viewed through an adjustable proscenium opening. It has been designed to accommodate the maximum number of people consistent with good visibility and audibility under these conditions. It has 895 seats which are arranged so that the audience is concentrated directly in front of the stage in an intimate relationship with it. The stage is to be fully equipped with a flying system and a trapped floor incorporating two lifts, one to provide an orchestra pit and the other to receive stage wagons and lower them flush with the stage floor. The immediate off-stage space consists of a rear stage and a single side stage with a scene assembly area between the two.

Provision is made in each main auditorium to receive disabled people in wheel chairs and access to the auditoria is arranged so that they can be reached without the necessity to negotiate steps. The first four rows of seating in each auditorium, which some might consider uncomfortably close to the stage, are spaced more closely than the seats in the main body of the auditorium so that they can be sold on the day of the performance at relatively low cost to younger theatre-goers whose enthusiasm can contribute to the success of a performance.

The small studio theatre which is also provided is intended to serve as a research department to keep the theatre in touch with its future and to attract the enquiring young audiences who have a stake in that future. It will give new playwrights and directors the chance to prove their worth in a laboratory atmosphere and will provide opportunities for testing new techniques of presentation. The studio is a room approximately 60 feet square designed to be as flexible in use as possible. The room is surrounded on three sides by a gallery 8 feet above stage level beneath which actors can circulate to stage entrances between banks of seating. The seating itself would be in moveable units which can be arranged in a variety of ways to produce different stage layouts. There is a small backstage area on the fourth side of the room. A small entrance foyer is provided for the audience with access to the gallery level. Approximately 200 people can be accommodated, the actual number depending on the stage layout.

The auditoria and stages, if they are to function properly and be used productively need complex and extensive supporting accommodation. Scenery, costumes and lighting have to be prepared and stored in positions convenient to the stages, around which essential working space is required. Workshops for all technical departments are needed and must be strategically placed to avoid unnecessary transportation. Dressing rooms must be provided for the large company of actors needed to fill the wide range of parts to be played, and space is required to prepare and rehearse new plays and to re-rehearse plays already in the repertoire without interrupting the presentation of current productions to the public. (It is normal for one play to be rehearsed in the morning, another to be performed in the afternoon and a third to be performed in the evening – all on the same stage. Between these three presentations, each of which may require the attendance of a full crew of technicians, the entire setting and lighting may have to be changed.)

The dominant elements in the design are the upper auditorium and its fly tower poised over the main entrance on a diagonal axis inclined towards Waterloo Bridge. The fly tower of the lower theatre is a subsidiary element which serves to modulate the scale to that of the neighbouring buildings. Below these elements terraces recede in rhythm from the riverside and continue into the building forming the main foyers from which the majesty of the river panorama can be enjoyed. Outside, at the lower levels, the terraces link up with Waterloo Bridge and the existing system of walkways around the Royal Festival Hall, forming an extension of the riverside promenade which can be used and enjoyed by the general public. Higher up they provide external spaces, warmed by infra-red heating, for theatre audiences, places of relaxation for those working in the theatre, and essential emergency escape routes.

The combined entrance to the two main theatres faces the river and is accessible at car park level, road level and pedestrian terrace level, the three levels being interconnected by lifts and staircase.

II. THEATRE ORGANIZATION

(i) *Elizabethan Theatres* by R. A. Foakes

WHEN Shakespeare came to London between 1584 and 1592, he must often have heard the trumpets sound to announce a performance at a playhouse, and seen the crowds flock to it. Dukes and ambassadors, gentlemen and captains, citizens and apprentices, ruffians and harlots, 'Tailers, Tinkers, Cordwayners, Saylers, olde Men, yong Men, Women, Boyes, Girles, and such like' were likely to be among that audience, gathering to watch a spectacle that held something for each of them. Here was a splendid world of delight and instruction, offering poetry for the cultured, shows and a strong plot for the citizen, clowning and bawdy for the illiterate; and for everyone it brought to life, as no other medium then could, history, mythology, biblical story, and a whole range of earlier literature. Playwrights ransacked, as Stephen Gosson alleged, 'the Palace of Pleasure, the Golden Asse, the Œthiopian historie, Amadis of Fraunce, the Rounde Table, baudie Comedies in Latine, French, Italian and Spanish' to provide ever some new attraction. The Theatre was at once courtly and plebeian, aristocratic and popular, witty and vulgar, refined and ribald; it was a universal theatre, a meeting-place of all sorts of people, and a focus for all sorts of talent. It offered the writer a versatile stage, and actors who could sing, dance, tumble and fence as readily as they delivered their lines; and it gave scope to many kinds of writing. It challenged the popular compiler of chronicle plays to attempt poetic richness, and encouraged the sophisticated author, who knew his Terence and Plautus, to throw in a song or two, and some clowning, something for the crowd.

The stage was not only exciting in itself, but had a special prominence as the centre of a controversy between, on the one side, the church and civic governors of London, on the other side the court and aristocracy. If the actors seemed in their splendour to be kings indeed to the people, they were emissaries of the devil to puritan divines, who grew bitter as the churches emptied: 'Wyll not a fylthy playe, wyth the blast of a Trumpette sooner call thyther a thousande, than an houres tolling of a Bell bring to the

Sermon a hundred?', complained a preacher at St. Paul's in 1578. Fulminations against the Theatre as 'Satan's synagogue' or 'the nest of the Devil' did not affect its popularity, and the Church tried what it could do to restrain play-acting; so the Bishop of London, advising Sir William Cecil to prohibit plays for a year in 1564, added dryly, 'and if it wer for ever, it wer nott amisse'. The Church had the support of the Mayor and Aldermen of the City of London, who were continually seeking injunctions against 'common plaiers of interludes'. They complained that the actors drew large assemblies to view plays, and crowds were dangerous as tending to vice and disorder, and as liable to spread infection, especially in time of plague. Their pressure was successful to the extent that the public theatres were built in suburbs to the north of the city, or south of the River Thames on Bankside, in areas that were out of the jurisdiction of the city authorities.

Against these, the actors had powerful allies at Court, where Queen Elizabeth liked to see a play or two on festive occasions especially at Christmas, when it was usual for one or more companies to be called to perform before her. Their chief protectors, however, were the lords whose name and livery they took to give them prestige and good standing in an age when players not 'belonging to any Baron of the Realme' were condemned in the statutes as rogues and vagabonds. The relationship between a company and their patron may not always have been very close but he could intervene strongly on their behalf, as the Lord Admiral and Lord Chamberlain did through Privy Council for their companies in 1598, causing a third company to be suppressed. What the actors gained by such patronage may be glimpsed in letter written by James Burbage and five others to the Earl of Leicester in 1572, in which they ask him to

> vouchsaffe to reteyne us at this present as your household Servaunt and daylie wayters, not that we meane to crave any further stipend or benefite at your Lordshippes handes but our Lyveries as we had and also your honors License to certifye that we are your household Servaunts when we shall have occasion to travayle amongst our frendes as we do usuallye once a yere, and as other noble-men Players do and have done in tyme past.

So in attacking or protecting the stage, the highest authorities were involved, bishops, mayors of London, the Queen and great lords who could exercise some control through Privy Council. The profession of acting or of writing plays had a special prominence because of this, and held its own risks. Plagues or disturbances might cause all playing to be prohibited, and force actors to travel far into the provinces; the city authorities might find some new means of harassing them, such as forcing them to contribute to the upkeep of the poor; but also the most benevolently inclined lords and the Queen herself were susceptible to the influence plays might have on the public, and were liable suddenly to become the stage's worst enemy if they suspected a play of engaging in political or religious matters. Actors and authors would then be disciplined, playing suppressed, and authors perhaps committed to prison, as, among others, Ben Jonson and John Marston were later to suffer imprisonment in this way. At the same time, to be an actor, author, or, as was not uncommon, both, was to engage in a profession capable of bringing glamour, prestige, popularity, and wealth. A letter-writer lamented in 1587, 'Yt is a wofull sight to see two hundred proude players jett in their silkes, wheare five hundred pore people sterve in the streets'; but many must have found the players a fine sight. Shakespeare became one of them, wore the livery of several lords, and eventually took his place at the head of the list of actors granted four yards of red cloth for liveries to walk in the coronation procession through London in 1604. He had reason to be proud.

During Shakespeare's early years, great developments were taking place in play-acting. There was a long tradition of playing by adult companies of men, performing in inn-yards, on scaffolds, or in halls and private houses; and an equally long tradition of acting by schoolboys, especially by the boys of the schools of St Paul's Cathedral and the Chapel Royal. Before the 1570s there seem to have been performances on Sundays and holidays, perhaps without any settled regularity. Frequent regulations forbidding playing during time of divine service or the late afternoon show that plays were commonly staged on Sundays, chiefly in 'great Innes, havinge Chambers and secret places adjoyninge to their open stages and gallyries', as one order puts it. As early as 1545 a proclamation speaks of plays being 'commonly & besylye set foorthe', and the city regulations extended in 1566 to forbidding Robert Fryer, a goldsmith, from staging plays for the public in his house before 4 on Sundays and festivals. The presentation of

plays was evidently widespread, but, except for private performances in the houses of the great, or at court, was confined to
non-working days.

The first building constructed for dramatic performances was
erected by James Burbage, an actor, in 1576; he called it, simply,
The Theatre. It was a structure developed from the inn-yard or
from the arenas long used to exhibit bear-baiting, with tiers of
galleries extending round a central area and stage exposed to the
open sky. In the same year, Richard Farrant, new master of the
Children of the Chapel, leased a part of the old priory of Blackfriars,
and converted it into an indoor theatre, where his boys proceeded
to perform before the public. He seems to have done this to
compete with the Children of Paul's, whose vicar choral, Sebastian
Westcote, had been cited by the Court of Aldermen in the previous
year because, as they said, he 'kepethe playes and resorte of the
people to great gaine'; his boys perhaps acted in buildings of the
school. A little later, about 1577, another public theatre was
built, the Curtain.

These events mark the beginning of a full-scale professionalism
in the theatre. Its further development over the next twenty years
falls into three phases, and Shakespeare emerges as a fledged actor-
dramatist in the third phase. The first extended through the
1580s. During this period the standing of the adult players was
enhanced when a group of actors was selected in 1583 to form a
company under the Queen's patronage; this new company took
prominence because of the talents of its leading players, especially
Richard Tarleton, the great clown. The children's companies
were active until 1584, when the Children of Paul's seem to have
ceased playing for a time. The Children of the Chapel appeared
occasionally after this date until 1592, and then vanished until
1600. In 1587, however, the Children of Paul's returned to
playing for three years. It is doubtful if plays were as yet given on
more than two or three days a week, but performances certainly
were offered on days other than holidays. Already in 1578 John
Stockwood spoke with horror in a sermon of 'the gaine that is
reaped of eighte ordinarie places in the Citie whiche I knowe; by
playing but once a weeke (whereas many times they play twice
and sometimes thrice) it amounteth to 2000 pounds by the yeare';
and in 1583 the licence for the Queen's Men permitted them to
play at two inns, the Bull and the Bell, on holidays, Wednesdays
and Saturdays.

Tarleton died in 1588, a jester much loved and much mourned; and this blow to the Queen's Men was followed by another when the company became involved in the Martin Marprelate controversy in 1589. The actors seem to have become too vehement in their attack on the puritans, who had begun the affair with a series of anonymous pamphlets purporting to be written by Martin and denouncing episcopacy. Playing was prohibited in November, because the actors had dealt with 'matters of Divinytie and of State unfitt to be suffred', as the Privy Council minute puts it. Thereafter the Queen's Men are traceable in the provinces, with only an occasional appearance in London; and in May 1594, Philip Henslowe noted in his *Diary* that the company 'broke & went into the contrey to playe'. The Children of Paul's were also involved in this controversy through the writings of their principal dramatist, John Lyly, and their acting was suppressed altogether in 1590.

There is not much evidence of the repertory of the Queen's Men during these years, but it included chronicle plays, classical romance, and pseudo-moralities like the two extant plays by Robert Wilson, an actor in the company; one important dramatist, Robert Greene, sold much of his work to them. It was probably a more popular repertory than that of the boys' companies, for their chief draw, Tarleton, was famous for his ability to play 'knave and foole'. The children, acting in indoor theatres, charging higher entrance fees, and drawing a narrower and more select audience, had thrown up no outstanding actors, but gave scope to the scholarly talents of university-trained writers like John Lyly, who produced witty comedies on classical themes. Lyly was writing by 1584, and may be referred to in Stephen Gosson's *School of Abuse* (1579) as the author of 'two prose books played at the Belsavage, where you shall find never a word without wit, never a line without pith, never a letter placed in vain'; certainly this is an apt comment on those plays of his which remain. He was the major dramatist of the decade, and Shakespeare studied his work with great profit. Nevertheless, it would be wrong to draw too simple a contrast between the sophistication of the children's companies, and the crude vigour of the adult players, between the expensive 'private' theatres and the cheaper 'public' playhouses. The tastes of the audiences at these were not so different as to prevent authors like George Peele and Christopher Marlowe, from writing for both; and, in addition, all the companies had enough in common to be welcome at Court to play before the most select audience in the realm, and to be able to entertain in the provinces audiences that were probably less sophisticated than any in London.

The decay of the Queen's Men and the suppression of the Children of Paul's coincided with the ascendancy of other adult companies, marking a second phase in the growth of a full-scale professional theatre. Two of these companies were to emerge quickly as outstanding. First were the Lord Admiral's Men, who played under the patronage of the Lord High Admiral, Lord Howard; they appeared as a group in 1585, and Edward Alleyn, who was then a member and had acted earlier, acquired a major share in the control of the company in 1589. Alleyn seems to have been one of the great actors of the English stage, a man praised by Thomas Nashe in 1592 as the finest ever: 'Not *Roscius* nor *Æsope,* those admyred tragedians that have lived ever since before Christ was borne, could ever performe more in action than famous *Ned Allen.*' The second company was the group known as Lord Strange's Men, who played under the patronage of Ferdinando Stanley, later Earl of Derby. Their early history is obscure, but possibly by 1588, certainly from 1590 to 1594, they were working in liaison with the Admiral's Men, at times as one combined company. In 1594, after the death of Lord Derby, the companies separated, many of the former Strange's Men taking the patronage of the Lord Chamberlain, Lord Hunsdon. Richard Burbage, a slightly younger man than Alleyn, was their leading player: he may have acted in the 1580s, but first comes to notice in 1590, when he was probably with the Admiral's Men. It would be pleasant to think that he learned his craft from Alleyn, whose standing as the leading actor of the age he inherited in the first decades of the seventeenth century, after Alleyn, still not forty years old, had retired finally from the stage about 1605.

These two companies seem to have had the main use of the true theatres, as distinct from inn-yards and the like, available in London. James Burbage (father of Richard), a poor actor in the early 1570s, married a wealthy woman and used her money to build the first theatre. After 1585, the Curtain, operated by a Henry Laneman, was used as an 'easer' to the Theatre by an agreement between the proprietors who pooled and equally divided the profits. By 1586, possibly much earlier, a theatre at Newington Butts was in use. Then in 1587, Philip Henslowe, who seems, like Burbage, to have acquired money by marriage, contracted with a grocer, John Cholmley, to build what was to become the Rose Theatre. This was erected by 1588, and by 1592 had passed into the sole ownership of Henslowe. As James Burbage saw his son become a leading actor and sharer in the Chamberlain's Men before he died in 1597, so Philip Henslowe saw his stepdaughter, Joan Woodward, marry Edward Alleyn in 1592, and from that time on Alleyn became a son to him. The close relationship between the leading actor and sharer in the company's stock and the theatre owner may have been a stabilizing factor in the history of these two companies. During their period of association, the Strange's and Admiral's Men played at the Curtain, the Rose, and, for a brief period in June 1594, at Newington Butts, which by then may have come into Henslowe's control.

Other companies were active during these years. The Earl of Pembroke's Men, who were ruined by the great plague of 1593 which stopped all playing in London between February and December, the Earl of Sussex's Men, who seem to have broken up in 1594, and the Queen's Men, before their removal to the provinces, all had some connection with the activities of the Admiral's and Strange's Men. Plays belonging to Pembroke's Men seem to have passed to Sussex's Men, who acted briefly with the Queen's Men in April 1594 before both companies broke up. Some of their plays came into the repertory of the newly formed Chamberlain's Men in 1594, among them *Titus Andronicus, The Taming of a Shrew* and a version of *Hamlet,* while others were taken over by the Admiral's Men, like *The Jew of Malta,* and *Friar Bacon and Friar Bungay.* From this year, 1594, which marks the end of the second phase of development, the Admiral's and Chamberlain's Men dominated the London stage, at any rate until the turn of the century.

Of these two companies, the Admiral's Men had a longer continuity and fame at this time, largely through Edward Alleyn, but also, perhaps, because most of the plays of the best writers of 1587–92 were written for them, or passed into their repertory – plays by Marlowe, Kyd, Peele, Lodge and Greene. Marlowe wrote one play for the Children of the Chapel, and so did George Peele, but the rest of their work was sold to adult companies, usually to the Admiral's Men; Greene wrote mainly for the Queen's Men, but his plays came into the repertory of Strange's

Men or the Admiral's Men by about 1592. The new writing talent of the so-called 'University Wits' was thus chiefly deployed for the adult companies that rose in the decay of the Queen's Men and the Children's companies. These men, who, except for Thomas Kyd, were graduates, wrote for the stage perhaps partly because they lacked patronage, or could not scrape a living by poetry, but also because the emergent companies of the late 1580s were competing for plays. Robert Greene seems to describe how he came to write plays in his pamphlet *Francesco's Fortunes* (1590), where, in the person of Francesco, he tells how he 'fell in amongst a company of players, who persuaded him to try his wit in writing', and so he wrote a comedy, 'which so generally pleased the audience that happy were those actors in short time, that could get any of his works'. These 'sweet Gentlemen', who, in the words of Thomas Nashe writing in 1589, 'vaunted their pens in private devices, and tricked up a company of taffata fooles with their feathers', brought to their craft a new poetic energy and command of language, a new maturity of design and power of thought, and a new insight into character. They brought also an academic training to their work, which is as sophisticated in its kind as Lyly's is in his own vien. Their plays, especially those of Marlowe, are the earliest English plays which are still widely read and occasionally revived on the stage.

The plays of these writers had their greatest theatrical success while Edward Alleyn, who played Orlando in Greene's *Orlando Furioso,* Tamburlaine, Doctor Faustus, and Barabas in *The Jew of Malta,* was at the height of his powers. Well before Allyen retired from the stage for some years in 1597, Greene (1592), Marlowe (1593), Kyd (1594) and Peele (1596) were all dead. It was during their great burst of creative activity that Shakespeare appeared as an actor and playwright. The first certain allusions to him and his writings are found in pamphlets of 1592. In that year Thomas Nashe referred in his *Pierce Penniless* to the character of Talbot in *Henry VI*; Robert Greene misquoted a line from *3 Henry VI* in his *Greene's Groat's-Worth of Wit,* and complained of Shakespeare as an 'upstart Crow', a man who had pilfered the writings of others, or who had presumed equality with established authors, or who was a mere actor pretending that he could 'bombast out a blanke verse' as well as university-educated poets – several interpretations of Greene's doubtful words are possible; and finally, Henry Chettle defended Shakespeare as 'excellent in the quality he professes'. Such testimony from his contemporaries establishes that he had 'arrived' by this time.

In the same year, 1592, Philip Henslowe began to record his share of the daily takings at his theatres, and to list the plays performed, in his account-book, better known as his *Diary*, which is now in the library of Dulwich College. Among the plays he noted as performed by Strange's Men early in 1592 were a *Henry VI*, probably new on 3 March 1592, 'tittus and vespacia', and *The Jealous Comedy*, probably new on 5 January 1593. The Earl of Sussex's Men, acting at the end of 1593, performed a *Buckingham* and 'titus & ondronicus'; and the Admiral's and Chamberlain's Men, acting together briefly in June 1594, are recorded as staging 'andronicous', *Hamlet*, and *The Taming of a Shrew*. In 1594 also, a quarto of *Titus Andronicus* was published, its title-page reading, 'As it was Plaide by the Right Honourable the Earle of Darbie, Earle of Pembrooke, and Earl of Sussex their Servants'. In the same year a quarto of *The Taming of a Shrew* as played by Pembroke's Man appeared, and in 1597 *The True Tragedy of Richard Duke of York*, a play now thought to be a bad version of *3 Henry VI*, was ascribed to the same company. The relationship of *Titus and Vespasia* to *Titus Andronicus* is not known, and that between *The Taming of a Shrew* and *The Taming of the Shrew*, though close, remains indeterminate; *The Jealous Comedy* may have no connection with *The Comedy of Errors*, and *Buckingham* may be nothing to do with *Richard III*; but there is left enough evidence to show that Shakespeare was at work at the very latest by the beginning of 1592, and probably for some time before that. It also seems likely that his progress to the Chamberlain's Men was via Pembroke's and Sussex's Men. Through a connection, perhaps as actor and writer, with these companies he would have come into association with Strange's Men, who were acting a part of *Henry VI* in 1592, and with the Admiral's Men. Then, when Strange's and Admiral's separated after playing as a combined group in June 1594, he joined the new company that succeeded Strange's Men and took the patronage of the Lord Chamberlain, Lord Hunsdon.

So Shakespeare, coming to London as the old style of adult playing by the Queen's Men, referred to as 'Vetus Comœdia' already in 1589, was in decay, and as the boys, after achieving their finest work in acting Lyly's plays, were suppressed, attached himself to a company that soon brought him into connection with the prominent Strange's and Admiral's Men. These, financed by the only builders who had established their own theatres in close connection with a company, and possessing the leading actors in Alleyn and Burbage, were the inheritors of the achievement of the adult and boys' companies of the 1580s; and after 1594, their wealth and their talent stabilized in family relationships, they came to have something of a monopoly. Shakespeare came to maturity in the third phase of development from the building of the Theatre in 1576, the post-Marlovian phase, after emerging in 1594 to work with the up-and-coming Richard Burbage in the Chamberlain's Men.

During the next six years the Admiral's and Chamberlain's Men had little serious competition to face; no Children's companies or 'private' theatres were operating, and not much is heard of other adult companies. A new theatre, the Swan, was built in about 1596 on Bankside by Francis Langley, who drew a number of the Admiral's Men, and a few actors probably from the Chamberlain's Men, to play there as the Earl of Pembroke's Men in 1597. But the venture was short-lived, for the Privy Council prohibited all playing after a performance at the Swan of a lost play by Nashe, *The Isle of Dogs,* in July 1597; it was apparently a play 'contanynge very seditious and sclanderous matter'. Langley's company promptly returned to the Rose to play in Henslowe's theatre, and were absorbed into the Admiral's Men again. Henslowe quickly obtained a licence to start playing again, but Langley did not, and an order of Privy Council in February 1598 calling for the suppression of a third company may show that he staged plays for a time without permission. This order of the Privy Council shows that the Admiral's Men and the Chamberlain's Men were the only companies licensed to perform plays at this time. Their predominance is reflected in the way they took turns in appearances at Court in connection with the Queen's Christmas festivities until 1600, when an Earl of Derby's company also played there. It is reflected also in the prosperity which brought to each company a new theatre. Cuthbert Burbage, the elder son of James, took over, on the death of his father in 1597, a troublesome dispute with the owner of the ground on which the Theatre was built, and solved it by taking down the building, transporting it from Shoreditch piece by piece across the river, and setting it up again on Bankside, presumably with much renovation. This new, or renewed, theatre was called the Globe, and its appearance near the Rose, which was also south of the river, caused Henslowe and Alleyn to plan a new stage for their company. In 1600 they opened the splendid new Fortune theatre in Finsbury; they had moved across the river in the opposite direction to the Chamberlain's Men, instructing their builder to copy the Globe in many details, and clearly setting out to match their rivals.

The two main companies competed not only in their theatres, but also in their repertories. They each inherited part of the stock of the old Sussex's, Pembroke's and Queen's Men, and until 1594 they played the same kinds of play, as Henslowe's records confirm. It is probable that they continued to do so, though not much is known about the repertory of the Chamberlain's Men apart from Shakespeare's plays, whereas Henslowe's lists provide a great deal of information about that of the Admiral's Men. However, Shakespeare's plays reveal some evidence of competition. At first he seems to have built on the work of his contemporaries and predecessors, trying his hand at chronicle-history, at Senecan tragedy, and at various forms of comedy, and imitating now Marlowe, now Lyly or Greene. After 1594, when his status as a leading member of his company is confirmed by his acting, together with Richard Burbage, and the famous clown William Kemp, as payee for Court performances, he continued to write several different kinds of play, sometimes in response to successes at the Rose. His creation of Shylock may have been provoked by a revival of *The Jew of Malta* by the Admiral's in 1595–6. They had a play on the theme of *Julius Caesar*, a *Henry V*, and a *Troilus and Cressida* before Shakespeare wrote his; and they replied to his *Henry IV*, or rather to his portrait of Falstaff, with their *Sir John Oldcastle*. The rivalry of the companies extended even to personal oppositions, as revealed by Henslowe's records of loans to discharge Thomas Dekker from arrest by the Chamberlain's Men in 1599, and to enable William Bird to pursue a lawsuit against Thomas Pope, a member of Shakespeare's company.

The affairs of the two companies may have differed a good deal in detail, and after the building of the Globe, they had a different organization. But before 1599 both companies consisted of a number of sharers, who each owned a share in the joint stock of plays, properties, costumes, and the like; they employed other actors, possibly some with a high standing as master actors, some hired men, some boys. They worked in a theatre owned by a financier, James Burbage or Philip Henslowe, who took half of the receipts in the galleries at each performance as his perquisite. Relations between owner and company were doubtless close, and Henslowe came to act as banker, moneylender, and general helper to the Admiral's Men. However, this company lost its family link with the owner when Alleyn retired from the stage in 1597. Although he returned to it from 1600 to about 1605, he devoted himself more and more to his properties, taking a large share with Henslowe in ownership; they built the Fortune as partners. The Chamberlain's Men kept and strengthened the link between owner and players. Richard Burbage, who continued to act until his death in 1619, and his brother Cuthbert, the inheritor of the Theatre, made a new arrangement with the company when they built the Globe. They kept only a half share in the lease and profits of the playhouse for themselves, and admitted five leading players, one of them Shakespeare, to equal shares in the other half. So a body of the sharers of the acting company obtained an interest in the ownership of the theatre itself; and this no doubt contributed to the strength of Shakespeare's company during the later part of his career.

Nevertheless, Henslowe's accounts contain much that is relevant to a consideration of Shakespeare as an actor and dramatist. Most plays of this period are lost; many were never printed, or were printed anonymously, and few authors seem to have troubled about the publication of the plays they wrote after they had sold them to a company. Ben Jonson was the first to gather his works together and oversee their printing in 1616; Shakespeare's plays had to wait for some of his fellows to bring them out seven years after his death. It is doubtful whether all printed texts survive, and certainly most manuscripts do not; they remained in the company stock until destroyed by time or the decay of the theatres, or, often, by some accident, such as the fire which burnt down the Fortune in 1621, reducing to ashes playbooks and costumes. There would be little evidence even of the titles of missing plays if Henslowe's *Diary* had not survived to show how men wrote for the Admiral's company, singly or in collaboration, to show what they wrote (the *Diary* indicates that Michael Drayton was the author of *Sir John Oldcastle*, printed anonymously in 1599, and had a hand in 23 other plays now lost), and to offer the only proof that some men wrote at all (Charles Massey is an example). It is useful to cite the *Diary* here because the early association and later rivalry of the Admiral's Men and Chamberlain's Men make it probable that their repertory systems of presentation and their methods of obtaining plays were roughly similar.

Henlowe's lists show that the Admiral's Men played a daily repertory, probably excepting Sundays, and with longer breaks during Lent, when acting was forbidden, and in summer, during the long vacations, when the company sometimes travelled in the country. Performances were in the afternoon, and there was normally a change of play every day. Even a very successful play, like George Chapman's *Humorous Day's Mirth* (*Comedy of Humours*), first acted in May 1597, was not performed more than twice in one week. No play received more than thirty-two performances in all, and twelve to fifteen indicate a respectable success. This meant a huge turnover of plays: between June and December 1594, fifteen new plays entered the repertory, and another fifteen during the following year. Not many of these remained in the repertory for as much as a year, though some were revived after a lapse of time. A dramatist sold his work outright to the company for comparatively little, £5 being a typical figure in the 1590s, and the company seems to have withheld plays from publication, as more of an asset unprinted, at least until their first run was over, and often for a much longer period. In such conditions, playwrights multiplied, and collaboration was common. Among the authors who wrote for Henslowe at this time were Chapman, Dekker, Henry Chettle, John Day, Samuel Rowley, Michael Drayton, Thomas Heywood, Henry Porter and Ben Jonson. Some, like Rowley, Jonson and Heywood, were also actors; and some other actors in the company, like Charles Massey and John Singer, wrote an occasional piece for the stage. Many seem to have written loyally for the Admiral's Men, but Ben Jonson changed allegiances several times, Chapman went over to writing for the Children's companies when these were revived after 1600, and it seems that authors were free to sell to whom they pleased. At the same time, it was natural for actors like Samuel Rowley or Shakespeare, who had a stake in one company, to write mainly for their own group.

The repertory of the Admiral's Men shows an enormous variety of plays, on British history, real and mythical, on recent French history, comedies set in Greece, France and Italy, plays on biblical themes, the new comedies of 'humours' of Chapman and Jonson, romantic comedies like Dekker's *Shoemakers Holiday*, a 'pastoral tragedy', and tragedies on themes ranging from *Agamemnon* to *Cox of Cullompton*. It also included a fair number of plays, presumably comedies, with titles like *Crack me this Nut*, *The Fountain of New Fashions*, *Christmas Comes but Once a Year*, *What Will Be Shall Be*, and *As Merry as May Be*, some of which are reminiscent of Shakespearian titles, *Twelfth Night* or *What You Will*, *As You Like It*, *Much Ado about Nothing*. The range is remarkable, and reflects another feature common to this company and the Chamberlain's Men, that they were able to perform all kinds of plays, and entertain all kinds of audiences; it also points to the mixed character of the audience at the public theatres in the 1590s. Both companies might be called on to play in private at the house of some lord; for instance, Henslowe recorded a payment in March 1598 to 'the carman for caryinge and bryngyn of the stufe back agayne when they playd in fleatstreat pryvat', and the Chamberlain's Men acted *Henry IV* before the Flemish ambassador in private in 1600; perhaps on each occasion they had already acted on the public stage before an audience ranging from gallant to groundling during the afternoon of the day concerned. Both companies were accustomed to acting at Court, and both knew what it was to travel in the country, and amble, as Dekker put it, writing of Ben Jonson, 'in leather pilch by a play-wagon, in the high-way'.

Wherever they performed, much of the attraction of the actors and their plays no doubt lay in their flamboyance, in the richness and splendour of fine costumes, hangings, and stages that were already in 1592, according to Thomas Nashe, 'stately furnisht'. There is plenty of evidence for the splendid appearance of the players and stage in Elizabethan theatres, which have so often been regarded as 'bare'. Henslowe noted frequent expenses for very elaborate costumes for plays, and among other documents left by him and Edward Alleyn are lists of properties and costumes in the stock of the Admiral's Men in 1598. The items include a hell-mouth, two steeples, Phaeton's chariot, a tree of golden apples, various tombs, an altar, a canopy, two mossy banks, a dragon, a lion, a great horse, a frame for beheading, and the cauldron used in Marlowe's *Jew of Malta*. The lists also mention the city of Rome and the cloth of the sun and moon, perhaps both painted cloths for hanging at the rear of the stage. The theatres themselves presented an attractive appearance. The stage façade

I Picture-Frame Theatre: model of the Lower Theatre of the proposed National Theatre, London.

II Open-Stage Theatre: The Mermaid Theatre, Puddle Dock, London, with the stage set for *Galileo* by Bertolt Brecht.

III Thrust-Stage Theatre: The Stratford Festival Theatre, Stratford, Ontario.

IV Arena-Stage Theatre: The Arena Stage Theatre, Washington, D.C.

V Modified Open-Stage Theatre: The Octagon Theatre, Bolton.

VI   Platform-Stage Theatre: the auditorium of the The Haymarket Theatre, London, from a print dated 1807.

VII   Modified Open-Stage Theatre: model of the Upper Theatre of the proposed National Theatre, London.

VIII Booth Stage: from an unascribed painting in the Drottningholm Theatre Museum, probably Flemish and dated about 1660.

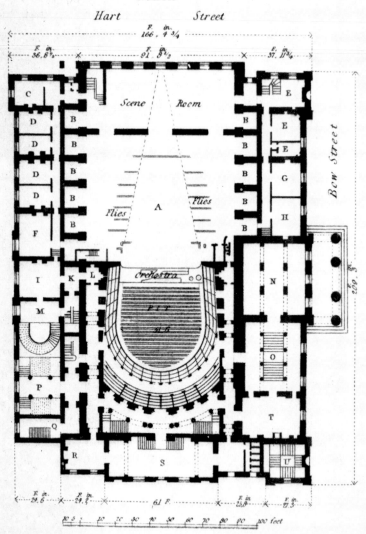

A. The Stage.
B.B. Recesses for Scenes.
C. Managers Room.
D.D. Womens Dressing Rooms.
E. Mens Dressing Rooms.
F. Store Room.
G. Stage Managers Room.
H. Green Room.
I. Royal Saloon.
K. Ante Room.
L. Kings Box.
M. The Kings Staircase.
N. Entrance Hall.
O. Principal Box Staircases.
P. Entrance to Boxes.
Q. Lower Gallery Staircase.
R. Bar for Refreshments.
S. Saloon.
T. Vestibule.
U. Stairs to Lower & Upper Galleries.

IX   Covent Garden Theatre, from a plan dated 1826.

X   Classical Theatre: the theatre at Epidaurus.

XI   Neo-Classical Theatre: The Teatro Olimpico, Vicenza.

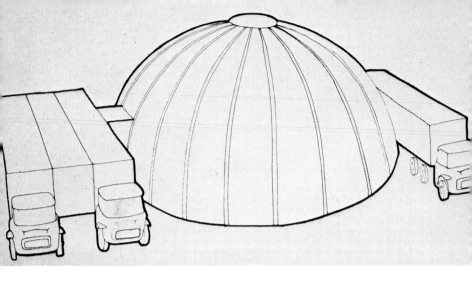

XII Working drawings of the proposed Welsh Mobile Theatre.

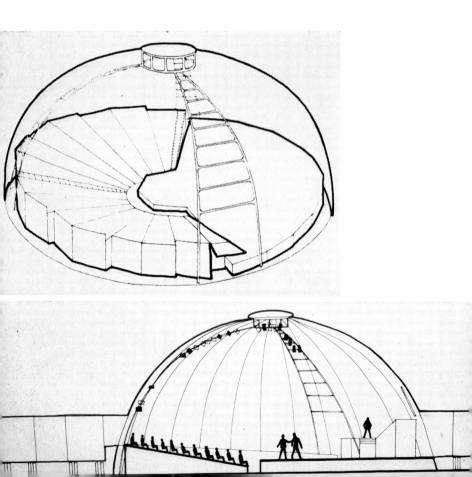

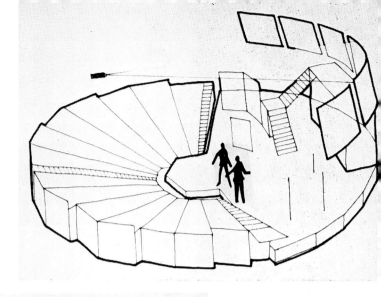

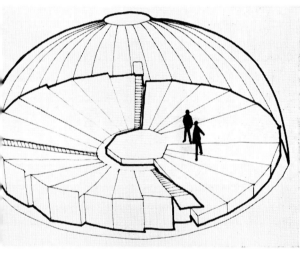

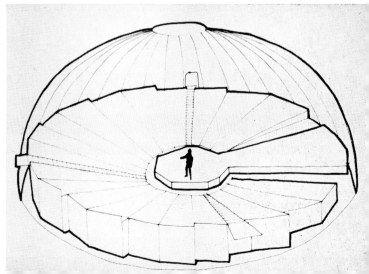

XIII Garrick: by Benjamin Wilson, published 1754.

XIV John Philip Kemble: by Sir Thomas Lawrence, 1800.

XV Edmund Kean: by Wageman, 1818.

XVI Henry Irving: by F. Armytage.

XVII Johnston Forbes-
Robertson: ? 1897.

XIII–XX EIGHT
HAMLETS

XVIII Jean-Louis
Barrault.

XIX   John Gielgud: 1934.

EIGHT HAMLETS
continued

XX   Laurence Olivier:
1936.

XXI Cliff and Beach Scene (10 pieces) by P. J. de Loutherbourg (1740–1812).

XXII A Setting for *The Wonders of Derbyshire*, or *Harlequin in the Peak*, 1779; by de Loutherbourg.

XXIII   Entry of Bolingbroke into London, a Scene from Charles Kean's production
of *Richard II* at the Princess's Theatre, 1857; from *The London Illustrated News*.

XXIV   Scene from Henry Irving's production of *Dante*, 1903.

XXV Model of setting for *The Duenna* at The Lyric, Hammersmith, by George Sheringham, 1926.

XXVI Scene from The Moscow Arts Theatre production of Gorki's *The Lower Depths*, first produced 1902.

XXVII Act II of O'Casey's *Silver Tassie*, designed by Augustus John, The Apollo Theatre, London, 1929.

XXVIII   *Hamlet,* 1937: Scenery by Randle Ayrton, Production by B. Iden Payne.

XXIX   *Hamlet,* 1948: Scenery by James Bailey, Production by Michael Benthall.

XXX   *Hamlet,* 1956: Scenery by Michael Northern, Production by Michael Langham.

XXVIII–XXXI   *Hamlet* at the Royal Shakespeare Theatre.

XXXI   *Hamlet,* 1958: Scenery by Motley, Production by G. Byam Shaw.

The Steps by E.
Gordon Craig; 1905

XXXII The Steps
I.

XXXIII The
Steps II.

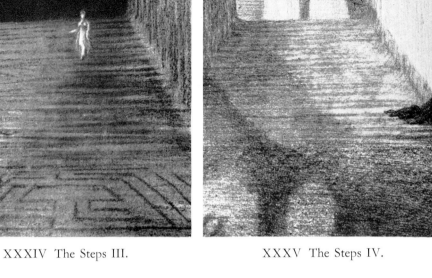

XXXIV The Steps III.   XXXV The Steps IV.

XXXVI *Hamlet*, I. ii, by E. Gordon Graig, 1910.

XXXVII *Hamlet*, I. iv, by J. Svoboda, at the National Theatre, Brussels, 1965.

XXXVIII
Gorki's *The Last One*, by J. Svoboda, at the National Theatre, Prague, 1966.

XXXIX   Model of *King Lear*, I. i, by Noguchi, for the Shakespeare Memorial Theatre, 1956.

XL   Harold Pinter's *The Homecoming,* by John Bury, at the Aldwych Theatre, London, 1965.

XLI Episode from *Kordian* directed by Jerzy Grotowski, at the Theatre Laboratory, Opole, from a performance in 1963.

XLII The Use of Stage Space for *Kordian;* as in a circus there is much simultaneous action

acteurs

spectateurs

" KORDIAN "

XLIII Samuel Beckett's *Play,* designed by Jocelyn Herbert at the National Theatre, London, 1964.

was richly ornamented ('painted' was the word used by Gabriel Harvey and Edmund Spenser), with its gallery or balcony over the stage doors on either side, and canopy supported on two columns over part of the great platform area extending into the middle of the arena, where the groundlings stood to watch and listen. The columns supporting the canopy were marbled, or perhaps gold at some theatres, if we may trust the testimony of Thomas Heywood in his translation of Ovid's *Art of Love* (? 1600), who speaks of

> The golden ensignes yonder spreading fare,
> Which wafts them to the gorgeous Theater:
> See what thin leaves of gold foile guild the wood,
> Making the columns seeme all massie good.

The canopy itself was painted on the underside like a sky, 'nail'd up with many a star' as Thomas Middleton said, a 'heaven' to match the 'hell' under the stage. The mainposts of the framework supporting the three tiers of galleries surrounding the stage area, and the columns bearing the canopy, were, at the Fortune Theatre, adorned with figures of satyrs. The stage itself was hung with an arras or painted cloth; so Ben Jonson testifies in his Children's play for Court-presentation, *Cynthia's Revels* (1600), in which a boy walks on the stage in the Induction pretending to be a gentleman come to watch the play, and speaks with other children acting as stage-hands,

> Slid, the boy takes me for a piece of *perspective* (I hold my life) or some silk cortaine come to hang the stage here! sir cracke, I am none of your fresh pictures, that use to beautifie the decaied dead arras at a publike theatre.

In addition to elaborate properties, painted cloths, splendid costumes, and a richly decorated stage façade, it is known that special hangings were used to mark, for instance, a tragedy, as, in the Induction to *A Warning for Fair Women* (1599), a play belonging to the Chamberlain's Men, History says

> The stage is hung with blacke: and I perceive
> The Auditors preparde for *Tragedie.*

It would be surprising, then, if part of the attraction of the theatre was not its spectacle; the stage itself must have seemed magnificent to the groundlings, but the plays too might provide

E.T.—5

much visual splendour. So in *The Trumpet of War* (1598), Stephen Gosson describes how 'in publike Theaters, when any notable shew passeth over the stage, the people arise up out of their seates, & stand upright with delight and eagernesse to view it well'. The plays of the public theatres have numerous shows and processions, often quite elaborate, like the following, from the successful *Old Fortunatus* by Dekker, played by the Admiral's Men before the Queen, probably over Christmas 1598–9; Fortunatus lies under a tree, and there enter

> a *Carter,* a *Sailor,* a *Monke,* a *Shepherd* all crown'd, a *Nimph* with a Globe, another with *Fortunes* wheele, then *Fortune*: After her fowre *Kings* with broken Crownes and Scepters, chained in silver Gyves and led by her. The foremost come out singing. Fortune takes her Chaire, the Kings lying at her feete, shee treading on them as shee goes up.

Such a lavish show was not to be seen in all plays, but most have processions, council-scenes, battle-scenes, duels, a play within the play (like *The Spanish Tragedy* and *A Midsummer Night's Dream*), a trial, a dance or masque, or a display of some kind.

The large, open stage projecting into the arena was suitable for such shows, and in addition to this area, the dramatist had a balcony, at least two doors, a central curtain, tent or alcove, the exact nature of which is not yet certainly established, and the two pillars supporting the canopy to use if he wished. The 'hell' under the stage could also be employed to good effect with the aid of trapdoors, as in *Hamlet*, where the Ghost speaks from under the stage. But for all its splendour, its possibilities of spectacle and of effects like fireworks, or descents from the 'heavens' (Henslowe installed a throne there in 1595), the stage was basically a simple one, with a permanent, largely neutral, background, the interior façade of the theatre itself. There was no proscenium arch to the stage, and the greater part of the acting-space could not be curtained off; so one scene followed another with no break in performances that took place in open daylight. The main visual effects were embodied in the appearance and movements of actors or managed by portable properties; further dimensions of visual splendour might be suggested by a poet's verse, which, as Shakespeare supposes in the prologue to *Henry V*, could piece out the imperfections of the stage, and tempt an audience to think their 'wooden O' transformed into 'the vasty fields of France'. In general, plays were sufficiently independent of machinery to be staged readily elsewhere than in at Court, or within a private house.

(ii) Traders and Artists: 1952 by Richard Findlater

The modern theatre is only eighty years old. Towards the end of the last century far-reaching social changes transformed the stage and its status in the community. The concentration of a rapidly multiplying population in the towns, the decay of agriculture and rural life, the spread of elementary education, the development of transport, and the rise in living standards all helped to dissolve the old social and cultural patterns, and fostered the creation of a vast entertainment industry. Anti-theatre inhibitions were weakened, and vast new middle class audiences, brought into London by the development of bus and rail services, were recruited to the ranks of Satan. From the seventies onwards, playhouses multiplied in London and the provinces, the stage became an outlet for surplus capital and the source of immense profits, and the theatre became respectable. Public school boys and university graduates found it possible to work in the service of organized illusion with a clear conscience. At the universities, official opposition dissolved, and the A.D.C. and the O.U.D.S. were founded; amateur actors from the middle classes began to penetrate the ranks of the professional stage; and, as theatre periodicals and books began to multiply, editors of the daily press appointed men of intellectual standing as critics of the drama. The Church veered round, with considerable reluctance, to recognition of the stage as a moral force in the nation's life. Men of letters treated the stage with a new respect, as a possible instrument of social change and personal profit. Matthew Arnold's celebrated call of 'The theatre is irresistible; organize the theatre' was the sign of a change of heart, and though the call was not answered, the idea of establishing a national theatre was canvassed for the first time. Shakespeare was discovered, belatedly, to be a practising playwright, and there was a serious attempt to reconstruct the conditions under which his plays were staged. Meanwhile, the development of electric light, the rapid technical advances, the behaviour of the new audiences, and the change in the drama transformed the arts of the stage.

Although the puritan opposition had relaxed by the turn of the century, it did not disappear: the tradition died hard. For though the theatre was gradually accepted as a respectable institution, its function was clearly limited – it was to provide fun. On no account was it to be taken seriously. The theatre had become genteel, but it must be impotent. Playwrights must keep their place, for they were entertainers not preachers, and no trespasses would be forgiven. The pressure of this Philistinism helped to save the commercial drama of the new entertainment industry from any intellectual taint or hint of heresy.

But in the *avant-garde* puritanism reasserted itself in a different way, with dangerous results for the future health of the drama. Many theorists of the 'new drama' were intellectual puritans, who sought to use the theatre as a pulpit. They distrusted the exhibition of personality on the stage; they attacked the extravagance of romantic acting; they derided the theatricalism of their predecessors. The 'playwright's theatre' of their dreams was to be free from red plush, emotional contagion, and other trappings of the sinful Victorian playhouse; drama was to be real and earnest, stripped of the bait of entertainment, and the play-actor was to be disciplined and educated. One result was the curious joylessness of the repertory theatre, which embodied the new drama; blind to the wider horizons of the theatre, too many disciples of Shaw and Granville-Barker treated playgoing as a duty, not as a pleasure. This side-tracking of the Ibsenites by inherent puritanism is one reason why the rebel naturalism of the Théâtre Libre had such feeble issue in England, and why Grein's Independent Theatre failed to transform the contemporary stage. The Vedrenne-Barker slogan of 'truth as opposed to effect' was often adopted with unfortunate results: it showed a fundamental confusion between theatrical and non-theatrical 'reality'. This was the beginning of an attack on the theatre which continues today – the perennial attempt to make it into something else, into a church or a parliament or a museum, to replace the actor by a puppet, a tumbler or a pool of light. This sublimated puritanism in intellectual high places is one of the chief obstacles to establishing a healthy national theatre: it is found in criticism, scholarship, politics, and architecture.

Moreover, the changes in the trade were by no means an unmixed good. It is true that – in England, at least – in order to be recognized as an art, the theatre had to succeed as a business – to paraphrase Irving's words. And the suppression of the patents and the liberation of the drama from the absurd categories of 'legitimate' and 'illegitimate' entertainments were necessary preludes to reform. But it was the misfortune of the theatre that the installation of free trade should have come at a period of rapid economic expansion, before a new theatre art had time to grow. In its new prosperity the old craft foundations were undermined. The actor's social status and pay improved, the level of public taste rose, the insulation of the stage ended, but because of the long tradition of ostracism and *laisser-faire* a vacuum was left unfilled. The circuit system broke up, and with it the methods of training young actors in the stock companies. Theatrical life became over-centralized, and the independence of the old provincial Theatres Royal vanished when they became the shelters of London companies touring carbon copies of West End successes. The Shakesperean companies perished, and with them the Shakespearean technique. With the end of the repertory system the annual turnover of productions was drastically reduced, and most of the new plays offered considerably less opportunity to the actors. More playhouses were run not by actors, but by agents of London syndicates. The evil effects of the change were partly concealed by the dominion of the actor-managers, who provided a continuity of policy and employment, but by 1914 their day was over.

In accepting the theatre, the middle class had transformed it. Middle class manners altered the relationship of the actor with the audience, and the actor assumed the middle class persona. Although great romantic actors such as Irving worked in the new era, the theatre lost a dimension of expression, as well as a self-regulating craft.

Though by 1914 it was as profitable to write plays as to write novels, it was much more difficult for the writer to gain experience in the drama. Though the theatre had become respectable, it was still not protected or subsidized: the tradition of *laisser-faire* held firm. Many playhouses came under irresponsible control, and the new managers, concerned with selling show business at a profit, turned them into factories of fun. Inevitably, the theatre failed to meet the challenge of the new age, and lost customers and artists to the cinema and the music hall. During the 1914–18 war nearly all the London playhouses and many of the large provincial theatres passed into the hands of unscrupulous profiteers and speculators. Rents were trebled and standards quartered, and with the death of the last great actor-managers – Tree (1917), Alexander (1918), and Wyndham (1919) – all hope of stemming the flood vanished. It was a triumph for free enterprise in the arts, and for the British tradition.

At the turn of the century there were signs that the bogeys of the past might be defeated, and a living English theatre might have been established as a centre of intellectual and artistic life if the lessons of the Continent had been followed. But though writers and artists were ready to turn to the stage for the first time in generations, though the long divorce between the theatre and her sister arts might have been healed, there was no means of incarnating their ideas and visions. The economic forces of the 'free' English stage and the playgoing traditions of an anti-theatrical people were against them.

Today there is the same danger – a danger more urgent than before – that the advances of the last ten years may be wiped out by the evils of the unholy trade; and that because of a mistaken fear of state interference and a misplaced confidence in the free market, the chance of a renaissance may be lost again for generations.

*   *   *

Art is kept alive, not by the established trade in it, but by the desperate efforts of art-hungry individuals to create and re-create it out of nothing for its own sake.   SHAW

A theatre, if it is to do public service should be given the freedom of the city, released from rent, rates, taxes, the cost of light and police, and the necessity of advertising.   HARLEY GRANVILLE-BARKER

During the past seventy years, theatre rents have increased, sometimes up to a thousand per cent, production costs by 600 per cent, and prices of admission by only 50 per cent; while entertainments tax, income tax and supertax have helped to kill free management and creative enterprise. The margin between profit and production cost has steadily decreased since the heyday of the Edwardian actor-manager, and it is still diminishing, for costs are still rising, apparently beyond control. Many playhouses are anachronisms, like the system under which they are rented, and the industry is working on obsolescent equipment, which cannot be renewed because of the vicious inflation of land values and the vicious indifference of many landlords. The trade is breaking down: and since 1945 the process of disintegration has accelerated. That is the most important fact about the theatre today.

When the Bancrofts introduced the ten shilling stall at the Prince of Wales in 1874, they set theatre prices at a new and dangerously high level. The increase was necessary to pay for higher salaries and royalties, greater comfort and efficiency, better plays and productions: it also helped to raise the prestige of play-going, and to make the threatre safe for the middle classes. Yet not only did the introduction of the expensive stall help to banish the working class from the theatre and set the middle class in authority, but it put a price on admission which left no margin for advance. What else could the Bancrofts do, in a competitive trade, when they wanted to improve their commodity, but make the consumer pay? But there is a limit to the amount that an Englishman is willing to spend on a good seat at the play, and the Bancrofts reached that limit almost at once. The managements of today are paying for their enterprise. For the price of seats has been pegged for years at an impossibly low level, though to the English public it may seem still outrageously high.

Seventy years ago, a manager might rent a moderate-sized West End theatre for a moderately long lease at £50 a week: today he would probably have to pay anything up to £500 a week, with no assurance of tenure. In 1800 there was no entertainments tax: today he pays about a sixth of his takings to the state, win or lose. In 1880 income tax was at 8d. in the pound, and there was no surtax: today the managers lose at least half their hypothetical profits to the tax collector. In 1880 there was no minimum wage for actors and no Esher Standard Contract, for there was no Actors' Association or Equity: actors, stage-hands and technicians were underpaid and overworked. The small-part player got £2 where today he gets £15, and the star got £60 a week where today he may get £300. In 1880 the manager spent a fraction of his budget on publicity: today it is one of the major items. Star producers were unknown seventy years ago: today they get a cut of the takings and a preliminary fee of several hundred pounds. The costs of electricity, paint, timber, dresses, furnishings, paper, and other materials have risen to dizzy heights, with the costs of labour and administration. Yet the theatre stall of a West End theatre costs from thirteen to sixteen shillings only, an increase of about 50 per cent on average. And in spite of this increase the manager only gets ten to thirteen shillings (thirteen and six on a sixteen shilling seat), after paying entertainments tax. Nearly half the rest goes to the lessees. The enormous profits of a Bancroft, a Wyndham or a D'Oyly Carte (who left £174,535, £197,035 and £240,817 respectively) are no longer possible.

So the playgoer gets, in effect, for an increase of 50 per cent a commodity which has probably cost seven times as much to produce: and he will not pay any more. At the national theatres he can, it is true, buy a seat in the stalls for 4s. 6d., but only at the expense of the actor's salary and the range of the repertory; and it is worth noting that although the 'commercial' stall has increased by only 50 per cent the Old Vic seat has increased 400 per cent in the last forty years. Ten shillings was once the maximum price; today it is the minimum price for a stall, a minimum which is, in my opinion, impossible to maintain.

Why have theatre costs increased at such a rate? And why does so much of the public's money go to politicians and speculators, rather than to managers and artists? For the answer one must look at the long history of *laisser-faire* and at its effects on the contemporary organization of theatre business.

Between the wars the London theatre was dominated by speculators who milked it of its profits without worrying about the state of the drama or the welfare of the stage. They came into the West End to make money, and they made it as fast as they could, in giving the public what they thought it ought to want. They made their money without risk, at the expense of the artists on the boards and in the offices of playhouses – the managers as well as the actors, the impresarios as well as the theorists of the drama. In other industries the same phenomena were seen, of the reckless distribution of profits rather than reinvestment in capital equipment and technical research, but the gamblers of Shaftesbury Avenue – many of them responsible figures in other national industries – were distinguished by their irresponsibility, greed and inefficiency; their ignorance and sloth: their cowardice, vulgarity, and the criminal neglect of their own resources. This is the immediate cause of the predicament of the theatre today, but the roots of the disease go much further back. Most of these men have disappeared, and today a more responsible clique has succeeded them; it is led by men, like Emile Littler, with practical experience of the theatre, and its record is golden beside that of the pre-war pirates. But though personalities change, the system of landlord control remains, though its dangers may be disguised by the virtue of its present controllers.

The modern playgoer takes the system of presenting plays for granted. He does not find it strange that the Pantheon, to take an imaginary title, should stage in the course of a year a comedy thriller, *Hamlet*, an American farce, a documentary, and a Pirandello revival; that the changing fortunes of these plays should be controlled by six different partnerships; that he should never see, if he is a regular patron, either Mr Neverlose, the lessee, whose name appears on the programme; or Mr Box and Mr Cox, by arrangement with whom, it seems, the piece is presented; or Athos, Porthos and Aramis, who are actually putting on the play in association with D'Artagnan. The playgoer is accustomed to pay sixpence for his programme, and sixpence to leave his coat in the cloakroom; he often agrees to pay much more for an ice or a beer than he would in the working world outside; and he accepts with infinite patience the general discomfort of the house and disinterest of the staff. These are the penalties of much London playgoing.

Yet in 1880 the Pantheon would be known for its policy of presenting one kind of play, for a permanent company of players, and for the personality of its manager. The customer would know that he could expect to see, say, a good light comedy; that in the cast he would see the same players who appeared in the last play and the play before that; and that the manager would probably be acting on the stage or standing in the foyer, seeing that the show was running smoothly and that the house was satisfied. There were no multiplications of Boxes and Coxes, no arrangements and associations of Musketeers. The man who leased the theatre presented the play and probably directed it as well. Programmes were free; the cloakrooms and saloons were part of the playhouse service; and even though conditions often fell far short of the ideal, the theatre was run as a personal enterprise under direct control.

It is unlikely, moreover, that the manager of the Pantheon owned more than one other London theatre, if he owned any. Yet today one group of business men control, or are closely connected with, over half the metropolitan playhouses.

Seventy years ago, the manager could 'nurse' a new play on

half-full houses for weeks until business improved. Today he may have to close down if he is not doing 60 per cent capacity business by the second week of the run – if he can last that long – and another manager moves in. The man with the theatre has the power. His overheads have increased, but his risks are small. It takes a much longer run to balance the manager's books: the landlord's profits are less uncertain.

The trouble is that playhouses are treated as units in real estate deals, not communal assets as valuable as public libraries and museums. And it is the landlords and lessees who get the lion's share of the public's money, not the actors, authors and managers. Under a free system such as ours the only sure profits are to be obtained by the ownership of the 'bricks and mortar', and in the last forty years a little colony of parasites flourished on the leases of many London theatres. Mr X buys a lease at £50 a week, and sub-lets it to Mr B at £70 a week; Mr B sub-lets it at £100 a week; and so the process went on. It is in this way that the level of London theatre rents was forced up without any relation to the level of prices or costs, for these were irrelevant to the 'bricks and mortar' magnates. So it is not surprising that theatre owners have made a great deal of money, and that they have reinvested some of their surplus capital in the producing managements; or that ambitious managers have entered the bricks and mortar business, and created their own system of social security. Industrial expansion in a free field has thus inevitably resulted, as in other industries, in a concentration of capital, the close association of production and distribution, and the consolidation of monopolist power.

The theatre 'manager' of seventy years ago is now, as such, a salaried official of the lessee or landlord. The Pantheon is a temporary shelter, rented by any fortunate manager with capital and a play on his hands. And the lessee takes no part in the play's presentation or production, except to guarantee himself a share of its takings. It is the producing management – now usually a limited company – which takes all the risks. It buys the play; finds the 'angel' who will supply the capital; hires a producer; engages the cast; and – its most important and most difficult task – rents a playhouse. It is – in theory, at least – a contractor of labour without a permanent factory. All the year round, a queue of productions waits for a London theatre to 'go dark', and the independent manager probably waits longest. Members of the

West End group may have special privileges, though there is no evidence of a closed shop. And even for them, management is a gamble: they cannot make long-term plans, for they never know when a theatre will fall vacant or what theatre it will be or how long, once in, they can hold their tenancy.

The lessee of the theatre is usually assured by agreement with the management of about 30 per cent to 40 per cent of the takings, on a fixed scale arranged according to costs. It is agreed that the play should be withdrawn when takings fall below a certain figure, at which either party can give notice. The lessee also takes the proceeds of programmes, cloakrooms and bars, and remits entertainments tax in a weekly cheque to the state. This sharing system has, it seems, largely replaced direct renting, especially inside the main London group. Under either system, producing managers have to accept the lessee's terms.

The running costs vary widely according to the site, the number of sets and stars, the size of cast, the policy of the lessee, but £1,500 a week is an average sum for a straight play with a small cast and two changes of scene. The 'rent' is the biggest item in the budget for the management; and there are author's royalties, producer's royalties, star royalties. The lessee contributes to the cost of current advertising and technical staff, and usually meets front-of-house expenses, as well as the theatre's maintenance. The preliminary costs may be about £3,000 for a rehearsal period of three weeks, on half-pay rehearsal salary for the cast, fees for producer and designer, and the cost of sets and dresses. A musical may cost as much as £30,000 to stage; and it is not uncommon for ambitious productions to run many months before the costs are paid off and the books are balanced.

This means, of course, that a very high level of box-office takings is necessary, especially during the first weeks of the run. At the Court Theatre season of Vedrenne and Barker, it was considered to be a guarantee of success when the house was taking £600 a week: on that figure a run could safely be prolonged. The renaissance of the nineties was only possible, in Shaw's words, because of 'a supply of theatres which could hold nearly twice as much money as it cost to rent and maintain them'. But soon the costs began to rocket, and today plays taking three times as much a week might be doomed. Because of such increases, the virtual blackmail of managements by many lessees, the general waste and anarchy of the system, today it needs a much greater capital reserve to present plays than at any other period in the theatre's history. The freedom to produce plays is as limited as the freedom to start a national newspaper. No management, however good their intentions, can afford to 'nurse' productions for any length of time or to risk many experimental pieces. To play safe is the policy of survival in this free-for-all. Managers pick plays with not too many characters or scene changes, and with the well-tried ingredients of popular success, which they expect to pack the house within the first fortnight of the run. They import Broadway successes, revive the long-runners of pre-war days, or present the safer plays of contemporary authors, and fill the cast with stars. This policy is of course endorsed – and indeed enforced – by many landlords.

The safest bet in provincial management is to avoid legitimate plays altogether, and to present leg-shows, musical comedies, nude revues, and spectacles. Only about 10 per cent of the productions touring the country are those of 'straight' plays: most of Britain's theatres still cater for customers who want to relax and look at pretty costumes and beautiful girls. It pays to lower the sights, and take the least line of resistance: and why should managers do otherwise in an uncertain trade? One amazing feature of the unholy trade is that some managers persist in risking first-class productions because they believe, apparently against all the evidence, that the public will always respond in time. But such managers are exceptional, and their laudable altruism is proportionately rare. Experiment doesn't pay. Even with tax exemption, the Company of Four has lost as much as £20,000 a year at the Lyric, Hammersmith.

There is no room under this system for minority tastes. As Mr Benn Levy has pointed out, 'unless 300,000 or 400,000 people want to see a play it cannot be done – 50,000 people are not sufficient to support it'. Yet 50,000 readers give an author a handsome return, by modern standards: 'If 5,000 people want to read a book the publisher does reasonably well.' Moreover, 'not only is it necessary for 300,000 or 400,000 people to want to see a given play; it is necessary that they should want to see it at the same time. It is no use for them to straggle in sparsely over a year or eighteen months because by that time the unfortunate manager would be in Carey Street.'

The crazy economics of presenting plays are further confused by the anomalies in the administration of entertainments tax, first instituted in 1916 as a wartime emergency measure, and never since surrendered by the state. The theatre pays the full rate of tax on all seats sold from the first day of the run, irrespective of the success or failure of the production. It is not the profits, but the gross box-office receipts, that are taxed, and it is possible – indeed it is common – for the Exchequer to make a big profit out of a three week run on which the management may have lost several thousand pounds. The entertainments tax, as it stands, penalizes both promoters and artists and favours the bad play at the expense of the good.

Its evils have been partly alleviated by the exemption of non-profit-making companies. Between the wars the amateur movement grew up virtually tax-free, for exemption was granted to productions staged for charity or by non-profit-making organizations. But it was not until 1934, for example, that the Old Vic claimed exemption as an institution 'not conducted or established for profit'. In 1942 it was decided to exempt all companies which were properly constituted as non-profit-making and which presented 'partly educational' plays. This category proved impossible to define, and in 1946 the Customs and Excise was given the power to exempt from tax those companies with a partly educational *policy*. There are now over 7,000 companies liberated from the burden of tax, who receive a rebate of 15 per cent of their gross takings otherwise exacted by the Customs. Most of them are amateur groups, but they include several non-profit-making satellites of the big business managements, which are in effect permitted to present 'commercial' plays to balance their budgets over a year's work, provided that they plough back their profits into the presentation of 'educational' new plays and revivals. This amounts to an indirect subsidy to the high theatre by the state.

This remission of tax has had highly beneficial results on the drama and the stage during the last decade. It is by means of its non-profit-making subsidiary, Tennent Productions, Ltd., that H. M. Tennents has done such valuable work for the English theatre, that the plays of Eliot, Fry, Priestley and Bridie, and other minority works, have been presented in the West End, and that ambitious Shakespearean revivals have been staged. It helps to keep the Old Vic prices low, and West End managers can accumulate capital reserves which would otherwise go to the state or, in an untaxed theatre, line the pockets of the backers and landlords. But it is none the less a negative, niggardly, piecemeal compromise, which leaves immune the central evils of theatre economics. Moreover, it is unjustly applied: exemption should be granted to play-producing societies and theatre clubs, penalized by the confiscation of a seventh of their scanty income. It is absurd that such decisions should be at the discretion of officials of the Customs and Excise. It is only a partial return of the state's plunder. And in some ways it may serve to exaggerate the evils of excessive costs today, for theatre-owners may demand higher rents with impunity, and exempted managements can bid higher for stars and plays. At present the Arts Council assessors are, it seems, alertly on the lookout for unfair practices, but there are obvious dangers in the situation. And after all, it is capital that the independent theatre manager needs, much more than an amnesty from taxation. It is inevitable that the big commercial managements, who have capital, should dominate the field.

(iii) The Federal Theatre Project by Elmer Rice

The stock market crash of late 1929 was followed by the worst economic depression the United States has ever known. By the time Franklin D. Roosevelt assumed the Presidency in 1933 the state of affairs was catastrophic. Tens of millions of Americans had, through no fault of their own, lost their jobs, their homes and their savings. Many were living in colonies of improvised shacks known as Hoovervilles and queueing up for handouts on municipal bread lines. The Roosevelt administration, in an attempt to remedy this situation, inaugurated a vast programme of public works that provided employment for millions, and by 1935 conditions had begun to improve.

However, things were still very bad, and nowhere worse than in the theatre; for theatre-going is for most people a marginal activity, and one of the first to be dispensed with when the budget must be cut. All over the country theatre attendance had shrunk, hundreds of theatres had been forced to close their doors, and thousands of theatre workers were destitute. Men and women of high professional standing were reduced to the status of vagrants, unable to find employment and forced to eat the bitter bread of public or private charity.

At this time I was attempting, in association with a group of actors, designers and directors, to organize a co-operative non-profit repertory theatre. We needed a working capital of $100,000, but after months of effort we had succeeded in raising only $7,000 and were about ready to give up. As a last measure I went to Washington, with the faint hope of persuading the Federal Emergency Relief Administration to underwrite what was, after all, a plan for putting people to work. My request was quickly refused, but Jacob Baker, to whom I had made it, asked me to have a talk with Harry L. Hopkins, then in command of the entire relief programme.

Hopkins told me that both President Roosevelt and Mrs Roosevelt were keenly aware of the plight of workers in the arts, particularly in the theatre, and wanted very much to find a way to help them, but though numerous individuals had been consulted, no one had yet submitted a plan that seemed workable. He asked me if I had anything to suggest. I replied that I had not given the problem any thought, because I had not known of the government's interest in it, but that I was sure of one thing, namely, that if a theatre project were to be created, it could not be based entirely upon New York, as was the commercial theatre, but would have to be organized on a regional basis. Hopkins replied that that was exactly what he wanted to hear and urged me to think about it and submit a plan to him.

I did think about it, and a few days after my return to New York I wrote Hopkins a long letter, which I take the liberty of reproducing here, substantially in full, not only because it was partly responsible for the establishment of the Federal Theatre Project, but because it describes my dream of a theatrical Utopia: a dream that will never be realized, but that I shall always go on dreaming.

Dear Mr Hopkins:

I am going to set out here the broad outlines of a scheme which I believe to be both desirable and workable. As a premise, I am taking it for granted that any such programme must be designed to meet the following requirements:

1. High standards of quality;
2. Low prices of admission;
3. Security and permanence of employment for workers in the arts;
4. Decentralization; and adaption of regional projects to local community needs.

I propose the following plan of action:

1. The creation of a Governmental agency to buy or lease existing theatres, in 100 large communities throughout the country. These buildings are now dirty, frowsy, neglected. Put your unemployed architects to work (using local talent whenever possible) to remodel and modernize these theatres. Wire them for sound, put in cooling plants and comfortable seats, overhaul the stage machinery and the lighting systems, add a pleasant refreshment room and an exhibition hall suitable for shows of painting and sculpture, scrape off the gilt and the gingerbread. Put your unemployed artists to work freshening and redecorating the auditoriums, painting murals in the lobbies and rest rooms, designing curtains. This will entail the immediate employment of masons, carpenters, house painters, electricians, technicians and construction people of all sorts. In six months or a year, every large community in the country will have a bright, modern, comfortable community theatre, suitable for plays, music, motion pictures and art exhibitions.

2. Put into each of these theatres a permanent stock or repertory company, recruited mainly from the ranks of the unemployed, but carefully selected on the basis of talent. As far as possible, get the thousands of out-of-town actors, who are now crowding the streets of New York, to return to their home communities, emphasizing the idea of using local talent. Wherever established and worthwhile community theatres already exist, use these as the nucleus for the community project. Use local unemployed musicians to form a small orchestra to play incidental and entr'acte music. Budget all your operating costs, including salaries, on the basis of a minimum season of forty weeks. On the basis of 100 communities, permanent employment would be provided for 2,500 actors, 800 musicians and 5,000 theatre employees of all other categories. To this must be added part-time work for thousands of persons employed by scenic studios, manufacturers of costumes and properties, printers, advertising agencies and the like; and a living income for numerous playwrights and composers.

3. Create a rounded programme of art activities to be handled, in each community, by someone with a thorough knowledge of the professional theatre and high standards of taste, working in consultation with the leaders of local schools and cultural organizations, for the aim should be to meet the needs and requirements of the community. But there should be no compromise with quality, and whether the play is a Shakespearean tragedy or a modern farce, it should rank high in its own category, and should be excellently acted and mounted. Every effort should be made to encourage local playwrights to draw upon the life around them and the rich folk

material of America. Local artists should be permitted to exhibit their work; local soloists to give recitals. Educational and scientific motion pictures should be exhibited as well as pictures which, for one reason or another, are not shown in commercial theatres. (This may well result in the production of more adult pictures.) Plays for children and adolescents should be given at low prices, in the late afternoon and on Sunday morning. There should be lectures, debates, forums and symposia, dealing with drama, literature, painting and the other arts. For all performances, seats should be available at 25c. In no case should the top price exceed $1.50; wherever possible it should be $1.00.

4. In the larger communities, string quartets, small orchestras, small choruses and dance ensembles should be organized, which will augment and supplement the dramatic programme. Cycles of programmes consisting of the vocal and instrumental works of such composers as Beethoven, Schubert, Mozart and Bach should be given, as well as programmes of folk and popular music. Whenever regional music exists, it should be fostered and encouraged. For the smaller communities, musical units should be organized to make circuits of four or more cities in a particular region.

5. In addition to the permanent acting companies, the old, visiting-star system should be revived. Many well-known actors would be delighted to have an opportunity to appear each year, in fifteen or twenty cities, in fine plays, under dignified auspices. And audiences would flock to see, at small cost, the finest actors of the day. To put the thing concretely: imagine such a community theatre in Omaha, in which one could see, for a dollar, John Barrymore in *Hamlet*, George M. Cohan in *Seven Keys to Baldpate*, Helen Hayes in *What Every Woman Knows*, Walter Huston in *Desire Under the Elms*, Edward G. Robinson in *The Racket* and Wallace Beery in *Shore Acres*. I am not suggesting the creation of jobs for Hollywood stars, but by utilizing the eagerness of these actors to be seen on the stage, it is possible at once to ensure the livelihood of thousands of less-known players and to bring the best that the theatre has to offer to drama-hungry communities which have had to be content with third-rate road companies, shoddy stock companies or puerile amateur groups.

6. Although each theatre should be an independent community project, the entire programme should be co-ordinated, on a national basis, by some agency which can act as a clearing house and by means of which standards may be established and duplication and waste avoided.

7. I believe that, properly organized and administered, 20 per cent of these theatres should be self-supporting within two years, and 50 per cent to 75 per cent within four or five years. By pooling

revenues and expenditures in a central agency, the surplus in the self-sustaining enterprises would take care of the deficit in the others.

This does not pretend to be a bill of specifications. It represents a policy and an attack. As a general approach, I believe that it is sound artistically, economically and socially. If the Government will really get behind this project, and if it is done in the right way, it will be the greatest contribution to American culture that any Government has ever made.

And so indeed it would have been! The cost would have been substantial, of course. To inaugurate the programme I outlined perhaps $100,000,000 would have been needed, and perhaps as much again to underwrite it until it became self-supporting. But it would not have been too high a price to pay for the establishment of a nation-wide organization dedicated to the popularization of the arts of the theatre. Compared to the hundreds of billions spent upon weapons of destruction, most of which become obsolete before they are even completed, the amount that would have been required for the theatre programme is infinitesimal.

At any rate, those of us, all over the country, who were interested in getting some relief for the artists who were victims of the depression, were summoned to Washington for a conference with Hopkins and Mrs Roosevelt. As a result of this meeting four projects were set up: Art, Music, Writing, Theatre. Hallie Flanagan, director of the Experimental Theatre at Vassar College, was selected as national head of the Theatre Project. A better choice could hardly have been made, for she is a woman of high ideals, great capacity for work, and a wide knowledge of the drama and of the theatre. I was asked to organize and direct the New York region of the Project. After some hesitation, I accepted; had I known what was ahead, I should probably have declined.

The task of launching the Art, Music and Writing Projects was relatively simple. Artists were put to work painting murals in post offices and other public buildings. Musicians were organized into ensembles of various sorts that gave concerts, usually free, in school buildings or outdoors when weather permitted. Writers were set to work on the composition of guidebooks, a job that really needed doing; eventually they turned out a series of informative and readable volumes, covering practically every state in the Union; some were subsequently issued by commercial publishing houses. All these activities could be undertaken with a minimum of organizational work, a small executive staff, and little expenditure for the materials or overhead.

The Theatre Project was in an entirely different category, . . . to begin with, physical plants had to be made available: halls in which to rehearse plays and theatres in which to perform them; workshops for the manufacture and assemblage of scenery, costumes, properties and electrical equipment. Space also had to be provided for casting directors, play readers, designers, typists and publicists. And, of course, finding qualified specialists required an enormous expenditure of time and energy.

These organizational problems were aggravated by the financial limitations within which the Project had to work. The Projects came into existence primarily as a means of taking unemployed workers in the arts off the relief rolls and putting them to work. Consequently the amount allocated for executive personnel, and especially for materials, was only a small fraction of the total cost of the Project. Even when established theatre workers could be found, capable of handling the directorial and managerial jobs and willing to accept the nominal compensation provided, it was not easy to fit them into the rigid framework. And of course even the simplest theatrical production calls for a substantial expenditure for equipment and accessories. It took considerable ingenuity to find ways of cutting costs and of doing without.

Even with the good will and co-operation of the ruling powers, it would have been hard enough to cope with these conditions; but the hostility and obstruction of influential elements, both inside and outside the government, made the difficulties almost insurmountable. In the first place, in Congress, which was the source of appropriations, there were from the beginning many vociferous and persistent opponents of all the art projects. Some of these dissenters were motivated by considerations of economy; some by a suspicion that all the arts, but particularly the theatre, were allied to the machinations of Satan (or Stalin); but mostly they belonged to the anti-Roosevelt faction, to whom all manifestations of the New Deal or the 'welfare state' were anathema. So the Projects, regardless of their purpose or achievements, were always used as a horrible example of the workings of the Rooseveltian philosophy. (As Philip Guedalla once said: 'Any stigma to beat a dogma.')

Further, the Projects were set up under the authority of the

Works Progress Administration and all organizational activities were governed by its regulations. Every expenditure had to be approved, which meant that every roll of canvas, electric lamp or false moustache had to be separately 'requisitioned' by the directors of the Project and steered through the not always clear 'channels' of the regional WPA office. Attempts to expedite procedures were not always successful, for a good many of the Works Progress Administrators (mostly businessmen who had been reluctantly drafted into the public service) were hostile to the principle underlying the Project or annoyed at having another burden added to their already heavy load.

Outside governmental circles the opposition was equally formidable. Wealthy and influential taxpayers did not attempt to conceal their dissatisfaction with the large-scale expenditure of public moneys for the support of vagabond players, most of whom were presumably Communists or they would not have been unemployed. Nor were they hard put to find space for expression of their complaints in the columns of the powerful anti-Roosevelt press, which lost no opportunity to denounce wastefulness, vote buying and what was quaintly called 'boondoggling'. But most painful of all, at least to me, was the opposition of many leaders of the professional theatre, who argued that the Project's performances at nominal prices were taking business away from them, shortsightedly refusing to see that the Project was making it possible for millions of young people to become interested in the theatre and thereby creating a vast audience for the coming decades.

Within the Project itself all sorts of political and emotional cross-currents were constantly in action. At various times, often simultaneously, I was charged with running a non-union shop and with being dominated by the unions; with favouring Communists and with excluding them; with discrimination against Jews and Negroes. My devotion to the cause of civil liberties was quite generally known, but people with political axes to grind seldom bother about facts.

From the foregoing it might well be inferred that the Theatre Project was doomed to disastrous failure. But surprisingly enough, from an over-all point of view, it turned out to be a brilliant success, thanks to the soundness of its underlying principles and to the skill and devotion of hundreds of its workers. It was clear from the beginning that many of the things hoped for by its inaugurators could never be realized. No money was available and no authority existed for governmental acquisition and renovation of theatres – it took the utmost ingenuity on the part of the New York staff to get the use of any theatre whatever. Nor was it possible to break up the log-jam in New York and send people back to their own communities, where many of them had homes and friends, and where they could have participated in local activities of the Project. There was no money available for transportation; and had there been, the WPA regulations would have made it impossible to transfer relief 'clients' from one jurisdiction to another. And so it went, right down the line, with this or that item in the theoretical programme eliminated or curtailed by fiscal policies, governmental routines, and the usual administrative reluctance to break with tradition.

However, many of the objectives were attained. Foremost, from a humanitarian or social point of view, was the provision for some 10,000 unemployed theatre workers of opportunities for engaging in their professional activities and advancing their careers. In the New York region alone, in the course of three or four months, some 4,500 persons were put on the Project's payroll: about 60 per cent were actors, about 15 per cent technicians of various sorts, the rest playwrights, box-office employees, ushers, cleaners and so on. The effect upon the morale of most of these individuals, many of whom were rapidly succumbing to despair, cannot be overestimated. While the pay they received (the maximum was about twenty-four dollars per week) was barely above subsistence level, the restoration of their self-respect was beyond monetary appraisal. Many, many workers in the theatre today, some of the highest rank, remember with gratitude the help they received from the Federal Theatre Project when they most needed it.

But it is the theatrical record that concerns us here, and that is really extraordinary. In the first place, the regional scheme was strictly adhered to and by the time the Project was in full operation theatre units were performing in forty states. The able leaders of existing community theatres, from the North Carolina Playmakers to the Pasadena Community Theatre, were called upon to lend their experience and influence to the organization of regional units. Resident companies were established in large cities, touring companies in rural areas. A second main item in the programme that was fully achieved was the presentation of good theatre at nominal prices (or without charge) to millions of Americans who either were unfamiliar with the theatre or could not afford to patronize commercial playhouses. According to Mrs Flanagan, something like 63,000 performances were given by the Project in the three and one-half years of its active existence, and the total attendance was over 30,000,000. When admission was charged, prices ranged from twenty-five cents to one dollar; yet the total receipts were in excess of two million dollars.

(iv) *The First Annual Report of the Arts Council of Great Britain: Drama; 1945*

It has been the task of the drama department to begin building up a permanent theatre organization on the basis of the work done during the war. As the most striking and original feature of this work was the touring, which was started to serve the factory hostels and finally spread to small towns, some of which had been theatreless for twenty years, the first preoccupation of the department was to devise the best system for perpetuating this work. Broadly speaking, the aim has been gradually to replace nation-wide touring organized from headquarters by the provision of companies at self-contained centres. It has been necessary to plan this activity on different levels, according to the size of each town to be served, and to choose centres and a method of organizing them *ad hoc*, as theatres or other buildings become available.

In October, 1945, a small cinema in Salisbury, which had been used as a garrison theatre during the war, was opened by the Council and renamed the Arts Theatre. It now has a resident company which plays there for ten days in every month and uses the theatre as a base from which each production can tour the smaller towns of Hampshire and Wiltshire. During the rest of the month, the Salisbury Arts Theatre is let for amateur activities and for concerts, or it presents other small touring companies under the Council's auspices.

In March, 1946, a similar centre was opened at the Coventry Technical College, which had been a regular 'date' for CEMA tours throughout the war. The system here is the same. This company will eventually be linked with another, based on a beautiful old theatre in Kidderminster which has been acquired and restored by an enterprising group of citizens with some assistance from the Council. There are plans for still other centres and for variations of the system in many small towns where promising buildings are available.

Strenuous efforts have been and are still being made to raise the standard of the smaller repertory theatres and to enable them to give wider public service by encouraging or forming small circuits or federations. The object is to achieve better productions by getting away from the system which makes it necessary to present a new play every week. The broader-based organization of such federations should also make for efficiency and higher standards all round, and should enable each one to form subsidiary companies to tour the smaller places in its region. A number of the most enterprising weekly repertory theatres now associated with the Council are actively planning such expansion. For example, it is hoped shortly to link Colchester with Ipswich, where local initiative and enthusiasm is about to provide a small theatre, again with the Council's help and encouragement. The Amersham Repertory Theatre has arranged an interchange of productions with a new organization which is about to start operations in Guildford. Plans for a considerable expansion of the Perth Repertory Theatre are being worked out and will be put into operation shortly.

It will, of course, be some time before these plans become general. A limited number of small town tours are being continued in the meantime. The Great Newport Company from the Arts Theatre have toured Lancashire with a new Dutch play which was later seen at their headquarters in London. Reunion Theatre Guild have undertaken a tour of *The Devil's Disciple* in South Wales and it is hoped that they will eventually establish a permanent centre there.

This small town work presents two very serious problems. The first is the lack of adequate halls or theatres. Most public halls have been built without any regard to proper stage facilities. Companies working from some of the established centres are often unable to play in places where they know their work would be welcomed, because the stages are so inadequate that the standard of presentation for the whole circuit would have to be lowered if the productions were made to fit them. It is hoped to devise special plans to meet these cases. The second difficulty is the lack of sufficiently well qualified actors and actresses prepared to undertake such arduous work in peace time. This may be partly remedied by linking the centres with good repertory theatres or federations of repertory theatres.

Two new repertory companies associated with the Council have been set up this year. In September, 1945, the Glasgow Citizens' Theatre, after two years' experimental work, was established on a broader base in the Princess's Theatre in the Gorbals. Its influence is already being felt in the theatrical life of Scotland and the company is undertaking tours to other Scottish towns, both large and small.

The Theatre Royal, Bristol, the Council's first enterprise in the management of a theatre, has now become the home of the Bristol Old Vic Company, whose first productions have aroused great enthusiasm. A new plan is in operation here, the Old Vic Company running each play for two weeks in Bristol and one week in either Bath or Weston-super-Mare. The vacant week in Bristol is at present being filled by the very interesting productions from the Lyric Theatre, Hammersmith, toured by the Company of Four.

In London and the largest provincial cities, three new companies associated with the Council have recently started operations. Associated Artists, with John Clements as producer, has been touring a new historical play, *The King-Maker,* before bringing it to London, where it is to form part of a repertory of three plays. Sherek Players, whose policy is the presentation of new English plays, with a bias towards those of special contemporary interest, has toured *Frieda,* by Ronald Millar, and this again will be one of a London repertory programme. Theatre '46, which is hoping to specialize in documentary plays by new writers as well as new versions of the classics, gave an experimental season at the Scala Theatre, London, in March, 1946.

Mr Martin Browne's Pilgrim Players started a season at the Mercury Theatre, London, in the autumn of 1945, with plays in verse by contemporary poets. The plays might be thought to have a limited appeal, but in fact one of them, *This Way to the Tomb,* by Ronald Duncan, with Benjamin Britten's music, has proved a widely popular success. Martin Browne has had the courage of his convictions in launching this metropolitan season, but he has not deserted the countryside where a second company of Pilgrim Players continues to work.

Tennent Plays have produced a series of fine revivals. The Haymarket season closed in the summer of 1945 after adding *A Midsummer Night's Dream* and a brilliant production of *The Duchess of Malfi* to the repertory. At the same period, Thornton Wilder's play, *The Skin of our Teeth*, was produced for the Company by Laurence Olivier, with Vivien Leigh in the chief part.

The Tennent Plays Board has been largely concerned in the experimental programme at the Lyric Theatre, Hammersmith, run by itself, Glyndebourne and the Arts Theatre, Cambridge, as the Company of Four. This is another interesting experiment in theatre organization. Each production runs for four weeks at Hammersmith and also visits four provincial centres: at present Brighton, Bristol, Cambridge and Cardiff.

Basil Langton's Travelling Repertory Theatre opened another Hammersmith season at the King's Theatre, in healthy rivalry, in February, 1946. The repertory included popular classics and two interesting new plays. Monday nights were given over to concerts.

The Old Vic have concluded a triumphal year at the New Theatre and have shown that the enthusiasm aroused by their first full London season in the autumn of 1944 was no passing thing. It has led to an important event in the dramatic life of Great Britain, the amalgamation of the Shakespeare Memorial National Theatre Committee and the Old Vic, a combination of forces which is warmly welcomed by the Arts Council. Ambitious plans for the development of a truly National Theatre are now being worked out.

(*v*) *Report on the needs for Drama in England outside London for the Arts Council of Great Britain: Summary of Recommendations; 1965*

The facts considered by the Committee show for the supported companies a situation of some strength. There are more companies in better buildings, with higher standards both in performance and play choice than there were five years ago. Although the enterprises are mostly small in scale their wide distribution, in spite of gaps, means that the live drama is slowly becoming accessible to more and more of the population. They are all locally sponsored, and their close links with their communities give them the opportunity to develop, as theatres, in individual ways, and to become the centres of a wide range of activities. In effect there has come into being a new form of theatrical provision for the provinces, different not only in quantity but in kind, from the struggling 'weekly reps' of a generation ago.

Two facts, however, give cause for concern. Firstly, all this has taken place against a background of serious decline in the older form of provision, the touring system. It is true that repertory theatres now far outnumber touring theatres; nevertheless the provincial public needs both, to house different types of performance. The Arts Council has a special interest in the matter in that its supported companies of opera, ballet, and touring drama need the large theatres of the circuits in which to play.

Secondly, so far as the repertory theatres are concerned, there is strong reason to believe that the positions gained will only with great difficulty be held unless substantial help is forthcoming in what is, in the Committee's opinion, a crucial stage in their history. This help is needed in the provision and improvement of buildings, in the strengthening of local relationships and, above all, in the maintenance and improvement of standards by the strengthening of the supported companies and their direction. This help must come primarily in the form of money, although other forms of encouragement are important.

Help can come from three sources: (a) Local Authorities; (b) business and private benefactors; (c) the Arts Council.

Local Authorities

The Committee believes that the principal sphere of Local Authority help should be in the provision and improvement of buildings and the strengthening generally of local relationships, particularly in the sphere of education. There appears to be an increasing and most welcome willingness on the part of Local Authorities to accept responsibility for the acquisition of theatres or the building of new ones. The major companies are, or will shortly be, well housed; but even here money is badly needed to improve the buildings at Bristol, Liverpool and Sheffield to adapt them to current requirements. In the case of many of the remainder, new buildings or major reconstructions are needed and in some cases are planned. The result, in standards and size of audiences, for the new theatres at Nottingham and Coventry has been obvious and immediate. Nottingham audiences trebled when the new theatre opened, and continue to average nearly 80 per cent of capacity: the Belgrade in Coventry is playing to nearly five times more people each week than the previous Midland Theatre Company in the Technical College.

However, the present method of financing some of these operations gives serious cause for concern. It can hardly be satisfactory for companies to be repaying to local rate funds the total cost of building their theatres out of subsidies provided by the Exchequer, and disbursed by the Arts Council for the improvement of their work. This is transferring money from one public pocket to another. The system adopted causes confusion in the public mind and adds fuel to local squabbles, at a time when ratepayers and their representatives are tentatively showing a willingness to help. A Local Authority will claim credit for providing a theatre, and it will not be generally realized that the total cost plus interest will be paid back by the theatre over a period. If a subsidy is given with the Authority's other hand, to help meet a part of this obligation, the giving of it will be stressed by the local opponents as a sign of loss and failure. The system clearly requires full consideration at both national and local levels.

The Committee suggests (i) that a fund be provided nationally, from which contributions could be made to Local Authorities contemplating the building or improvement of theatres to serve as an encouragement to action, and to help in the avoidance of local controversy; (ii) so far as the Local Authorities' contribution for building or improvement is concerned, if it is necessary to avoid any suggestion of concealed subsidy in municipal bookkeeping, the annual subsidy should automatically be fixed as the equivalent of the repayment figure to the local rate fund in each year until the debt has been repaid; (iii) that the making of a contribution from the suggested fund should be conditional on terms of the tenancy agreement between the Authority and the company being satisfactory, including the assumption by the Local Authority of proper responsibility for maintenance of the building.

Over and above the building question, which the Committee

considers to be a first priority, there remains the whole matter of expenditure by Local Authorities on Entertainment and the Arts, which was very fully discussed in the 1963/64 Arts Council Report. The Committee can only reiterate that few Authorities have yet availed themselves to any effective extent of the powers given to them by the Act of 1948 to help the Drama, and a change of policy here would have a most telling effect on the theatres in their areas. It may be that in some towns in which the Local Authority has provided, or is about to provide, a theatre, difficulty may arise if they are also asked to subsidize the work of the company. Provision of the building, on proper terms, should come first. Once it has become established and an object of local pride, the climate for revenue subsidies tends to become much more favourable. There are, however, many Authorities which do not have, or are not likely to have, theatres in their areas, but whose populations benefit from supported theatres in neighbouring areas: County Council, Councils of smaller Boroughs, Rural District Councils. These can certainly be looked to for grants and a number in fact already make them but mostly on a very small scale. Every effort should be made to encourage them to increase this help. It should be noted however that the 1948 Act does not apply to County Councils but help can be received from them under the Education Acts.

The Committee also welcomes the interest of a number of City and Borough Councils in the acquisition of existing theatres but considers that there is an urgent need for thought as to the uses to which they should be put. Mixed programmes raise problems requiring a fuller consideration than has been possible here. Such consideration might include a recognition that the standard formula of a permanent repertory company may not be the inevitable solution for certain towns, that some diversity in their programmes may be needed, and that these theatres may be a further step in the breaking down of the divisions between commercial and non-commercial and between repertory and touring managements. Provided that a satisfactory system can be devised there may well be justification for a change in the present policy and for subsidy to be given by the Arts Council to the theatre management itself and not only to visiting companies. The knowledge that some grant towards operating costs would be received could be a decisive factor in persuading a Local Authority to acquire its theatre.

Business and Private Benefactors

With regard to business and other private benefactors, their provisions have, up to now, been small and spasmodic. The Committee appreciates the difficulty in persuading industries and businesses to recognize any obligation here, particularly when the theatres concerned receive substantial public money. They welcome the setting up by the Institute of Directors of an Arts Advisory Council. There is evidence nevertheless, that the existence of a theatre of quality in a provincial town is a factor in attracting people engaged in industry to move and live there. Tax allowances for contributions to properly constituted theatres which are recognized as charities would of course be an encouragement to industry and commerce to make such grants.

The regular supply of information to this Arts Advisory Council should stress the importance of the theatre outside London and point out the advantage to a commercial concern and to its staff and their families of a theatre in its locality.

The Arts Council

Responsibility for the artistic strength of what is done in the repertory theatres has been and should continue to be mainly the responsibility of the Arts Council. This is not only a matter of giving money but of encouragement and guidance in the full sense of the Arts Council's Charter. The help in this sense given over the years, particularly by the Arts Council officers, has been a major factor in the attainment of the present position. It has been of great value in placing local theatres in touch with metropolitan sources and standards and has strengthened the hands of theatre directors working in isolation, responsible to a lay Board. It is difficult for the present small staff in the Drama Department to maintain enough contact with all the theatres and to fulfil adequately their function as assessors. In the Committee's view the staff should be increased.

Nevertheless, the basic need is for money for the companies themselves. The Committee are perfectly satisfied that there is little or no possibility of waste or extravagance in the budgets of any of the enterprises they studied. As Appendix B Drama 2 of the Arts Council Report for 1963/64 shows, the subsidy element for these theatres from all sources averaged out over all the companies is now 24 per cent of income by trading.

This addition to box-office takings has, over the years, made all the difference not only between survival and extinction but between adventurousness and playing for safety, between quality and mediocrity. The Committee consider that the time has come for a substantial increase in Arts Council subsidy. This would in turn result in an increase, if not an exactly corresponding one, in audience and takings. The achievements of the last ten years, as revealed in the Committee's Report, suggest an opportunity which can only be taken if additional strength is given in the measure now recommended. The situation will not be met by small annual additions to the present subsidy figures.

The sums required should, in the Committee's view, be in the following ranges:

For the major theatres, subsidies should be increased from up to £17,000 as at present to around £50,000 per annum. This would enable salaries of the order of £60 per week to be paid to directors and principal members of the company and allow for occasional special engagements which may have to be at a higher figure. This meets the unanimous view of the Drama Panel that the top figure of £50 per week suggested by certain directors is not enough, taking into account the financial and domestic disadvantages for an actor working in the provinces, and that these theatres should be in a position to offer more to an actor than he would receive in London. Actors commonly have flats or homes in London which they cannot give up for comparatively short provincial engagements – this means that they have to find double rent, be separated from their families and are cut off from the possibility of increasing their earnings by casual radio or TV engagements. This is true wherever they are working. Equally important, the subsidies recommended would allow the whole salary structure of these companies to become more realistic to ensure that actors in the intermediate and lower ranges, as well as managers, designers, technical and administrative staff could be engaged at adequate salaries to ensure the employment of people of the right quality. It would also allow certain new appointments to be made, for example public relations officers to build up and win new audiences. Such grants would also enable these theatres to be more bold in their policy and choice of programme and to raise the standard of presentation. These sums would result in a total subsidy to this class of theatre of £350,000 per annum and, in the Committee's view, it should be made for the year beginning April 1965, as all the major theatres are in a position immediately to make effective use of it.

Of the remaining repertory theatres, some fourteen urgently need and could immediately (i.e. from April 1965) effectively use subsidies of £20,000 each compared with their present figures of around £6,000. This would enable salaries to the directors and leading actors of possibly £40 per week to be paid and commensurate increase in the intermediate and lower ranges, as well as for managers, designers and other staff. The result would be an immediate improvement in their programmes of plays and their presentation. For this group a total sum of about £280,000 would meet the situation for a year, but after that, this figure should be increased to £400,000 to be spent on grants of up to £30,000 to such of these theatres as have justified it, by their development, real and potential, and the quality of their work. These factors should determine the size and pace of the increases.

For the thirteen smaller theatres whose grants at present range from £750 to £4,000 the Committee considers that these sums should be increased up to £10,000 in the cases where further growth seems possible. The total requirement for this group is £130,000. Their claim to such increases must be dependent upon proof of their ability to move into a higher category, and failure to show that they can do so will raise doubts as to their qualification for continued support.

With regard to touring companies, an increased sum should be earmarked for their support, but the precise amount cannot be assessed until further investigation of their position and their relationship with certain Local Authority theatres has taken place. It should be of the order of £100,000, to cover touring by the National Theatre, Royal Shakespeare Theatre, English Stage Company, as well as the specifically touring companies.

A sum of £53,000 will be required to meet the needs of the training schemes and New Drama referred to in Section 5 of the Report (New Designers £17,000; Producers, Managers, Technicians £8,000; New and Neglected Drama £28,000). For the extension of the Transport Subsidy scheme, £15,000 would be required. In the opinion of the Committee, these schemes have been of quite exceptional value, not only in the provinces, but to the theatre of this country as a whole. The Sub-Committees of the Drama Panel responsible for these activities consider that an increase to the figure mentioned above would allow for the necessary development in this work.

Finally, it is the Committee's view that a sum should be provided to cover likely needs for new companies which may come into being in areas where there are at present no theatres and to cover possible extensions in the number of activities of the supported touring companies. This should be in the region of £40,000 per year.

In all these calculations, except for the fourteen theatres in the second category, where a further substantial increase would be required in 1966/67, the Committee consider that national percentage increases of up to 10 per cent would be required to keep pace with rising costs.

Subsidies at the rates suggested would mainly be spent on salaries though they would immediately add something to the present meagre allowances for scenery and costumes. Nevertheless the resultant salary ranges would still not be excessive in relation to what is paid in other professions or in other branches of the theatrical and entertainment industry with which the provincial theatres are in competition for artists. Subsidies in the range contemplated would:

(1) Enable larger companies to be engaged making possible a choice of plays from a wider repertoire;

(2) Enable actors of talent and experience to join these companies and to commit themselves to long-term contracts. Repertory theatres will always be invaluable training grounds but provincial towns should have companies which are not entirely composed of young and raw actors;

(3) Help to ensure that the key figures, the directors, managers and designers, are of the right calibre. There is a strong case for payment of greatly increased salaries for these positions in certain of the theatres other than the major ones, to attract the right man in towns where there is a possibility of development;

(4) Enable companies so to arrange their work by increased rehearsal periods and by the adoption in appropriate cases of the true repertory system, that a higher standard can be achieved. The Committee are strongly in favour of the extension of the true repertory system wherever it proves practical.

It is the opinion of the Committee that if the companies are assisted in this way to operate more effectively the audience's response will be immediate and box-office takings will be increased. This has been taken into account in assessing the amount of subsidy needed.

How far these takings can be further increased by a rise in seat prices is a difficult question. Can these increases be at a higher rate than the fairly steady rise which has in fact taken place over the past ten years or so? New theatres with greater amenities often make it possible to raise prices fairly steeply. Leaving this factor aside the Committee cannot recommend any immediate and substantial rise. The whole conception of these theatres is that they should be places which all sections of the community can visit. Provincial people are not accustomed to paying the metropolitan prices which they themselves will readily accept for occasional visits to London. There is also reluctance on the part of the touring theatres to increase their own prices beyond a certain level and repertory theatres, in spite of their smaller size and seating capacity, have largely to keep in step. However, there should be regular reviews of seat prices by the supported theatres.

Summary of financial recommendations

	1965/66	1966/67 +10 per cent except *
	£	£
Seven major theatres	350,000	385,000
Fourteen theatres in the second category	280,000	400,000*
The thirteen smaller theatres	130,000	143,000
Touring	100,000	110,000
Training and New Drama	53,000	58,300
Transport Subsidy	15,000	16,500
Provision for new companies	40,000	44,000
	953,000	1,156,800

The sums proposed are substantial, but only in relation to the size of the present grants. These grants have been enough, but only just enough, to allow more than thirty or so theatres to establish themselves and strike their roots, some over a long period, the great majority since the last war. This has been achieved with very small resources and at the cost of self sacrifice on the part of many artists. The Committee believes that assistance on the scale suggested would now give the provincial theatre the strength and stability which it needs to make its important contribution to the life of our towns and cities and the enrichment of our theatrical tradition, in a way which is appropriate to the times in which we live.

(vi) The Difficulty of Getting Things Done Properly; 1964
By John Arden*

It is becoming more and more clear to me that it is impossible for workers in the British theatre ever to finish their job properly. I am not referring to playwrights—we can sit with a script on our desks for as long as we like, messing about with it and titivating it; but once it has passed into the hands of a company, the pressures of time and money will combine to ensure that it will be presented in a manner so slapdash and unconsidered, that if it were a ship to be put to sea or a building to be lived in, a prosecution for dangerous negligence would inevitably follow.

This is in no sense a criticism of actors and producers – they are equally aware that their talents are continually wasted and their energies frustrated by shortage of time and the necessity of pushing forward with work that they know to be only half-prepared. I do not believe that a new play of any size or complexity can possibly be put on without at least six months' preliminary work – most of it between the author, director and designer. The actors should never receive their scripts until every problem of interpretation of the essential meaning of the play has been thoroughly examined and at any rate partially solved.

I am moved to write this article after having had a new play presented by the Glasgow Citizens' Company. Now this company have done extremely well with what must have been a difficult play to present: but they had only three weeks in which to rehearse

* I would like to make clear that this article was not intended as a specific criticism of the Glasgow Citizens' Theatre or of any of the individuals involved in the production of my play there. On its original publication in *The Guardian* it did, I believe, give some offence. I very much regretted this, for I had meant it to be understood as a commendation of the Citizens' Company for presenting *Armstrong's Last Goodnight* so well, *despite* many difficulties, which were not of their own making. These difficulties were, and still are, endemic to the production of new plays in local, subsidized theatres: and have little or nothing to do with the professional skills of directors, actors, designers and technical staff. (John Arden 1968)

it, and not much longer in which to prepare for the rehearsals. This is not their fault – usually they have only a fortnight. It is the fault of the system that in this case subsidises with public money what is virtually the Scottish National Theatre but so restricts the subsidy that any more expansive system of work would put all the actors out of employment in a month.

To take two small examples of what I mean. An actor was cast in the part of a sixteenth-century ecclesiastic. I wrote the part in an appropriate Scots speech of the period. After three weeks of rehearsal – two days before the first night – it became evident that the actor (an Englishman) could not manage the accent sufficiently well to convince a Glasgow audience. So we had to make him a Frenchman. This was historically plausible, but clearly the character of a Scots priest in Scotland requires an entirely different approach from that of a French priest in Scotland.

There was no time for the actor to adjust his reading, so we had to be content with a change of accent and the hope that the audience would not notice. They did not notice – at least I don't think they did. But if they were used to seeing plays where such details as the social backgrounds of personages were seriously considered, they should have done.

A second problem was the set. As the scenery for the previous production occupied the stage throughout rehearsals, our set was not built until within 36 hours of the curtain going up. We then realized that a basic misconception in the design (as much my fault as anyone else's) meant that, by the highest standards, the whole thing should have been taken down and rebuilt from the floor up. But there was no time, the highest standards were of necessity ignored, and a hurried job of chopping and patching was carried out, which pleased nobody, least of all the designer.

The theatre today is full of talented people who seek only an opportunity to exercise their craft with some sense of fulfilment and responsibility. The sort of frustration I have described above is not confined to the provincial stages. The work done at the National and Aldwych Theatres bears similar signs of irrelevant pressure and haste. The nation seems to agree in principle that the theatre is an art which we need and should be prepared to pay for: but there is as yet no understanding that to pay for shoddy theatre and to be content with it is almost worse than to pay for none at all.

If such circumstances are discovered in, say, the armed forces, there is a row in Parliament and individuals find themselves called to account. We hear a great deal these days from politicians about efficiency and modernization: I would be more impressed by these protestations if I thought they were applied to other aspects of national life than our ability to administer nuclear megadeaths or to fill an inadequate road system with unsafe motor vehicles. I was told recently by a German producer that he regarded Britain as theatrically the most stimulating country in Europe. I found it painful to disillusion him. Is it too much to hope for that in a few years' time there will be no need to do so?

(vii) *West End Managements and the Playwrights; 1958* a letter from Robert Bolt

I would like to claim that I wanted to enter the West End in order to get the best acting and direction for my play, but, of course, the best acting and direction are not confined there. A West End production is a form of success, and I wanted it for all those vanities and greeds that success is held to satisfy. Also I wanted it because only there could a play earn enough money for me to leave off schoolteaching and become a professional. These, not very edifying, were my motives and, while I don't suppose I am alone in them, they are of no social significance – unless the obvious fact that a writer ticks in the same way as most other people is of social significance.

And perhaps playwrights *ought* not to want to get into the West End. Have not the centres of theatrical vitality been outside the commercial enclave? When did the West End do anything other than reap a debased harvest from the true seed sown by others?

I think there is truth behind these rhetorical questions, but that something remains to be said. I don't know how the Moscow Arts and New York Group theatres were financed but I do know that they played so often to such small houses that under the conditions obtaining now, here, they couldn't have functioned. In our Experimental Theatres (I mean such theatres as the Oxford Playhouse and Royal Court) excellent productions of plays whose importance nobody denies frequently attract fractional audiences which do not meet the costs of the theatre. The theatre-goers, and even the theatre-lovers, who should be filling the seats, are in the West End; or perhaps at home reading about it.

This does not mean that these theatres are doomed to fail; it means that their Directors are doomed to look out for a 'hit', a *Lysistrata* or *Look Back in Anger* to pay for productions which have run at a loss. This 'hit', the audience being given (and it *is* given; the Experimental Theatres have not succeeded in building up adequate audiences of their own) is likely to be not very dissimilar from the best concurrently offered in the West End.

I am very far from concluding that these theatres have no function here. *Look Back in Anger* was given life by such a theatre and I doubt if any West End management would at that time have done it. But when *Look Back in Anger* happened the West End *saw* that something had happened. Just as there is a strong external pressure on the Experimental Theatre to find a 'hit' so, I believe, there is a strong internal pressure on the West End to find plays that are more than show business.

This brings me to the second rhetorical question and the point where I can make use of my own recent experience. The managements mean it when they say they want new plays by new playwrights. When such a script is rumoured to have arrived in someone's office, copies are sought for very vigorously indeed. And it is a new kind of play that is wanted. Of a competent and witty play attracting large audiences a manager said apologetically, 'Of course, it's only the *old* stuff.' The internal pressure to find the new stuff is sometimes mere irritated bewilderment, as when a very experienced manager, asked if he thought his current play would 'go' replied from the heart 'Who the blazes knows *what's* going to go these days?' But at other times it is simple excitement and pleasure that the London Theatre should be getting on the move once more. My suggestion is that our Art Theatre and our Commercial Theatre may be moving a little closer than is sometimes admitted.

Now all this is very comfortable and I imagine the fury it may provoke in some of your readers whose experience does not bear it out, no-longer-young playwrights who have beaten their fists for years perhaps on those unresponsive doors. You ask me: 'Is it really possible for good plays to get stuck in managers' offices and die there?' I think it happens less often than is supposed, that every off-beat play which has a success (*Look Back, Entertainer, Seventeenth Doll*) makes it less likely; but it does happen.

Before guessing how it happens I had better give my own history. I have written eight plays. The first three were for radio (and I would recommend to anyone the BBC as a loyal if slightly stodgy patron whose requirements are not so different from, and perforce less exacting than, those of the stage). The next five were stage plays, and my agent dissuaded me from showing the first three of these to managements at all. It hardly needs saying that this was much against my will; such technical faults as my plays embodied seemed to me lesser on any serious count than the faults of heart embodied in several plays then running, and anyway was I expected to write a masterpiece before . . . etc., etc. The last two plays were shown to managements and both were bought and produced.

And here I think we come to it. Of the many plays that seek production in the West End the majority are at a glance unworkable and these are rejected quickly. (I don't believe that scripts lie about for long simply unread; the market is too keen.) The ones that get hung up are plays which tempt the manager by their quality but have some fault of pace, development, characterization, or dialogue which makes him nervous. These are the plays on which he takes out an option for six months, hesitates a month, takes out another option and so on and eventually returns. This is the experience which makes authors old before their time and it only happens to good, or goodish, scripts. But I think the root of it is usually to be found *in* the script.

Do I then propose that the author accept the manager's willingness to produce his play as an infallible measure of its quality? Of course not; plays are receiving production all the time which are not only faulty in heart but riddled with faults of technique also. But these tend to be examples, decadent examples, of the 'old stuff', the last rather desperate scrapings from the bottom of that particular barrel. It is to be expected that managers should be more wary, more demanding, of the new stuff, for as yet they don't know where or what its strength is – except in the fact of its not being the 'old stuff'.

What I do propose is that authors should not waste time exploring 'complicated and various' channels, but should use it in improving their plays. (That rings very priggy; but the work of an unknown author is usually open to improvement by himself because, though he may be an equally skilled craftsman with authors whose work is regularly produced, he is always tempted

to think: 'It doesn't matter anyway; no one will ever read it.')
I make this proposal not because cultivating 'contacts' is
immoral, it isn't, but because it is uneconomical. By whatever
efforts the manager is brought to the water, if there is a serious
fault in the play he won't, finally, drink.

And against this I should be surprised if the managers in their
present mood allowed a thoroughly workable play on a worthwhile
theme to lie dormant for long.

Having said that I must immediately make a partial recantation.
Such a play *could* lie dormant I think if it were deliberately
written without 'parts', without, we may as well say it, 'star parts'.
And any nameless playwright who wants his work to hold his
audiences off with composed formality rather than drawing them
in by the warmth of powerful personalities in powerful situations,
may well be in for a thin time. For if the manager can secure a
star cast he will, and then there is a danger that the play will be
forced into an inappropriate convention; and if he cannot he may
lose confidence in the script altogether. Clearly a gulf could open
here between author and manager, though it is not impossible
that, given a strong lead from the Experimental Theatres, the
West End would modify its preoccupation with casting. I know
of no one in this country who is yet writing for an effect of full
alienation and my misgivings on this are for the future.

For the present I am convinced that the unknown author's
effort is most likely to be fruitful when it is directed to his script
which, when it is ready, should be marketed in the most obvious
way, through an agent, who should be as tough as possible –
artistically tough that is, not commercially tough. If I may return
to my own experience again: I think my agent was right to stencil
out those first three plays. The managements are used to
promising scripts, near misses, and to have had three such going
the rounds would have done me harm rather than good, even had
they been more promising, and nearer misses than they were.
What is wanted, with an eagerness verging on rapacity, is the
script that is more or less on target.

There was a gap, covered by extended options, between the
purchase and production of *The Critic and the Heart,* of 16 months,
and the production when it came was comparatively modest. I
think there were two reasons for this; firstly the play itself was
in various ways not strong enough, secondly and arising from
that, it did not attract stars of the first magnitude.

You ask me if I regard *Flowering Cherry* as my best play. I'm not sure, but it is certainly my most ambitious and from a manager's point of view the most risky in theme and treatment, and its history exemplifies well the script-hunger of the West End. It was read and bought by Frith Banbury, Ltd., the joint managers with H. M. Tennent, Ltd., almost within hours of their receiving it. It was sent at once to Sir Ralph Richardson and Miss Celia Johnson and within a few days both sent favourable replies which within two or three weeks hardened into definite acceptances. From then on it was, for me at any rate, plain sailing, though it is worth noting that H. M. Tennent, Ltd., and the Haymarket managers gave sufficient importance to the play to support in its favour some inconvenience and I think loss, connected with the change-over from *The Chalk Garden*.

Also, and contrary I confess to my expectations, I was active at every stage of the production; auditioning, rehearsals, scene setting, and throughout the out-of-Town run. Naturally all these people do not sit at the feet of an untried author panting to materialize his every suggestion. But, for example, I was questioned and consulted in detail and repeatedly by the producer Frith Banbury; the management brought the production from Liverpool to Oxford before sending it back north to Leeds for no other purpose than that the author should be able to attend a run of performances; and from the stars I met with none of that arrogance and indifference to my intention which is part of theatrical folklore but on the contrary, courtesy and a willingness to listen.

Does all this sound like a man seduced, preparing now to write fat parts in box sets and generally be a good boy? Well, that's the danger of course – just as the danger of being in an under-privileged minority is that one will grow to like it. As with a greater conflict in a wider arena, the conflict between Art and Commercial Theatre may be partly caused by the conviction of both camps that it must be so.

(vii) Broadway Theatre Myths; 1965 by Thomas Gale Moore

The theatre is an anachronism. Once the only form of dramatic entertainment, it now survives as a handicraft industry. What the assembly line did for automobiles, movies and television have done for drama. Like hand-woven sweaters, theatre has become a luxury that can be afforded only by a very few. And because its essence is live actors performing before a live audience, attempts to mechanize it are vain. Costs per spectator, and consequently ticket prices, will always be higher than movie admissions – and the aesthetic results more uncertain than in film. It is therefore a myth to suppose that the live theatre will ever be 'popular'.

A number of other beliefs about the theatre are likewise myths. Articles proclaim that the 'theatre is dying' or 'costs are pricing the theatre out of existence'. The latter death-knell is usually accompanied by statements that 'scalping is driving the audience away' or 'ice is draining income that would make the theatre affluent'. Often the claim is made that 'only comedies or musicals can succeed' or that 'playwrights are coerced by producers into writing plays with small casts and few scenes'. Some of these assertions have a superficial plausibility; others are half-true. None are accurate.

'It is later than Broadway thinks,' Howard Taubman wrote of the 1962–3 season. In fact, Broadway's death has been frequently predicted. Despite statistics which appear to support such obituaries, the data on gross receipts, performances, and profits belie them. Some facts which substantiate pessimism are that productions on Broadway have dropped from a high of 264 in 1927–8 to 60 in 1963–4, new plays have slumped from 183 to 35, and new musicals have dropped from 53 to 15. The contraction in the theatre has not, however, been continuous. Broadway openings fell rapidly in the thirties because of the Depression but, buoyed by a population seeking release, they rose slightly during World War II and the Korean War. The trend, however, is downward, and if it continues, by 1970 there will only be about 43 Broadway premieres; by 1980, under 34.

What are the best criteria for evaluating Broadway's health? Persons concerned with the richness of a season judge by the number of premieres. The fact that a New York audience is the final test for new plays supports this thesis. Broadway is the source of most properties used in summer, community, amateur, and university theatres; it directly feeds Hollywood and TV; its scores and librettos help sustain the record industry. From the point of view of our national theatre and other entertainment media, Broadway's contraction has been unfortunate. At its peak, over 200 new plays and musicals a season were made available for national production; in the fifties, these diminished to fewer than 50.

To the casual theatre-goer the number of openings must seem like an irrelevant statistic; he is far more impressed with the range of his selection. If, as happened during a typical week in February, 1927, 27 plays and 17 musicals were playing, the theatre-goer was more likely to find what he wanted than if, as in February, 1963, there were only 15 plays and nine musicals. On this basis, however, there has been less shrinkage in total theatrical activity than in openings.

During the thirties, the musical theatre was especially hard hit. In February, 1934, there were only two musicals running compared to 17, seven years earlier. Because Americans like girls, music, and dancing, the musical stage came back strongly after those bleak days, but it has never attained its pre-Depression level. Serious theatre and bread-lines went together: the non-musical stage, while contracting from 1930 to 1934, suffered less than musicals, and the number of straight plays on Broadway has remained static since the New Deal. The total number of productions running each week is larger today than in the thirties. While total productions per season have contracted 80 per cent since the twenties, the number of shows playing – during an average week in February – has declined only 50 per cent.

Other criteria for evaluating Broadway's health are relevant to special groups. Performers, stage-hands, and front-of-the-house personnel are concerned with the number of work-weeks per year. Feast alternating with famine has been their lot. Total performances – a measure of work-weeks – fell to half the mid-twenties' level by 1933–4, aggravating a chronically bad employment situation. Throughout the thirties and into the War, the yearly total of performances remained low and fully-employed actors scarce. Theatrical activity boomed as the War went on, pushing performances to a peak exceeded only during the late twenties and early thirties. This peak has not since been topped. In recent seasons, the work-weeks have been low: between 8,000 and 9,500 performances were given – the same level as during the Depression. Job opportunities, though no worse than in the grim thirties, are no better.

The earnings of proprietors, producers, and playwrights depend on box-office. After 1930, the decline in receipts – they fell 60 per cent – was so steep and abrupt that many theatre owners lost their property. The Shuberts were unable to pay interest on their bonds and went into receivership. Since the disastrous 1933–4 season, total gross has inched upward, mostly because of the musicals. But when inflation is taken into account, average receipts per show per week have remained static since the Depression.

Why, then, do people invest? The angels who back Broadway shows do not put up $100,000 solely because they love the theatre. Almost all hope to get their money back with a profit. As the partnership is usually drawn up, the backers get the operating surplus – the difference between weekly costs and box-office gross – until their investment is repaid. Only about one out of five shows recoups its investment; then the angels get half of the operating surplus as their share of the profits. The longer a show runs, the larger the take. Frequently, with a flop, the 'profit' takes the form of a tax loss.

The profit to investors depends on production costs and operating surplus as well as length of run. Average runs have doubled since the twenties, but the average production cost has tripled. On the other hand, gross receipts have advanced more rapidly than operating costs and, consequently, operating surpluses have climbed over the past 35 years. The net result is that average profits have probably remained constant. Certainly the proportion of plays which recoup their investment has remained constant.

Averages can conceal more than they reveal. Not all shows run twice as long as in the twenties. In fact, while a few productions run for years, many close immediately. The hit or flop alternative has become less avoidable. In 1927–8, 12·8 per cent of the plays lasted less than ten performances (most of these ran for a full week); but in the three seasons following 1957, 23 per cent raised their curtains less than ten times, many closing after one or two nights. In 1927–8 no play ran more than 440 performances; but in the more recent period, 12 plays – 10 per cent of the total – lasted for more than 450 performances. In the twenties, many plays persisted for two, three, or four weeks. By the late fifties, however, plays either shut promptly or had a substantial run. In our current situation, it is obvious after several nights whether or not a production will cover its operating expense. If not, it promptly closes. According to *Variety*, the most expensive one-night stand in history took place 6 February, 1965, at the

Broadhurst theatre when *Kelly* folded after its premier performance for an estimated loss of $650,000.

With investment per play considerably higher, and failure assuredly faster, the theatre is a riskier venture than before. While on the average it may be as profitable as ever, if one figures in the diminishing value of money, investors lose more with a flop and earn more with a hit than they did before the Depression. Backing plays can be lucrative. Mr and Mrs Howard S. Cullman earned about $2,000,000 on 300 productions from 1938 to 1961; Arthur Cantor, who invested in 41 shows between 1957 and 1961, counted 25 hits which earned about 50 per cent profit on his investment of $103,000. According to one study, an investor who supported *all* the shows between 1948 and 1958 would have earned 19·5 per cent annually. Unfortunately, it is impossible to invest in all shows. Some producers finance their own productions, others have a coterie of backers and seek new money only when the property looks doubtful. New producers will accept money from any source. However, neither situation is usually profitable.

While the statistics do not indicate a Broadway renaissance, neither do they suggest that Broadway is dying: profits are good; the number of plays showing at any time is up since the Depression; box-office has climbed. Yet actors find employment on Broadway scarce, and each season offers fewer new plays.

Factors Affecting Broadway

In the late twenties and early thirties, three things decimated the theatre: the depression, sound movies, and radio. The sharp drop in the national economy cut attendance drastically, and the worst season in modern history was that of 1933–4. By the end of the thirties other industries had regained their pre-Depression levels, but not the theatre.

With the introduction of synchronous sound track, movie grosses at downtown New York theatre doubled. By February, 1929, *before* the Depression, Broadway box-office receipts began to decline. By 1931, when the film houses were at their pre-Depression peak, sales for musicals had fallen off 80 per cent. As might be expected, talkies had less effect on straight plays. Box-office peaked there two years after the musical theatre had started to slide. And, although straight plays never regained their pre-1930 level, the reduction in earnings was considerably less than it was for musicals. Besides changing the entertainment habits of millions, sound revolutionized Hollywood. Picture companies turned swiftly to the great reservoir of Broadway for writers, actors, and directors.

Thus the talkies had two effects on the New York theatre: audiences deserted to the movies and personnel deserted to Hollywood. If the former effect had been dominant we should have expected a reduction in Broadway ticket costs to recoup audiences. In fact, theatre rentals were reduced from about 45 per cent of gross to about 30 per cent. But instead of lower ticket prices, charges increased. Between 1926–37 – in the face of a 60 per cent reduction in tickets sold – ticket prices climbed 5 per cent for musicals and 21 per cent for plays even after adjusting for changes in the value of money. Production and operating expenses shot up: from the late twenties to 1940 these advanced 43 per cent. A major factor was competitive bidding against Hollywood for talent.

Radio added to the stage's troubles. Although it was a poor substitute for live drama and a medium which appealed to that mass audience which never came to the theatre, radio, like Hollywood, deprived the stage of needed talent. Helen Hayes, for example, was wanted in New York, in Hollywood, and on the networks.

In the long run it was the combined effects of supply and demand that cut weekly attendance in half. By 1940, an individual in search of entertainment could listen at almost no cost to *Stella Dallas* or *The Shadow*; he could see *Gone With the Wind* for 75c and most other films for less. Only the best talents could lure him to Broadway, where he would spend $2.20 or $3.30. But good talent was scarce and therefore producers offered fewer shows.

One might think that TV too has hurt Broadway. But, surprisingly, TV has had little effect. By 1955 almost every city in the country was within reach of a station; yet during the years 1945–55 there was no downward trend in either attendance or box-office receipts. If TV has affected any market, it is the movies. Even the TV talent drain has been largely from those who would otherwise make their careers in film.

Ticket Prices
While the post-war stagnation of Broadway has often been traced to the rise in ticket prices, most of this increase can be attributed

to simple inflation: the *real price* of tickets has gone up very little, 15 per cent for a straight play, 8 per cent for a musical. Compared to the thirties, today's seats, in dollars of 1963 purchasing power, actually cost less: in 1934–5 the average for the best seat at a play was $7.54; in 1962–3 it was $7.50; in 1929–30, the best seat for a musical cost $10.82, in February, 1963, the cost was down to $9.18.

The movement in ticket prices reveals the underlying cost trends affecting Broadway. Prices for plays rose from the 1927–1928 season until the mid-thirties. Subsequently they declined, reaching a low point during the War. Post-war prices rose after 1954, and a real-price peak was reached in 1959–60. Prices have remained constant since then. Ticket prices for musicals have followed the same pattern, except that the peak came earlier (1929–30) and the bottom came earlier also (1933–4).

Rising Costs

Both production and operating costs ballooned between the late twenties and 1940. Simultaneously, theatre rent fell. In the twenties a producer kept only 50–55 per cent of the gross receipts; by 1940 he took 70–75 per cent.

Production cost figures are generally unavailable for the period around 1940. Yet we know from producers' records that cost doubled during the thirties and rose only 10 per cent during the forties. Actors' salaries for rehearsals tripled from before the Depression to 1950. During the same period the cost of scenery doubled, and outlays for costumes rose 147 per cent. Payments to designers went up 170 per cent in the thirties and directors, who had been receiving flat fees, were, by 1940 earning a percentage of the box-office in addition to a fee. These figures reflect an attempt by producers to upgrade their productions as a response to motion picture and radio competition.

Between 1940 and 1950, the 10 per cent increase in production costs was matched by a small drop in operating costs. The result was that the cost of a show remained unchanged from 1940 to 1953. But during the last half of the fifties, costs again went up, pushing ticket prices ahead of them. Much of this rise in expense is due to higher spending for publicity. Between 1955 and 1961, weekly advertising costs more than doubled. Expenditures for ads in the *New York Times* increased only 26 per cent; the rest of the increase was spent on billboards, TV, radio, magazines, and out-of-city newspapers. The big advertising push was made largely to increase pre-opening sales and to attract a non-New York audience. I have conducted a survey and found that theatre-goers claim rarely to be influenced by non-newspaper ads; much publicity money, then, may be ill-spent.

Almost as expensive as the growth in advertising expenditure has been the multiplication of incidental expenses, such as lawyers' fees, accounting costs, telephone, insurance, secretarial service, and transportation. Some of these expenses, such as transportation and telephone, reflect the use of stars, directors, and authors who are imported from great distances. But many of these 'small' expenses seem unnecessary. For example, late in the 1940s the Securities and Exchange Commission ruled that the limited partnership agreement used on Broadway was a sale of securities to the public and subject to regulation. The Commission assured producers that only a short set of papers would be required and that five days after filing, unless the Commission objected, backers could be accepted. Five days grew to six or seven weeks and the short set of papers multiplied. At one time the SEC even proposed that a plot synopsis be included in the bundle! Recently the SEC has required all those who have produced a show before to list the profits of past efforts.

In 1964, the New York State Legislature enacted a bill requiring producers to file more reports and keep more records. Thus new secretaries must be hired, more legal and accounting fees paid. The intent of the law is to protect innocent investors from rapacious producers; at the same time, the new bureaucracy costs money. In passing, it might be noted that legislation to protect investors in other areas has not been notably successful (see George J. Stigler, 'Public Regulation of the Securities Markets,' *The Journal of Business*, April, 1964).

Unions and Costs

There is a widespread belief both in and out of the theatre that feather-bedding and exorbitant labour demands have been responsible for increased costs. The major items contributing to the 70 per cent rise in weekly total outlay over the past 35 years are presented in table over page.

The fastest growing items have been directors' fees and the 'miscellaneous' bureaucratic entries just discussed. But directors were non-union during the period considered; and certainly the

MAJOR FACTORS CONTRIBUTING TO THE INCREASE IN TOTAL
PRODUCING AND OPERATING COSTS ON BROADWAY (PLAYS ONLY)

Factor	Percentage of total costs		Percentage rise in weekly expenditures (in constant dollars)	Percentage contribution to rise in total costs
	1927–9	1960–1		
Cast	39·1	30·5	32·3	27·3
Advertising	15·6	15·8	71·7	16·2
Playwright	10·0	9·3	58·6	9·1
Crew	5·7	6·2	86·2	6·4
Scenery & Props	12·0	5·7	−19·4	3·4
Directors' fees	2·4	3·2	129·8	3·5
Scenic Designers	1·3	1·2	51·0	1·1
Managers*	2·6	4·7	—	—
Costumes	2·6	1·9	27·4	1·7
Electrical & Sound	2·7	1·1	−31·3	0·5
Miscellaneous	6·0	20·4	474·2	25·6

* In 1927–9 this includes only stage and company managers. In 1960–1 it includes general managers as well. Because of difference in definition, comparisons between the seasons cannot be made.

miscellaneous expenses cannot be attributed to the unions. In fact, three of the four fastest climbing factors are unrelated to union activity.

Furthermore, increase in payment to unionized personnel can be explained by other factors. Although the average size of a Broadway cast has remained unchanged, the real weekly salaries to actors have increased 32 per cent since the late twenties. Meanwhile, weekly wages in manufacturing have more than doubled. One could argue that Actors' Equity has been a rather ineffective union.

There is more opportunity for automation backstage than onstage. Nevertheless, because each show presents unique problems, the possibilities for automation are limited. Most charges of featherbedding start or end with a story about the Theatrical Protective Union, Local 1, of the International Alliance of Theatrical Stage Employees (the stage-hands' union). Everyone knows tales about the stage-hand whose only job is to push a button in the second act but who cannot be asked to move a chair in the third. If we reduce these stories to statistics, we see that outlays for stage-hands have not risen excessively. Crew costs have risen 86 per cent over the past 35 years, which is still below the rise in manufacturing wages. And from the producer's point of view, crew cost is a small item, accounting for only 6·2 per cent of total expenditures during 1960–1. In the twenties, crew costs made up 5·7 per cent of expenditures. If, in the absence of unions, there had been no rise in the payments for grips, carpenters, electricians, etc., total outlays during the 1960–1 season would have been only 6 per cent lower. Other unionized employees, such as designers and stage managers, account for an even smaller proportion of total costs.

Slightly over 9 per cent of the increase in real total outlay can be attributed to earning advances made by playwrights. There is good reason to believe that this increase was due to movies, radio, and TV competition. The rise in earnings may be in part due to the Dramatists' Guild; however, the Guild sets only minimum terms and those for Broadway productions have remained unchanged since 1928.

Briefly, the unions have had a negligible effect on costs.

Ice

When the surcharge on tickets exceeds the legitimate ticket agency charge of $1.50 plus tax, or the tickets are purchased at a premium from a source other than an agency, the resulting excess payment is illegal: that's 'ice'. There has been more wild talk by theatre people about ice than any other topic. Estimates of its magnitude have ranged as high as $10,000,000 a year; various theatre problems, including the progressive decline in Broadway openings, have been attributed to it.

To secure hard figures on ice I took a survey in April, 1962, of audiences in seven Broadway houses, for a total of 18 performances; questionnaires were included in the *Playbills* and 26 per cent of the evening audience was represented by the returns. A few visitors to New York during the survey week were charged as much as $29 for a $9.60 seat to a Friday performance of *How to Succeed in Business Without Really Trying*. Some others paid $26 for a $7.50 seat to *A Thousand Clowns*. New Yorkers tended to make smaller illegal payments. The highest, $27, was paid for a Wednesday evening performance of *How to Succeed*. Out of town patrons made up only 30 per cent of the audience, but they accounted for more than 60 per cent of the total ice.

For *How to Succeed*, the biggest hit, the audience paid well over $80,000. At that time *Variety* listed the box-office receipts at $67,000. Earlier in the run, scalpers must have taken in more. Extrapolating from the surveyed shows, illegal receipts during the survey week must have been between $30,000 and $55,000. The New York State investigation committee charged that ice may be $10,000,000 a year. On the basis of the survey, however, the total would be between $1,500,000 and $3,500,000 – probably about $2,000,000 a season. Correspondence with the New York State Attorney General's Office failed to elicit any clues about the source of its estimate.

Both New York statutes and federal law prohibit the sale of seats at more or less than the printed price. That these laws have effectively prevented producers from discounting blocks of seats to brokers is generally overlooked. Before 1938, discounting was practised on a large scale. Leblang's agency, for example, many times purchased large sections of tottering shows to market the seats at less than the printed price, often as much as a 50 per cent discount. Students, old people, and those who were careful with their dollar haunted Leblang's lobby looking for bargains. After the prohibition of discounts, the only practical means of reducing prices has been to issue 'two-fers'. But with the change in the federal tax law, more flexibility in pricing will be possible.

The abolition of pricing restrictions – both up and down – will be beneficial to the theatre-goer. Weak productions will be able to market their seats at a discount and more tickets will be available for hits at short notice. The *real* cost for hits may go down (no under-the-table ice). Those who do not mind waiting will be able eventually to get seats at list, or below list. Without restrictive legislation, prices may be high at the start of a run and slowly decline as demand is satisfied. Gross box office receipts will more closely reflect money actually paid. The scalpers will have diminished.

Some believe they benefited from the law as it stands: the actors. Equity has strongly opposed scalping on the grounds that it cuts attendance. And certainly the more people who go to the theatre the better the job chances for actors. Theatre owners and producers generally favour ticket price restriction, although they are superficially hurt by a law which encourages ice. Some producers feel the public would object to a free market; a few may actually profit from ice which has an underground way of getting back into the box-office. Payoffs are made to theatre managers, and to box office personnel. Theatre owners and producers, who control the front of the house, always have the final say on ticket distribution. Any income earned through payoffs would not, of course, be shared with author, stars, backers, or tax-collectors. Thus it is possible for a producer to earn more through ice than he could if tickets were on a free market. (It should be noted that undoubtedly most producers do not profit from ice.)

(ix) *La Mama Experimental Theatre Club; 1967*
by Josh Greenfeld

On the east side of Second Avenue, between Seventh Street and St Marks Place, sandwiched between storefronts ('H. H. Budick, O.D., Eyes Examined', 'Automatic Laundry', 'One Hour Martinizing', 'Loans') are heavy metal doors with the sign: '122 Delivery Entrance'. Beyond these doors up a long steep flight of steel-lipped stairs and past another heavy metal door is a long, narrow loft which looks more like a place where one would store old furniture than unveil new plays.

The far long wall of the 25-foot-by-100-foot loft is peeled – or worn – down to its bare brick. Along the opposite wall are a kitchen counter framed with hand-lettered theatrical posters, a refrigerator, a hot plate, a pay telephone and, at a right angle to it, a single lavatory and a closet-sized dressing room. In the centre of the loft is an acting area and raking back from it on either side are 74 chairs with low tables beside them. Behind the last row of chairs stands a partition of old flats, masking a storage area of cluttered sofas and upended tables and a dressing area consisting of mirrors and stools. The effect is that of a maiden aunt's musty attic set upon by nieces and nephews during a summer vacation. This is the theatrical home of La Mama ETC and Ellen Stewart.

An audience at La Mama consists of 'members' only. One becomes a member by taking the trouble to find out where La Mama is, going there, and filling out an application form; in return, one receives a membership card. One cannot attend a La Mama performance at that time. Instead, whenever a member desires to attend a performance he must call and make reservations in advance. How does he know what is being presented? An ad appears weekly in The Village Voice announcing the bill, but giving neither the phone number nor the address of La Mama. How does a member know the phone number? It's on the membership card. But, of course, in order to have received the card one must first have gone directly to a theoretically unknown address. The process—which allows La Mama to function scrupulously within the framework of its charter as a private club – seems as involved as getting into certain unions, but some 3,000 card-carrying members, including Peter Brook, Peter Weiss, Jerome Robbins, Leonard Bernstein and Aaron Copland, seem to have mastered it.

'La Mama is now', says Paul Libin, an Off Broadway producer and La Mama member, 'like Off Broadway originally was. There is again a place playwright hopefuls can look to'.

Miss Stewart explains:

'An untried artist can be completely destroyed by non-objective criticism of his work. I started La Mama so there would be a place where a playwright could write, see and learn. Why should a new playwright be regarded on the same terms as an experienced playwright the very first time out – which is what most professional criticism does?

'After all,' she goes on, 'the ovum is a tiny egg and if a big hole is punched into it and the lifeblood is drained away the organism dies; in the same way the young artist can die.

'La Mama is concerned with actors, directors, all of theatre. But the playwright is the inspiration, the beginning, the germ. All things must serve him in their particular ways.'

Serving the playwright does not always serve an audience, and even some of La Mama's best friends sometimes feel like gritting their teeth before returning there. It is not just that Off Off Broadway plays tend to be off beat in content, form and language, or that they are usually no more than one-acters. It is that many of them – like most dramatic efforts anywhere – are simply not very good. Not long ago, one of The Village Voice drama critics, Joseph LeSueur, complained:

'The hit-or-miss quality of La Mama's work I've come to accept as inevitable. This means that I'm now as philosophical and cynical as the next theatregoer when I go to La Mama: I know the odds are against my seeing something I'll like and I know I have to take the bad with the good. I know too, that the situation isn't likely to improve in the foreseeable future, for the outfit's activities are governed by a generous, freewheeling policy of offering encouragement to just about anybody who thinks he's written a play. Still, I can't help wishing that the odds were a little more in the theatregoer's favour – a reversal, say, of the organization's present average of about a half-dozen misses for every hit.'

Acting levels at La Mama are also inconsistent. One cast may be composed entirely of experienced Broadway veterans, another wholly of Off Off Broadway neophytes. However, the touring La Mama troupe, under the direction of Tom O'Horgan, does maintain high standards of ensemble performance.

'But the important thing about La Mama,' says director Alan Schneider, 'is not whether the work is good or bad, but that Ellen Stewart helps keep theatre alive by constantly giving new playwrights productions.'

Most La Mama plays are typical of Off Off Broadway fare. What characterizes them is not so much a great and unifying artistic credo as the fact that they can be physically produced on postage-stamp stages. Off Off Broadway champions like to refer almost euphemistically to the 'human-scale' size of its coffee-house and miniloft theatres where audiences and actors, literally breathing upon each other of necessity, learn to effect a rare rapport, the *sine qua non* of a metaphysical happening.

'The difference between Off Broadway and Off Off Broadway,' says Ross Wetzsteon, another Village Voice critic, 'is the difference between an organization like Americans for Democratic Action and the New Left principle of "parallel institutions", the one trying to improve the Establishment, the other trying to replace or at least to exist outside of it.'

Off Off Broadway is not so much interested in 'making it' as in 'being it'. It does not consider itself a means – a mistake it assigns to Off Broadway – but rather as an end in itself. As for Broadway, Off Off Broadway would no more think of comparing itself to that uptown establishment than a *théâtre poche* in the Latin Quarter would expect to be likened to the Folies Bergères.

In fact, whenever Off Off Broadway fails to make its way up the prepositional scale and the economic ladder – as occurred last season when two bills of one-acters from La Mama foundered on Off Broadway – its champions regard the experience not so much as a failure as an object lesson: to return to the lofts and coffee-

houses where they belong and where they can thrive in musty
freedom.

Not surprisingly, Ellen Stewart characteristically insists upon
espousing an avant-garde esthetic: 'I'm interested in the New
Theatre, subliminal theatre that explores or seeks to manipulate
man's inner emotion. New Theatre plays – like those of Beckett,
Pinter, Ionesco, Brecht and Tennessee Williams's *Milk Train* –
may evoke extreme hatred or fear; one may dislike them, but one
is never unmoved by them.'

She likes to contrast New Theatre with what she disparagingly
calls Contemporary Theatre. 'Contemporary Theatre deals with
man's conscious receptivity; the new art, the New Theatre, the
new playwrights are interested in unconscious receptivity.'

Ellen Stewart's critical precepts are important because she
chooses every script La Mama presents. However, though she
professes that every play chosen is 'new' rather than 'contemporary', her standard is at once charmingly simple and
completely unassailable. 'If a play is talking to me personally,'
she says, 'if a script *beeps* to me when I'm reading it, we do it.'

'And if she thinks a play shouldn't be done, it won't be done
and you can't make her do it,' says playwright Melfi. 'She's very
emotional and mystical – and stubborn.'

The first stage in a La Mama production takes place when Miss
Stewart meets with the beeping play's be-beeper and tries to help
him decide upon a director. Thereafter she stays out of the way.
Casting for La Mama plays is always open – anyone can try out.
Notices of casting appear on the door of La Mama and are often
carried in the trade newspapers that serve as tip sheets to actors.

The playwright is in complete charge of the production process.
He is the final arbiter of changes and cuts. Some playwrights
steadfastly and resolutely stick to their original scripts; others
rewrite and make wholesale slashes.

At almost any given time, at least two plays, and possibly a
third, are in rehearsal. Because of the shoestring nature of the
operation, script duplication poses a constant major problem. If
the playwright can afford it, he pays for it; if not, Ellen does. But
not until attempts have been made to bootleg Xerox copies on
office machines in firms where La Mama actors or friends may be
working. If La Mama has a single crying need, ironically, it is for
its own copying machine.

Ellen does not believe new plays should have long runs. In

fact, she thinks long runs might tend to corrupt La Mama's principles by getting it involved in the success-failure hang-up. At first, La Mama changed its bill every week. Rising costs have since forced it to compromise on two weeks.

But even one week can prove a long run for a new playwright. One La Mama play drew but seven people on opening night. The show went on to play to a grand total of 87 people that week. 'But the playwright saw his play and learned from it,' says Ellen.

Miss Stewart never sees an opening night at La Mama – only the last night of a production. The moment any other performance starts, she steps out, through the heavy metal door, and takes a seat on the stair. She does so to prevent interruptions; it also gives her a good chance to catch up on her business. She holds whispered court there with actors who know her 'office hours', as she puts it, and she takes care of 'all my little ditties', which means dipping into her ever-present handbag pouch and taking care of her mail. On a typical night this might include responding to an invitation from Germany asking La Mama ETC to participate in an International Theatre Week; a letter from an Indian playwright whose work La Mama had produced while he was passing through New York; a postcard from a Hungarian who met her once in Zagreb asking how La Mama is coming along.

For La Mama is as international as its name implies. In addition to the New York operation and the repertory company's tour of the Continent, where its appearances in cities such as Paris and Copenhagen are regarded as major cultural events, La Mama plays are also regularly performed in translation by a resident troupe in Bogotá.

All of this activity, of course, costs money – last year's European tour, for example, more than $5,000. How does Ellen finance it? 'Well, there's a pawnshop down the block. And the bank will keep giving me new loans as long as I pay off the old ones,' she says.

The economics of La Mama are half Keynesian, but only half – pumps are constantly primed, but no wells are first dug. The rental for the Second Avenue loft – plus that for a rehearsal hall on East Ninth Street – comes to $325 per month. There are expenses for utilities, cleaning, postage, programmes, coffee and sugar, paper cups, etc. And there is the budget for each new production – set at $200 but usually exceeded. All together, monthly operating expenses run to more than $1,000.

La Mama's sole income is derived from the 'dues' of $1 per member, a maximum of $74 per performance – a figure which is rarely achieved consistently. La Mama is able to meet its deficits, according to Ellen, 'because we have a fat cat: me'. This spring, for example, the $1,000 honorarium she received as part of the Brandeis Award, given annually by Brandeis University for a distinguished contribution to the theatre, went directly to La Mama bill collectors. She refuses to estimate how much of her own money she has spent. Friends place the figure at more than $20,000.

But she considers herself no more dedicated than any of La Mama's playwrights. 'All I'm interested in is that they get the recognition and support they deserve,' she says. 'Meanwhile, they wear a shirt for a week, and they don't see much theatre and they walk wherever they go, and they don't eat every night – but they're all writing plays.'

(x) The Annual Financial Report of the Belgrade Theatre, Coventry, England; 1967

The Arts Council's contribution to the theatre consisted of an outright grant of £30,000 plus a guarantee against loss of £10,000. The actual loss was £8,692. Not only is this loss within the guarantee, but is calculated after providing for special items of equipment, such as the new bar in the restaurant lounge, which will improve the facilities and future income of the theatre.

In addition to their normal grant of £9,000 plus £3,500 for special publicity, the City Council made a special grant of £8,197 which eliminated the accumulated deficit carried forward at the beginning of the year. Nuneaton Borough Council made a grant of £250.

These substantial grants and the improved box-office of 47 per cent for the year compared with 41 per cent for the previous period, mean that the theatre for the first time in 7 years has no deficit to carry forward.

It is important that the revival of public interest in the theatre, as shown by the box-office, should continue.

THE FOLLOWING SHOWS WERE PRESENTED IN THE YEAR ENDED 31st MARCH 1967

	Number of Performances	% Attendance	% Box Office
LOCK UP YOUR DAUGHTERS	17	82	79
RAWICZ AND LANDAUER†	2	51	49
LOCK UP YOUR DAUGHTERS	7	63	56
CHERRY ORCHARD	7	49	33
FOL - de - ROLS†	16	30	24
PERIOD OF ADJUSTMENT	15	20	17
EH!	15	22	19
JANE EYRE	23	72	60
ITALIAN STRAW HAT	15	43	37
DIAL M FOR MURDER	15	43	39
SAILOR BEWARE	15	47	42
BLITHE SPIRIT	15	50	45
CYRIL FLETCHER†	7	19	16
CAROUSEL*	7	72	69
DAVID KOSSOFF†	1	45	44
CYRANO DE BERGERAC	23	53	47
THE CRUCIBLE	15	51	42
CLEO LAINE†	1	100	100
ONE FOR THE POT	15	68	58
LITTLE MALCOLM	8	38	29
JULIUS CAESAR	25	70	46
CURE FOR LOVE	18	39	35
OH! MY PAPA	23	50	43
PINOCCHIO	27	98	51
UNEXPECTED GUEST	23	65	60
THE FESTIVAL	15	61	54
GILBERT AND SULLIVAN†	1	90	89
LARRY ADLER†	1	24	23
HOBSON'S CHOICE	15	57	48
THE KNACK	15	68	58
TRIP TO SCARBOROUGH	16	41	36

† Tour.   * Amateur.

REVENUE ACCOUNT FOR THE YEAR ENDED 31st MARCH 1967

THE EXPENSES OF RUNNING THE THEATRE WERE:—

PRODUCTION	£	£
Employees		
Artists	21,585	
Backstage	18,181	
Stage Equipment and Materials	14,256	
Royalties and Music Rights	4,951	
Touring Companies	3,641	
Other Expenses	3,550	66,164
FRONT OF HOUSE		
Employees	16,730	
Tickets and Programmes	1,531	
Publicity	6,000	
Premises:		
Fuel, Light, Cleaning and Water	4,740	
Rent, Rates and Insurance	18,651	
Equipment, Tools and Materials		
Contribution to Renewals and		
Repairs Fund	8,800	
General Administration Expenses	5,062	
Other Expenses	5,374	66,888
		133,052

THESE WERE MET BY:—

	£	£	%
INCOME			
Box Office	64,341		
Tours	1,250		
Catering Gross Surplus	4,356		
Bar Gross Surplus	3,936		
Other Income	10,927		
	———	84,810	64%
GRANTS			
Arts Council – General	30,000		
– Special	300		
Coventry – General	9,000		
Nuneaton – General	250		
	———	39,550	30%
Arts Council Guarantee against loss (£10,000 available)		8,692	6%
		———	———
		133,052	100%
		———	———

(*xi*) *Theatre Staff* by Clive Barker

Theatres usually build their organizations to suit themselves, depending of the size of the theatre and the type and amount of work they do during the year: the following is a typical organization.

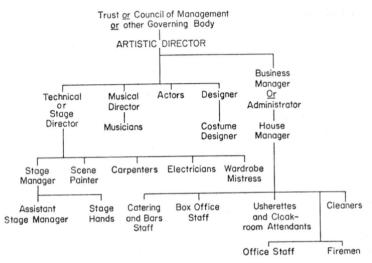

NOTES

1. Although subordinate to the Artistic Director, the Business Manager is responsible directly to the Trust for the theatre's financial control. He is not normally concerned with back-stage staff but, in the absence of the Artistic Director, will take over the running of the theatre entirely.

2. In most small theatres, the Business Manager and House Manager are one and the same person.

3. In some large theatres, a Press Officer works directly under the Business Manager.

4. Sometimes the Scene Painter is in fact an Assistant Designer and directly responsible to the Designer.

III. ACTORS

(i) The Art of Acting; c. 1778 by Denis Diderot

A BUDDING actor, or let us say a budding actress, asks you to
come and see her quietly to form an opinion of her talent. You
grant that she has soul, sensibility, passion. You cover her with
praises, and leave her when you depart in hope of the greatest
success. But what happens? She appears, she is hissed, and you
acknowledge that the hisses are deserved. Why is this? Has she
lost her soul, her sensibility, her passion, between the morning
and the evening? No; but in her ground-floor room you were
both on the same low level; you listened to her regardless of
convention; she was face-to-face with you; between you there
was no model for purposes of comparison; you were satisfied
with her voice, her gesture, her expression, her bearing; all was
in proportion to the audience and the space; there was nothing
that called for exaltation. On the boards all the conditions were
changed: there a different impersonation was needed, since all
the surroundings were enlarged.

In private theatricals, in a drawing-room, where the spectator
is almost on a level with the actor, the true dramatic impersonation
would have struck you as being on an enormous, a gigantic
scale, and at the end of the performance you would have said
confidentially to a friend, 'She will not succeed; she is too
extravagant'; and her success on the stage would have astonished
you. Let me repeat it, whether for good or ill, the actor says
nothing and does nothing in private life in the same way as on the
stage: it is a different world. . . .

I knew Pigalle [the sculptor]; his house was open to me. One
morning I go there; I knock; the artist opens the door with his
roughing-chisel in his hand; then stopping me on the threshold
of the studio he says, 'Before I let you pass, assure me you will
not be alarmed at a beautiful woman without a rag of clothes on'.
I smiled and walked in. He was working at his monument to
Marshal Saxe, and a very handsome model was standing to him
for the figure of France. But how do you suppose she struck me
among the colossal figures around her? She seemed poor, small,
mean – a kind of frog; she was overwhelmed by them, and I

should have had to take the artist's word for it that the frog was a beautiful woman, if I had not waited for the end of the sitting and seen her on the same level with myself, my back turned to the gigantic figures which reduced her to nothingness. I leave it to you to apply this curious experience to Gaussin, to Riccoboni, to all actresses who have been unable to attain to greatness on the stage.

If by some impossible chance an actress were endowed with a sensibility comparable in degree to that which the most finished art can simulate, the stage offers so many different characters for imitations, one leading part brings in so many opposite situations that this rare and tearful creature, incapable of playing two different parts well, would at best excel in certain passages of one part; she would be the most unequal, the narrowest, the least apt actress you can imagine. If it happened that she attempted a great flight, her predominant sensibility would soon bring her down to mediocrity. She would be less like a strong steed at the gallop than a poor hack taking the bit in its teeth. Then one instant of energy, momentary, sudden, without gradation or preparation, would strike you as an attack of madness.

Sensibility being after all the mate of Sorrow and Weakness, tell me if a gentle, weak, sensitive creature is fit to conceive and express the self-possession of Léontine, the jealous transports of Hermione, the fury of Camilla, the maternal tenderness of Merope, the delirium and remorse of Phædra, the tyrannical pride of Agrippina, the violence of Clytemnestra? Leave your ever tearful one to one of our elegiac arts, and do not take her out of it.

The fact is, that to have sensibility is one thing, to feel is another. One is a matter of soul, the other of judgment. One may feel strongly and be unable to express it; one may alone, or in private life, at the fireside, give expression, in reading or acting, adequate for a few listeners, and give none of any account on the stage. On the stage, with what we call sensibility, soul, passion, one may give one or two tirades well and miss the rest. To take in the whole extent of a great part, to arrange its light and shade, its forts and feebles; to maintain an equal merit in the quiet and in the violent passages; to have variety both in harmonious detail and in the broad effect; to establish a system of declamation which shall succeed in carrying off every freak of the poet's – this is matter for a cool head, a profound judgment, an exquisite taste – a matter for hard work, for long experience, for an uncommon tenacity of memory. The rule, *Qualis ab incepto processerit et sibi constet* [Let it continue as it began, harmonious with itself], rigorous enough for the poet, is fixed down to the minutest point for the actor. He who comes out from the wing without having his whole scheme of acting in his head, his whole part marked out, will all his life play the part of a beginner. Or if endowed with intrepidity, self-sufficiency, and spirit, he relies on his quickness of wit and the habit of his calling, he will bear you down with his fire and the intoxication of his emotions, and you will applaud him as an expert of painting might smile at a free sketch, where all was indicated and nothing marked. This is the kind of prodigy which may be seen sometimes at a fair or at Nicolet's. Perhaps such people do well to remain as they are – mere roughed-out actors. More study would not give them what they want, and might take from them what they have. Take them for what they are worth, but do not compare them to a finished picture.

(ii) Concerning that Gaiety of Disposition which is Essential to the Comic Actor; 1755 by John Hill

I am here to speak of a qualification to the actor, which many may think quite unconnected with his profession: his natural temper appearing to them a thing he is always to dissemble and conceal, in order to his assuming that of his character. But this is not altogether the truth, in respect to some kinds of temper; they are in vain drawn by the poet, if he who is to represent the characters does not himself possess them. Of these, gaiety of disposition is one. We see an instance of the truth of this in the character of Sir Harry Wildair. The stage, at present, affords no actor who has this gaiety, connected with the address and manner of a gentleman; and therefore we have not seen it acted tolerably, nay, scarce attempted, except by a woman.

Characters of politeness are as difficultly represented as those of gaiety, because, unless the actor be himself polite, he can no more come up to the intent of the author, or the expectations of the audience in them, than he can to that of the one or the other, in those of which the characteristic is gaiety, unless himself is naturally gay. These characters make a very essential part of all comedy; and indeed some are for making them the whole of it: they are for banishing the parts of footmen and clowns to farce, supposing that a polite audience cannot be entertained with the absurdities of people so much beneath them. It is possible that good comedies may be written without these characters: but we find the best poets of our own and other nations introducing them. However, still the principal attention is to be paid to the highest characters, and it will usually be the lot of the best players to perform them.

These are of different kinds, and in the choice of them, provided that choice is left to the player himself, is shewn his greatest judgment; and on that choice depends his greatest success. Altho' a natural disposition alone will not enable a man to play a part of the same turn, (for we have seen real fops in life make miserable ones on the stage) yet it is the most happy addition that can be made to real talents. He who is able to act all characters decently, will be sure to excel in those which express his own turn of mind. It is said no man ever wrote well upon a subject, who did not feel something of the character in himself: it is not true, that no man ever acted a part well, who was not in some degree, of the same turn in his own mind; yet it is certain, that no actor has ever played those parts in comedy which affect us most, so well as those who have been like them in reality. Mr Cibber, the best lord Foppington who ever appeared, was in real life (with all due respect be it spoken by one who loves him) something of the coxcomb; and the reason why Mr Woodward succeeds less in them, is, that he has not in real life the true character.

In general, people who have naturally exalted sentiments are the fittest for playing tragedy; and that sort of disposition which will fit the comic actor best for his business, is, what we call sprightly and joyous. This will diffuse itself thro' his whole manner, and will give what the poet always means to convey, tho' often in vain, to the player, and thro' him to the audience.

As the tragic performer should, as much as possible, divest himself of all passions in private life, so should, nay so must, in a yet more perfect manner, he who would excel in comedy. The desire of applause ought to be the only passion allowed to him, beside those immediately connected with his part. As he has the more of this desire, he will obtain more of this applause, and the applause itself will not only encrease the desire; (for in that, fame is like gold, the desire of more encreases with the quantity;) but this very incident will give him more of that joyous spirit, which is so happy in comedy, than all other things.

If there be any thing in the player's private affairs that troubles him, he must quite throw it off for the time, if he would reasonably hope for any applause. The fullness or the emptiness of the house must not be suffered to affect him; for if it be empty, is it not to his credit to play so that those who are present shall say it ought to have been fuller? A manager is more likely to be affected by this circumstance than one who only plays: but of this we can have no instance. The only manager who acts at present, fills houses by his appearance.

We do see actors affected by the emptiness of an house, but they are always the worst; for they have least understanding. A Lear shall play as carefully to an hundred people, as if there were two thousand; but the majesty of an Albany or a Cornwall shall be offended at it beyond measure; they shall insult the people who are present by their indolence, and take snuff, or talk of their beer-engagements in the most interesting scenes. We have seen this, but those who saw it have so resented it, that probably we shall not see it any more.

As, in order to our being properly affected by tragedy, the player is to feel the distress, and to be himself melancholy, so we never relish comedy truly, unless the player is pleasing himself as well as us in the performance; and this will never happen, unless he have a natural turn to gaiety and sprightliness; in such a man it is nature, and we are therefore pleased to the height. It was for want of this that the comic characters of the late Mr Delane, tho' he acted very justly, never perfectly pleased us: and it is owing to the full perfection of it that we are often so delighted with the comedy of Mr Woodward. While he acts the character called the Fine Gentleman, in Lethe, he gives us a reality, not a representation. We see that in damning the audience for a parcel of rascals and scoundrels, he delivers his very sentiments, and laughs at them for being pleased with it: here he is perfect nature; and in his Bobadil, and some other characters of that kind, it is easy to see that he is entertaining himself as much as his audience.

This sense of pleasantry, and thorough relish of the spirit and joy of the poet in his own breast, is the true inspiring deity, the Phœbus of the comic player: he cannot encourage it too much in

E.T.—7

himself, nor give his audience too frequent or too strong instances of it: but let him all this time understand the admonition rightly. His pleasure is to be that of the person who transacts the scene of jollity, not that of some idle person who looks upon it: we are to see it expressed in the vivacity, life and fire of his air, and the spirit with which he goes through every part, not by the simper on his countenance. This is an error too many have made in the comic scene, especially women; but they should be informed nothing is so absurd or disgusting. Have they not seen that the pleasantry of a jest in common conversation is lost, when the person who speaks laughs at it himself. Much more is it on the stage, where the actor is not telling a story, as is commonly the circumstance in the other case, but is personating one of the characters.

It is said, the merry fellows are the saddest fellows in the world; it is no where so true as in comic actors. We see in tragedy some so charmed with the thought of representing an hero, that they will smile throughout the part of a Cato or a Bajazet; and we have seen men so conscious of the importance of acting any. thing of length, that they have looked as grave as if upon the bench, through the whole of a Scandal or a Heartfree. These are absurdities sufficiently glaring: but the other, of constant merriment of face, is as disgustful. People of grave countenances do not play comedy naturally, therefore never well; for all that is right in them is forced, and being so, it cannot please: but to be a perfect comic player, a man must have all this natural gaiety of disposition, and know how to suppress it. There is an admirable grimace in what we know to be the forced gravity of a countenance; and in general, the tragedy rule is to be inverted, in order to succeeding in comedy. The one must weep himself, if he would make his audience weep; the other, if he would make them laugh forever, must commonly check and curb his own merriment.

This disguise of the thought is often a great merit; and often an artful inattention has the same charm. Many things in comedy strike us greatly, as they drop inattentively from the character. The author intends to express them thus; and if the actor, out of his great discernment, will chuse to look wise, and see the consequences, he takes off the whole joke. A smile of cunning destroys all here, and so does a smile of applause in many other passages. To succeed perfectly, the player must disguise to his audience, in a proper degree, his intent of raising a laugh, and his expectation of doing it. Thus we see that gaiety of spirit is the great advantage of the comic player, but that it will not have half its effect, if he does not know how to regulate it. It is like all other good things, the worst of all, when out of its place, luxuriant, or indulged too fondly.

(iii) *Rules of Acting* by Jean-Louis Barrault

What follows is not a lesson in dramatic art but simply a personal recapitulation of a few rules which are necessary to the actor. Being continually engrossed in the same work leads one not only to grant an excessive importance to secondary details but also to neglect the fundamental laws which govern true acting. Let us therefore try to recall a few of these obvious rules which one tends all too easily to forget.

The first rule which an actor must observe is that of making himself heard and understood. In fact this is not a rule, it is a matter of elementary politeness, and failure to conform to it is an insult to the spectator. Making oneself heard is within everybody's capacity and has nothing to do with special gifts or talents; it is purely a matter of training, barring of course cases of physiological incapacity.

The second rule rests on observation and imitation, and here natural gifts play a part; nevertheless one must bear in mind the fact that the faculty of observation can be developed by practice and training. There are at least two methods of observation: the objective and the subjective method. For instance, take a box of matches and observe it analytically; concentrate your attention on the content, the quality of the wood, the writing, the marks, etc. After a few minutes of this kind of observation, hide the box of matches and describe it objectively. Practise this method of observation on any object which may come under your gaze, and you will soon note that your sight becomes quicker and sharper. After this apply the same method to the observation of your fellow beings; scrutinize them, take them to pieces in the same way and you will find that this kind of observation will supply you with precious data for future characterizations.

Let us now pass to the subjective method of observation. This time you only take one match but you not only look at it, you feel it, and you say to yourself: 'I become wood or a memory of wood from a Swedish forest. What remains of this body? I am thin, very thin, and elongated, and the slightest pressure could crush me, break me into pieces; I should crack up, crinkle, but those who use me do not crush me but strike me on the box and my head becomes alight, for all my fire is in my head. I live in a congested state, my forehead burns, my ears are red. I am living under the shadow of cerebral haemorrhage, my fate is to die at the moment when I myself generate life, heat and light. My existence consumes me; I am a symbol of life and of death at the same time. That's perhaps why I am laid out in advance in a grave, side by side with my sisters and without the slightest room to stretch my feet. There is no room in our box, but perhaps those who make them are right, for I have been told that in serious cases of heart illness one must remain motionless, if not the result is a cerebral haemorrhage. That is what lies in store for us, etc. etc.' This kind of subjective observation develops the art of imitation. In order to be able to observe and to imitate one must have certain gifts, but in spite of those gifts one might not know how to observe and how to imitate, and that is where practice comes in. To know how to observe and how to imitate is the second rule of the actor; it is the rule of authenticity. The question of producing effects only comes later. Any attempt at producing an effect in the theatre unfailingly reminds one of the shopkeeper's last words, 'And now, Sir or Madam, shall I wrap it up for you?' But one must remember that these are not the words with which he greets you, they are his final words, meant to produce the effect he is aiming at, if he is a good salesman.

Once an actor can make himself heard and understood, and once he has so throughly observed a chosen character that he is full of him, and can easily imitate him, impersonate him or give him life, he comes up against the rule which can be summed up by the three vital questions 'Whence do I come, where am I going and in what state am I?'

There are various opinions as to the way one should answer these questions, but the actor must have a clear-cut opinion about them at any moment of the performance, even when he is in the wings or backstage. Let us take Scapin as an example. We are in Naples; Naples is a hot place; we are in the Mediterranean world, a world where one practises siesta. Scapin must surely practise siesta, he may even be the king of siesta. Scapin, like every other animal, eats, sleeps, makes love and plays. He is either relaxed or he is active. He is a master at relaxing. Where does he come from? The answer is easy; he has just been shaken out of his moist sleep by the lamentation of Octave and Silvester. Where is he going? Nowhere, of course. Why should he go anywhere? He has renounced all things, he says these things come to him by themselves. In what state is he? Sleepy, he will awaken progressively. His first tirade flows forth from the fumes of sleep and wine and is garlic flavoured. He who is generally so talkative lets the others do the talking. No useless efforts (he knows that he will need all his energy later; but this point will be discussed in connection with another subject). When the others have ceased chattering, he yawns, stretches himself and says, 'Here you are, quite as big as your father and mother and you couldn't discover in your brains or contrive with your wits . . . etc.' And he stretches himself again, and once he has done so he has a clearer mind. Hiacinthe awakens him completely. Scapin has a heart and he is not insensitive to young women, so he thinks to himself, 'she is not bad at all,' then he turns a bit of charm on her, and with that he is off. 'All right, I want to help you both,' he says, so Scapin gets started and will only stop at the end of the famous scene with the 'sac'.

The third rule, which we have just discovered, is vital, it is called the rule of verisimilitude. The fourth rule could be summed up with the words, 'What am I doing here?' It is a rule about environment. The plot is unfolding, the characters play their respective parts. Agrippine nags Nero who listens, get bored, thinks of Julia, ends by being angry and completely shuts himself off from his mother's presence. The more one progresses in the rules the more complicated they become. The question 'What am I doing here?' implies at least two alternatives. One, what am I determined to allow the other to see, and what am I determined to hide? This rule is very complex for a character because although he thinks he knows himself, he may know himself badly and may sometimes confuse good faith with bad faith. He attaches importance to things that have none, and he is suddenly caught up by things from which he felt protected. A character may think that he is walking in the light and be in darkness, and then the passion against which he is struggling may unsettle his equilibrium, distort his reactions and plunge him into errors. He may think he is walking with a steady step and he stumbles; he may think he sees clearly and he is blind. Now blind people find help in walking-sticks. A character who is at a loss as to what to do, might be greatly helped if he could find an object to which he could cling. During Agrippine's sermon, Nero plays with his coat which becomes his help, his refuge and also his means of expression. An actor who finds the object which connects him with the scene he is playing imparts concrete efficiency to his behaviour. To find the right object was the golden rule of Stanislavski; it is a most precious rule which has countless effects and it is one of the most important rules of realistic art.

The fifth rule is the rule of control, and it is also very important; it deals with sincerity and exactness. There is a prevailing belief that sincerity is automatically right; that is not always true. The actor might be sincere while at the same time the character he is portraying is not quite right within the performance. The reason is that the actor never identifies himself absolutely with the character he is playing, and that is normal since we are in the theatre, a place where life is re-created through art. The point is that it is the character who must be sincere, irrespective of the fact that the actor may or may not be so. The acting will be right if the character is constantly sincere. The closer the identification between actor and character the more sincere they will be. But there are situations in which total identification of the two would bring about disasters. The death of a character compels the actor who plays the part to disconnect himself from it and merely to project the picture of death out of himself, with as much sincerity as he can command. Death is an extreme case, yet there never is complete identification between actor and character. The actor must work within the play's setting, keep on remembering his relationship with the other characters of the play, remain aware that he is in a theatre, and that he must be heard, and that he must stick to the plot, keep an eye on the lighting, etc. The superimposition of the actor's person on that of a given character resembles those cheap coloured prints in which the colours overflow the contours of the drawing. Exactitude of performance depends on the sincerity of the character and on the power of control of the actor who must constantly ask himself the question: 'In spite of my sincerity is my character truly sincere?'

Such are the five main rules for the basic training of an actor. They are the foundations of his studies and art, and his talent can only blossom thanks to them. Just as in the course of primary, secondary and university studies we spend a great deal of time going through the same cycle or unlearning what we learnt with so much difficulty, we seem at this point to run the risk of coming up against rules which might seem to contradict the preceding ones. Yet, in fact they don't. In our young days we might have learnt that two and two make four, and later we might have been compelled to realize that it is not quite so; yet this rule does not lose its virtue or its efficiency. In fact, superior rules do not abolish efficient rules, they only refine them. In the same way poetic theatre does not nullify realistic theatre; on the contrary, it raises it to a higher level.

After these five elementary rules which are the basis of normal drama which is realistic, there exist more practical preconceptions. First, the rule of transposition. Once one has carefully laid down the foundations of one's work on truth (whether one is an actor, a producer or a stage designer) one can take the liberty of forgetting everything and begin anew. And so it happens that sometimes, guided by inspiration, one discovers a way of doing things which, although it does not a first sight rest on truth, contains nevertheless aspects which are the very essence of truth. That is truly poetic interpretation.

Let us now return to Scapin. We have previously described the way in which, according to logic, he ought to make his first appearance on the stage. The conception outlined previously was also that of Jouvet who produced *Scapin*, yet that is not the way in which he produced me when I played Scapin under his direction. Jouvet was a great producer and he knew how to invent and to transpose, while starting from reality. He thus invented how to make me appear as if from nowhere right in the middle of the reality of the stage. It was something like the appearance of the Prince of Valets. Truth was respected since the internal rhythm of Scapin remained slow, but the fact of turning his entrance into a kind of sudden emergence produced at the very beginning of the play a poetic tone which echoed from scene to scene. Even if *Les Fourberies de Scapin* [Scapin's tricks, or ploys] was a farce Jouvet was entitled to produce it as a poetic farce, yet in fact Molière did not call it a farce but a comedy and it is a comedy which contains a kind of poetry to which Jouvet was particularly sensitive. His invention about Scapin's first appearance on the stage follows the rule of transposition. In a transposition there is no apparent logic, there is a metamorphosis. Happy those who possess this sixth sense which transposes truth through poetry. There we have all the art and all the difficulty of Giraudoux's theatre!

Let us pass to another rule. I love horse racing but know nothing about it. Yet I feel that it is with the terminology of horse racing that I should discover my next rule. This new rule which concerns those who play big parts deals with the art of running a race. The actor who plays Hamlet, for instance, loses approximately two pounds in weight at each performance. If he starts too fast he will be short of breath in the second half of the third act; in order to avoid that he will increase his efforts, and will probably be flat out for the fifth. One of the great difficulties of Hamlet is its length. Right up to the beginning of the fourth act (the departure for England) the actor is carried forth by his own impetus without any time for cooling off; during the greater part of the fourth act, Hamlet is no longer very active and he cools off during the scene of Ophelia's madness. His head tired by a three hours' performance is bubbling with all the words, curses and sighs which he has just uttered and his will is liable to flag. The last effort of the fifth act, notably the Graveyard scene, is particularly painful. It some-times takes him a few minutes before he is again in full control of his reflexes. If *Hamlet* is a long-distance race, *Scapin* is the 800 metres, and everybody knows that 800 metres is a very difficult race to run. Once when I was in Buenos Aires I was curious enought to take my blood pressure before the start of the play and immediately after the scene of the 'sac'. From 7·11 it had gone up to 9·165. Every race must be run in its own particular way. The actor is like a jockey, he rules his character, or, like one of Goya's witches, he gets on his horse and plunges into the night for his infernal race. There are parts which require a fast start, a sustained tempo with some spurts here and there and then a slight slackening off as if one were travelling on one's acquired speed, in order to gather strength for the final speed burst of the end. Other parts require that the actor should keep his strength in reserve as long as possible until a given bend of the race. The actress who plays Phèdre must rein in her mount during the first act; she must in fact hold her back, and she must continue to control her during the second act (Hyppolyte's declaration). She lets her go in the third act—long strides, deep breathing, fluent diction, avoiding tensing up. Like that she will be prepared to give everything in the fourth act—muscular strength, heart,

nerves, senses and intellect. In the first two acts the fire is smouldering; it begins to crackle up with Hyppolyte's declaration, but it
only catches on under the wind of the third, and it only spreads
and brings down the building in the fourth. In the fifth, we have
the smouldering ashes. This way of running the race sets out the
worth of the part. Just as small unfinished patches in Despiau's
busts enhance the beauty of his work, in the same way it is useful
to slacken off for certain brief moments during which actor and
public gather strength for the best moment when they will get
drunk together. The problem of timing belongs to the rule of
control. There are very many rules of control for the actor, and
there comes to mind one which I find extremely difficult to apply:
it is the rule of relaxation. There are so many exercises to bring
about relaxation, but they are not easy to carry out and good
results are few.

It seems to me that one of the most important causes of tension
is timidity. It is possible to crave to get into somebody else's skin,
and to have the gift of changing personality in order to become a
character, but only when one is by oneself, and not before spectators. Timidity renders such an operation impossible. In the
presence of the public certain actors become nervous and tense
and lose the best part of their means. As they cannot relax, they
are likely to be unable to infuse the character that they are playing
with the sincerity, the authenticity and spontaneity which it
requires. In order to avoid these pitfalls, one must concentrate on
the most important rule of all, that of concentration and control
of the will. This is the foundation of the whole discipline of acting.
There are many excellent exercises for the development of the art
of concentration and control of the will which are the basic
principles of acting. The rest is silence, and that is, I think, true
for theatrical performances as well as for musical performances,
which only exist in order to cause silence to vibrate.

Concerning Emotion
Emotion is a state which the actor must never be conscious of.
One can only become conscious of an emotion which has already
passed, for the act of consciousness dissipates the actual emotion.
The actor only lives in the present and he continually jumps from
one present to another, carrying out actions which are bathed in a
kind of vapour which is the appropriate emotion. This vapour
is as much a part of his acting as juice is a part of fruit; but if he

becomes conscious of it, the vapour fades away and the acting dries up.

No actor could act his own genuine emotion. Actors who wish to make use of emotions are therefore compelled to fake them, but their tears, their trembling voices and shaking hands do not delude the discriminating public, which is the very one they try to please. 'I know that I please those whom I must please' says the Antigone of Sophocles.

One cannot say to oneself: 'I am moved', without ceasing to be so; one can say 'I was moved', or better still, 'I was probably moved'. In the present one can only say: 'He or she is moved', for one can only be aware of another person's emotion. It is therefore the public which has the strange joy of perceiving and enjoying the emotion lived by the actor. If the actor, whether he is moved or not, is himself moving, the public has nothing to say or think, it has only to enjoy the emotion. To sum up, one can say that emotions are very elusive phenomena little discussed in the theatre, where spectators and actors, although they move under their impact, are only concerned with actions. Whether the actor cries or not, does not matter; the essential thing is that he should make the audience cry. In the case of tragedy, which requires a great physical effort, too much emotion could be harmful. The more the tragic actor manages to convey emotions through rhythm, the less he will have to use his nerves to transmit it, and therefore the more, of course, he will remain in possession of his strength so as to use it in the difficult and tense moments of the play. When collective emotion in a theatre reaches an unbearable pitch, the spectators have a reaction which reveals their extreme tension and at the same time slackens it and renders it more bearable—they applaud. In such cases, the emotion is so strong and the illusion so perfect that the spectators are no longer quite sure as to where they are; they may have thought that Nero himself was on the stage, and in order to regain their equilibrium they applaud the actor who is playing that part. The applause is therefore a mechanism of defence against an emotion which was becoming too strong for comfort. The emotion is less a state than a reaction, and it is as such that it can interest us.

Let us see what kind of reaction it is. To act is to struggle, and to struggle implies the existence of two antagonistic forces. When at the climax of the struggle one of the two contending forces is on the point of being overwhelmed, it seeks refuge in a kind of

magical reaction which we call emotion. This reaction generally
assumes one of the following forms:

(1) It causes the complete disappearance of the force against
which it struggles.
(2) It can artificially transform this force by diminishing its
power.
(3) It causes its own disappearance.
(4) It transforms itself magically and turns itself into something
more dangerous than it was previously.

Thus, through an illusory disappearance or transformation of the
force which opposes us, we think that we can either escape or
conquer it, or we might hope to obtain the same results by the
disappearance or by the transformation of our own selves. For
instance, if I have to walk across a dangerous patch of ground, I
whistle and walk in a carefree manner as if I did not care about
anything. In reality I suppress the danger artificially. Suddenly an
armed aggressor springs on me; I faint and in reality I cause my
own disappearance. When I awaken I realize that policemen are
trying to bring me back to life; their behaviour shows that they
have a very low opinion of my frightened state. That makes me
feel ashamed; what can I do? I get angry and insult them; in truth,
I make myself more fearsome than I am in reality; in their turn
they too get angry and threaten to arrest me for insulting behaviour; I then rock with laughter. In reality, I metamorphose
them into friends or 'chums', I magically transform the atmosphere and I turn this whole incident into a farce. Back home, I fall
into a sultry mood; nobody can extract a word from me; I behave
like an amnesiac; my family concludes that I am sad. In reality my
whole being concentrates upon forgetfulness; I have successively
gone through fear, laughter and sadness. Dramatic characters
behave in just the same way, and their reactions in moments of
great emotion are the best illustrations of their character. Lorenzo's
fainting fit at the moment of the duel, Hamlet's shout of 'a rat,
a rat!' when he kills Polonius; Phèdre superimposing Theseus's
image on that of Hippolytus in the scene of the declaration, are
facts which enable us to know the souls of these various characters.

   Thus the actor need no more concern himself with emotions as
such, than he concerns himself with his perspiration in the course
of the performance. But he must, on the contrary, attach importance to emotions viewed as means of behaviour and actions, and

that will lead him to realize that characters never pause for one moment in the middle of their actions in order to offer gratuitous displays of feeling. They are involved in continuous actions and reactions; they argue, they plead, they discuss, they fight against others or against themselves, they delude themselves and others, sometimes in good faith, sometimes in bad faith, but they never stop. The spectator might try to analyse their behaviour, feelings and emotions, but for the actor who is caught in the middle of the dramatic game, there is nothing else but action.

(iv) *Macready's King Lear* by Westland Marston

William Macready's King Lear, as I saw it in his later days, when it had acquired a broader and more masculine outline than before, was, I think, his finest achievement in Shakespearian tragedy. With that poetic power of symbolism which was one of his especial gifts, there was, on his first entrance, in his accents, sovereignly imperious, and in his free, large movements (though the gait at times gave just a hint of age), the outward and visible sign, not only of Lear's strong and absolute will, but of the primitive, half-savage royalty that we associate with remote and legendary periods. He was still a hale and zealous hunter, not unwilling, indeed, to forego the toils of State, but bribed to do so, before the full need came, by prodigal love for his children. If he became, afterwards, 'a very feeble, fond old man,' it was ingratitude, not the weight of years, that had thus undone him. There were many fine touches of nature in the first act. One of these was especially suitable. Lear has repudiated his once idolized Cordelia; he would fain forget her and speak of his future plans. But, in striving to do this, his voice suddenly for a moment broke, then to the end of the sentence hardened into inflexibility. Very striking, too, was the King's demeanour just afterwards, when Kent remonstrates. His anger first showed itself in an omnious tone of warning which arrested and awed—

The bow is bent and drawn; make from the shaft;

then, as the faithful adherent persisted, it swelled into a mingling of amazement, scorn, and convulsive rage, that would have befitted a Caesar, flattered into the belief of his divinity, and swift to punish opposition as impious. The curse which ends the act

struck terror by its still intensity, and the change from wrath to
agony at the words—

> That she may feel
> How sharper than a serpent's tooth it is
> To have a thankless child,

almost excused the malediction. To specify all the striking details
of this great performance would need an entire essay. It may be
said, in brief, that as the boundless arrogance of Lear was the sin
by which he fell, so a revelation to the old man's heart—even
through his disordered wits—of the common ties of our humanity
was with Macready, the great lesson of the play. Thus he threw
into even unusual relief those noble passages in which the poet
contrasts the lots of rich and poor, of oppressor and thrall, or in
which he shows the nothingness of mortal man at his best, when
he encounters the forces of Nature or Circumstance. In the storm-
scene, where Lear's madness is yet incipient, and in the still more
terrible disclosure of the fourth act, Macready was on ground
(that of psychology), where, if we except a few inspired characters
of Edmund Kean, he seemed unapproachable. His dawning
insanity gleamed out in his almost parental tenderness to the fool,
as if he felt instinctively the bond between them. The recurrence
to a fixed idea, in his obstinate and, at last, passionate asseveration
that Edgar's 'unkind daughters' were the cause of his affliction,
might, for its air of penetration and good faith, have been set
down in the diagnosis of a physician. When complete aberration
set in, the signs of it were astonishingly true and various. The
keen, over-eager attention, the sudden diversion to new excitements, the light garrulousness, the unmeaning smile, or the
abstracted silence, denoted by turns so many shifting moods of
fantasy through which one torturing recollection, like a knell,
heard in brief lulls of winds and waters, broke ever and anon.
His gradual recognition of Cordelia, as the mists of delusion
gradually lifted and dissolved, was a worthy climax to such a
performance. Her well-known voice, her tender words, at first
fixed him as with a sweet but vague and bewildering consciousness:—

> You do me wrong to take me out of the grave.
> Thou art a soul in bliss, but I am bound
> Upon a wheel of fire.

> .   .   .   .   .   .

> You are a spirit, I know; when did you die?

Then, how fine was the struggle towards memory and definite perception! What effort, what despondency in the failure!

> I should e'en die with pity
> To see another thus.

And, finally, how true, how overpowering, the expression of yearning hope which he almost feared to test, as he sank trembling into her embrace!—

> Do not laugh at me,
> For, as I am a man, I think this lady
> To be my child, Cordelia.

It is in such a delineation as this that the actor (precluded from any great originality in the *conception* of the character laid down for him) becomes in his turn almost creative, by translating the poet's ideas into an appropriate language of looks, tones and gestures, which make that living and incarnate which was comparatively but abstract and intellectual. For such a rendering, patient observation is no less needed than sympathetic impulse. I have more than once heard Macready say, 'Patience is genius'—a sentiment which, I think, originally belongs to Montaigne. Yet patience, though a proof of the interest and fortitude which genius begets, can hardly be genius itself. The tragedian, I sometimes thought, did some injustice to his own spontaneity in insisting almost exclusively upon the value of hard work. The truth is, he found in mental activity not only a duty but a delight. His love of painting, his wide acquaintance with literature, the charm which psychology had for him, as evinced not only in his acting, where motive and character were so finely laid bare, but in the fascination of Browning's poetry, showed a warmth and extent of sympathy without which patience would have lacked its best incentive and yielded but frigid results. He was more of an enthusiast than he himself believed. One night the discussion turned upon Sir Walter Scott, and his inability as a dramatist, and why, with all his powers of characterization and situation in narrative, he had never written a play likely to move an audience. 'I suppose he did not choose,' said one of the party. 'Choose!' broke in Macready, warmly; 'it's no matter of choice. If he had had the true dramatic fire, he couldn't have suppressed it. So says Knowles, and I echo him,' thus showing that in his deepest convictions, his favourite patience, though sometimes a sign of genius, was no substitute for it.

(v) *The Hard Job of Being an Actor* by Constantin Stanislavski

Remember that my objective is to teach you the hard work of an actor and director of plays – it is not to provide you with a pleasant pastime on the stage. There are other theatres, teachers and methods for that. The work of an actor and director, as we understand it here, is a painful process, not merely some abstract 'joy in creation' that one hears so much empty talk about from the ignoramuses in art. Our work gives us joy when we undertake it. This is the joy of being conscious that we may, that we have the right, that we have been permitted to, engage in the work we love – work to which we have dedicated our lives. And our work gives us joy when we see that having fulfilled our task, put on a performance, played a rôle, we have contributed something worthwhile to our audience, communicated to him something necessary, important to his life, for his development, in short, I come back to the ideas of Gogol and Shchepkin about the theatre, words you have already heard many times from me and probably will hear again more than once.

Nevertheless the whole process of an actor's and director's work – including his performance – is one that requires enormous self-mastery and often also great physical endurance. This work cannot be replaced by vague, high-sounding words and 'temperament'.

What lies at the base of an actor's or director's creativeness is work, and not 'temperament' or any other popular cliché such as 'flights', 'down beats', 'triumphs'.

To the ordinary man in the street the most 'joyous' jobs might seem to be the dances of the prima ballerina in *Don Quixote* or *Swan Lake*. He does not know how much physical effort, concentrated attention, sheer hard work Madame Geltzer had to put into the preparation of her famous 'pas de deux' in those ballets, nor what she looks like when she is in her dressing-room after the dance is over. Perspiration pours from her and in her heart she reproaches herself for her failure to convey the slightest nuance in her performance.

That is true of dancing. Why should it be easier in drama or comedy? Yes, 'joy' exists and in creation is experienced by true artists after they have done a tremendous piece of work in any chosen and beloved field of work in which they have reached the goals they have set themselves.

But the artist is not worth his salt who simulates 'joy in creation', waves his brushes about in front of his easel, pretending he is 'painting' with such 'ecstacy' (that's another popular word among the modernists). At such times he is profaning his art. He is not trying to reproduce life on his canvas – life in its infinite manifestations – trying to catch the fleeting feeling or thought on the face of his model. All he is trying to do is become her lover.

The same is true of an actor on the stage. When you, as you did recently, present the 'joy in creation' instead of the subject and ideas of the play, you are just flirting with the public like actor-prostitutes. Not that! Never! Leave that to the decadent artist, the futurist, the cubist! The great Russian actors, painters and writers did not play fast and loose with life; on the contrary, they tried to show its revolting and its inspiring sides in order to *educate* their public.

Do not be afraid of that word in art.

I have talked at length to you on the general subject of the art of the theatre, because I want you not only to know how to play your parts better but also to learn how to *train* yourselves to become real artists. Whatever I have achieved has been at the price of tremendous effort, of years wasted in mistakes and deviations from the real line of art. I am turning over to you everything I have learned, all my experience, in order to keep you from making the same mistakes. You will have three times as much opportunity to further our art if you will follow me, choose to follow the path which I point out to you.

You are a new generation, come into the theatre since the revolution. I want you to learn again in practice what is called the 'Stanislavski Method'. There is no 'method' as yet. There are a number of propositions and exercises which I suggest actors should carry out: they are to work on themselves, train themselves to become master artists. What are the basic propositions of my 'method'?

The *first* is this: There are no formulas in it on how to become a great actor, or how to play this or that part. The 'method' is made up of steps towards the true creative state of an actor on the stage. When it is true, it is the usual, normal state of a person in real life.

But to achieve that normal living state on stage is very difficult for an actor. In order to do it he has to be: (a) physically free, in control of free muscles; (b) his attention must be infinitely alert; (c) he must be able to listen and observe on the stage as he would in real life, that is to say be in contact with the person playing opposite him; (d) he must believe in everything that is happening on the stage that is related to the play.

To accomplish this I shall propose a number of exercises. . . . They train these absolutely necessary qualities in actors. They must be done every day just as a singer practices or a pianist does his finger exercises.

The *second* proposition of the 'method' is: A true inner creative state on the stage makes it possible for an actor to perform the actions required of him in accordance with the terms of the play, whether inner, psychological actions or external, physical ones. I divide them arbitrarily like this to make it easier to explain them to you in rehearsal. Actually in each physical act there is an inner psychological motive which impels physical action, just as in every psychological inner action there is also physical action, which expresses its psychic nature.

The union of these two actions results in organic action on the stage.

That action, then, is determined by the subject of the play, its theme, the individual character and the circumstances set up by the playwright.

In order to make it easier for you as an actor to take action on the stage, put yourself first of all in the circumstances proposed by the playwright for the character you are playing. Ask yourself: what would I do *if* the same thing happened to me as happens in the play to the character I am playing? I call *if* jokingly a 'magic' word because it does so much to help an actor get into action. Having learned to take action for yourself, then determine what difference there is between your own actions and those of your character in the play. Find out all the reasons which justify the actions of your character and then act without considering just where your 'own' actions end and 'his' begin. The one and the other will merge of their own accord if you have followed the procedure I have indicated to you.

The *third* proposition of the system: True organic action (inner-plus-external, psychological-plus-physical) is bound to produce a fully felt performance. This is especially true if the actor can in addition find some attractive 'bait', as we saw in rehearsal.

Therefore the summing up is:

A true inner creative state on the stage, *action* and *feeling*, result in *natural life* on the stage in the form of one of the characters. It is by this means that you will come closest to what we call 'metamorphosis', always providing of course that you have properly understood the play, its theme, its subject and plot, and have shaped inside yourself the character of one of the dramatis personae.

(vi) *Acting as a Controlled Dream*
by Ralph Richardson, in an interview with Derek Hart

How easily do you find you are able to establish a relationship with your audience in the theatre?

The actor feels the temper of the audience very swiftly, almost the moment he steps on to the stage. And, of course, it is his business to control that temper. But I don't think actors really love their audience; they are more in the nature of a lion-tamer. Perhaps the lion-tamer loves the lions, I'm not certain about that; but the actor must dominate the mood of the audience.

How far do you identify yourself with the character that you're playing? Do you have to believe in this person absolutely? Is he based entirely upon your own resources, or on your observation of other people? How do you set about it?

When you've decided to take a part, you think of all the people like that character that you've ever met; it's surprising then how vividly you remember people in your past, that you think you've completely forgotten – some old schoolmaster, or somebody who ran a shop – memories come crowding back. You change their costume, make them up differently, in your mind, till you get nearer and nearer to the identikit as the police say, don't they, if you recognize someone – and so you try to form the identity of the person that you're seeking to portray. You never really get very far until you start to rehearse, to concentrate on the one subject; and then, gradually, if you're lucky, the image of this person comes to you, and you try to make yourself as like him as you can.

Once you've created a character to your own satisfaction, during the course of a performance, how far are you aware of yourself in relation to the character that you've created? In other words, are you fully inhabiting the character, or are you stepping aside and having a look at him from the outside?

Part of it is stepping aside and controlling it, that's the first thing. You're really driving four horses, as it were, first going through, in great detail, the exact movements which have been decided upon. You're also listening to the audience, as I say, keeping, if you can, very great control over them. You're also slightly creating the part, in so far as you're consciously refining the movements and, perhaps, inventing tiny other experiments with new ones. At the same time you are really living, in one part of your mind, what is happening. Acting is to some extent a controlled dream. In one part of your consciousness it really and truly is happening. But, of course, to make it true to the audience, all the time, the actor must, at any rate some of the time, believe himself that it is really true. But in my experience this layer of absolute reality is a comparatively small one. The rest of it is technique, as I say, of being very careful that the thing is completely accurate, completely clear, completely as laid down beforehand. In every performance you're trying to find a better way to do it, and what you're reshaping, the little experiments, may be very small indeed, and quite unnoticed by your fellow actors; but they are working all the time. Therefore three or four layers of consciousness are at work during the time an actor is giving a performance.

(vii) *A Dialogue about Acting; 1929* by Bertolt Brecht

The actors always score great successes in your plays. Are you yourself satisfied with them?
No.
Because they act badly?
No. Because they act wrong.
How ought they to act then?
For an audience of the scientific age.
What does that mean?
Demonstrating their knowledge.
Knowledge of what?
Of human relations, of human behaviour, of human capacities.

All right, that's what they need to know. But how are they to demonstrate it?

Consciously, suggestively, descriptively.

How do they do it at present?

By means of hypnosis. They go into a trance and take the audience with them.

Give an example.

Suppose they have to act a leave-taking. They put themselves in a leave-taking mood. They want to induce a leave-taking mood in the audience. If the seance is successful it ends up with nobody seeing any further, nobody learning any lessons, at best everyone recollecting. In short, everybody feels.

That sounds almost like some erotic process. What ought it to be like, then?

Witty. Ceremonious. Ritual. Spectator and actor ought not to approach one another but to move apart. Each ought to move away from himself. Otherwise the element of terror necessary to all recognition is lacking.

Just now you used the expression 'scientific'. You mean that when one observes an amoeba it does nothing to offer itself to the human observer. He can't get inside its skin by empathy. Yet the scientific observer does try to understand it. Do you think that in the end he succeeds?

I don't know. He tries to bring it into some relationship with the other things that he has seen.

Oughtn't the actor then try to make the man he is representing understandable?

Not so much the man as what takes place. What I mean is: if I choose to see Richard III I don't want to feel myself to be Richard III, but to glimpse this phenomenon in all its strangeness and incomprehensibility.

Are we to see science in the theatre then?

No. Theatre.

I see: scientific man is to have his theatre like everybody else.

Yes. Only the theatre has already got scientific man for its audience, even if it doesn't do anything to acknowledge the fact. For this audience hangs its brains up in the cloakroom along with its coat.

Can't you tell the actor then how he ought to perform?

No. At present he is entirely dependent on the audience, blindly subject to it.

Haven't you ever tried?

Indeed. Again and again.

Could he do it?

Sometimes, yes; if he was gifted and still naïve, and still found it
fun; but then only at rehearsals and only so long as I was present
and nobody else, in other words so long as he had in front of him
the type of audience I was telling you about. The nearer he got to
the first night, the further away he drifted; he became different as
one watched, for he probably felt that the other spectators whose
arrival was imminent might not like him so much.

Do you think they really wouldn't like him?

I fear so. At any rate it would be a great risk.

Couldn't it happen gradually?

No. If it happened gradually it wouldn't seem to the audience that
something new was being gradually developed but that something
old was gradually dying out. And the audience would gradually
stay away. For if the new element were introduced gradually it
would only be half introduced and as a result it would lack force
and effectiveness. For this isn't a matter of qualitative improvement but of adaptation to an entirely different purpose; that is to
say, the theatre would not now be fulfilling the same purpose
better, but would be fulfilling a new purpose, quite possibly very
badly at first. What would be the effect of such an attempt to
smuggle something in? The actor would simply strike people as
'jarring.' But it wouldn't be his way of acting that would jar
them, but he himself. He would grate on them. And yet a jarring
element is one of the hallmarks of this new way of acting. Or else
the actor would be accused of being too self-conscious; self
conscious being another hallmark of the same sort.

Have attempts of this kind been made?

Yes, one or two.

Give an example.

When an actress of this new sort was playing the servant in
Oedipus she announced the death of her mistress by calling out her
'dead, dead' in a wholly unemotional and penetrating voice, her
'Jocasta has died' without any sorrow but so firmly and definitely
that the bare fact of her mistress's death carried more weight at
that precise moment than could have been generated by any grief
of her own. She did not abandon her voice to horror, but perhaps
her face, for she used white make-up to show the impact which
a death makes on all who are present at it. Her announcement that
the suicide had collapsed as if before a beater was made up less of

pity for this collapse than of pride in the beater's achievement, so that it became plain to even the most emotionally punch-drunk spectator that here a decision had been carried out which called for his acquiescence. With astonishment she described in a single clear sentence the dying woman's ranting and apparent irrationality, and there was no mistaking the tone of her 'and how she ended, we do not know' with which, as a meagre but inflexible tribute, she refused to give any further information about this death. But as she descended the few steps she took such paces that this slight figure seemed to be covering an immense distance from the scene of the tragedy to the people on the lower stage. And as she held up her arms in conventional lamentation she was begging at the same time for pity for herself who had seen the disaster, and with her loud 'now you may weep' she seemed to deny the justice of any previous and less well-founded regrets.

What sort of reception did she have?

Moderate, except for a few connossieurs. Plunged in self-identification with the protagonist's feelings, virtually the whole audience failed to take part in the moral decisions of which the plot is made up. That immense decision which she had communicated had almost no effect on those who regarded it as an opportunity for new sensations.

IV. STAGE DESIGN

(i) Henry Irving's setting for 'Much Ado'; 1882
an interview reported by Joseph Hatton

'THERE ARE five acts in the play, thirteen scenes. Every scene is a set, except two, and they are front cloths; there is not a carpenter's scene proper in the entire representation. To begin with, there is the opening scene – the bay, with Leonato's palace built out twenty-four feet high – a solid-looking piece, that has all the appearance of real masonry. I am giving you these details now from a cold, practical stage-manager's point of view – fact without colour. Well, this scene – the outside of Leonato's house – has to be closed in two minutes and a half, discovering the inside, the ball-room, which extends right round the walls of the theatre. This finishes the first act.

'Now, the second act was rung up in eight minutes, showing Craven's beautiful garden scene – terraces, glades, and arbours – in which set the business of the entire act occurs.

'The next act opens in front of Craven's cloth – the terrace, which changes to the morning view of the garden, which, in its turn, is covered with the cedar cloth; thus accounting for three scenes. After the last one, in two minutes the change was made to the effective representation of the town at night; the riverside street; the quay with its boats moored; the houses on the other side of the river illuminated, Leonato's palace among them. This closes the second act.

'Our great anxiety, as you know, centred in the cathedral set. We calculated that a wait of eighteen to twenty minutes would be required to send the curtain up on that, no doubt, very remarkable scene. It was rung up in fifteen minutes, displaying Telbin's master-piece – the cathedral at Messina, with its real, built-out, round pillars, thirty feet high; its canopied roof of crimson plush from which hung the golden lamps universally used in Italian cathedrals; its painted canopy overhanging the altar; its great iron-work gates (fac-similes of the originals); its altar, with vases of flowers and flaming candles, rising to a height of eighteen feet; its stained-glass windows and statues of saints; its carved stalls, and all the other details that are now almost as well known in

New York as in London. What a fine, impressive effect is the entrance of the vergers!'

'Yes, you were telling me once, when we were interrupted, how you came to introduce this body of men into the scene; it might be worth while to mention the incident along with these practical details of the working of the piece.'

'It came about in this wise. I went into Quaritch's bookstore one day, and among other curious books I picked up an old, black-letter volume. It was a work on "Ceremonies," with four large illustrations. I went into the shop to spend four or five pounds; I spent eighty-four or five, and carried off the black-letter book on "Ceremonies" – all Italian. I was at the time preparing *Much Ado* for the Lyceum. In the picture of a wedding ceremony I saw what struck me at once as a wonderful effect, and of the period too – the Shakespeare period. The effect was a mass of vergers, or javelin men – officers of the church, I should imagine. They were dressed in long robes, and each carried a halberd. I pressed these men at once into the service of Shakespeare and his cathedral scene at Messina, and got that impressive effect of their entrance and the background of sombre colour they formed for the dresses of the bridal party. And it is right too – that's the best of it. Not long ago I was at Seville, and saw a church ceremony there, where the various parties came on in something like the fashion of our people on the stage; but we never did anything so fine in that way as the entrances of the visitors at the Capulets' in *Romeo and Juliet*. Do you remember the different companies of maskers, with their separate retainers and torch-bearers? . . .

'The last act of *Much Ado* was rung up in seven minutes, disclosing the scene where Dogberry holds his court; this is withdrawn upon the garden scene. Then we come to the tomb of Hero, never before presented, except by us, since, I believe, Shakespeare's own time. This scene, with its processions of monks, vergers, and mourners, and the few lines that are spoken gives us four minutes to make a remarkable change, back to the ball-room in Leonata's house, where the story is concluded.'

(ii) A Setting for Ibsen's 'Ghosts'; 1905
from a diary by Constantin Stanislavski

January 30, 1905
When Nemirovich-Danchenko first read *Ghosts* aloud to me,
Simov and Kolupayev [the Moscow Art Theatre's scene designers]
suggested the following mental images: a dark house (a sort of
Norwegian *Uncle Vanya*), with a view of mountains and plenty
of air. A rainy day. Many rooms. Portraits of ancestors. A lighted
fireplace in the dining room. Then there is the burning down of
the orphanage, a most interesting scenic effect. Several scenes and
visual impressions stuck in our minds: the pastor, the open fireplace (a welcome, unexpected detail). Mrs Alving's love for the
pastor. The traces of this and of her past make her interesting.
A comic scene over the insurance. Note: the pastor and the
woman who once was in love with him. The picture at the end
of the first act: the first attacks of the boy's illness, the conflagration, the contrast between the doomed boy and his mother, who
now loses everything. The fading out of a young life which cannot go on functioning. . . .

January 31, 1905. Stage Set Models.
We went to the scene shop: I, Simov, Kolupayev, Nemirovich-
Danchenko, Savistkaya, Moskvin, and Andreyev [an electrician
and apprentice designer]. Kacholov [Pastor Manders] and
Sulerzhitski joined us briefly.
    We set up the requirements for the designer. (1) The conflagra-
tion, the orphanage, a fjord, and a glacier must be visible to the
audience from all parts of the theatre. The sets therefore should
not be too low, although that would be conducive to creating the
right mood. (2) One must feel that it is a gray, rainy day, with
low-lying clouds, and hear the monotonous drip of the rain. (3)
It is necessary to show the whole dining room to the audience
and it would be desirable to suggest a series of rooms in an old
house. (4) The house is very old (Norwegianize the manor house
in *Uncle Vanya*); but the gloom of the house and its age should
be conveyed through bright rather than dark colours (which would
be too banal and medieval). Every corner reeks with the atmosphere of vice. (5) There must be a staircase leading to an upper

floor. (6) Portraits of ancestors are recommended. The walls should be crowded with them to suggest age. (7) The furniture should be upholstered in worn red velvet. (8) The sunrise must be clearly visible. (9) The principal moments for stage pictures (the acting areas for these must be prepared) are: the pastor conversing with the woman who once was in love with him (this in a cozy corner); the death of Oswald; the sunrise (finale); the drinking scene before he dies. (10) There must be a fireplace (a typical one). The conflagration effects must be experimented with – magic lantern, etc. The same is true of the rain and the sunrise.

We examined and compared similarities and repetitions among favourite Norwegian motifs. We picked out: (1) a rising staircase with an alcove under it, and a fireplace; (2) panelled windows; (3) low alcoves with divans; (4) Norwegian rugs, mats, and tables; (5) the walls and windows painted yellow, green, red (red doors); (6) a special design for the ceiling; (7) upper passageways with arches and balustrades (it is obvious that the rooms are low up-stairs). Also a special semi-circular landing at the foot of the stairs (this will suggest the naïve fancies of olden times and that is what we most of all want).

I went over each picture and everything I found that seemed original I copied architecturally in my notebook. Simov did the same. Tomorrow we shall compare all the designs. Perhaps we shall find something of interest. We shall assemble the models. So far we have found only a few individual angles, but the total picture of the room is still lacking, especially the arrangement of the furniture and a blocking scheme. So far, I visualize only several scenes on the stairs (conversation with someone above), and I see the alcove under the staircase and the fireplace.

Things haven't warmed up enough for our work to reach the boiling point. As I was leaving the theatre a few things occurred to me. (1) When the fire takes place in the orphanage, is the alarm given by a bell or by the distress whistle of a steamer in the fjord? (2) A steamer should go by and leave a trail of smoke as it would on a rainy day. (3) The firemen are volunteers. Perhaps Oswald, or one of the men-servants, may dash out hurriedly putting on his coat as he runs. (4) In the distance, sounds of building the orphanage, which is almost finished, are heard. (5) There must be a portrait of Oswald's father resembling Moskvin. (6) The carpenter plays the first scene at work. He has been sent for to repair a door.

February 1, 1905.

I, Simov, Kolupayev, and Andreyev. We assembled our models – none of them proved satisfactory.

Simov's first model has on the right an alcove with the staircase. Under this is an archway leading into the dining room, where there is a bay window through which we see the orphanage burning down. But it is not a success. The staircase, on which we counted so heavily, suggests more an entryway or vestibule. The alcove on the right certainly suggests a good mood. However there is no room there to stage a scene. There are no angles for the death scene or other intimate scenes. Nor is there any feeling of an old house which had belonged to a libertine.

Simov's second model, with long vaulted arches for half the length of the front of the stage, suggests an old boyar palace but not Norway. The fire next door cannot be seen. Still, the set does contain two or three comfortable corners in which scenes could be staged.

Kolupayev's model is overcrowded, and has no view of the fire. The over-all impression is that of an entryway.

My model is a variation on Simov's There are comfortable corners and other places for staging, a good view of the conflagration, but it has little general atmosphere.

Kolupayev's model is better adapted to playing but lacks interest. Andreyev fiddled around but did not turn up anything.

Nemirovich-Danchenko joined us but left without contributing anything. . . .

February 2, 1905.

Simov, Kolupayev, and Andreyev worked on the designs. I was detained by a rehearsal and came later. Again no inspiration, not even a hint. In accordance with my plan, they made a very shallow model, the stage scaled less than twelve feet in depth. We have never had a set in this shape. Very convenient for a *mise-en-scène* (this suggests we are near a solution). Yet we still cannot capture any mood. We are beginning to get nervous and fear that we have exhausted all our resources, have tried out every line and shape. This gives us a chill. We keep making combinations of a staircase, a dining room and a conflagration – all of which must be visible from every angle of the auditorium. Perhaps this is an insoluble problem. Nevertheless we are obliged to find the right model for the first act, that is to say: Norway, an ancient building, a sense of a sinful life led there.

All these torments and searchings, and tomorrow is the deadline, the last day to get the models into rough form, if the production is to be ready by the second week in Lent.

We decided to work from my latest model.

A torturing state to be in – to see various components in the mind's eye, to sense the atmosphere of this old-fashioned room, filled with ancestral relics, and yet not be able to translate it all into material form. I remember similar tortures while preparing the first and third acts of *The Cherry Orchard*. We had to create something never seen, never heard of, and I had to make a visual image of it. In the first act it was necessary that the whole audience should see the cherry orchard. Until you have the right design, you cannot begin to plot the action. The set is half the job. I gave up and went away because I felt my brain was tired and my imagination was going around in vicious circles.

February 3, 1905.
I, Simov, Kolupayev, and Andreyev worked from 1.00 to 5.30 in the scene shop.

Simov arrived to put the finishing touches on the model I had proposed. He made several changes of his own. For instance, I had thought the model original because it was all done in straight lines (we have used curves too often). But Simov again broke the straight lines by introducing curves. He was carried away with the view of the landscape and wanted the audience to be able to see it. The house now assumed the shape of a Russian letter 'L' [л] upside down. In order to open a vista of the landscape he found it necessary to angle the perpendicular line to the right, and that slanted the rear wall. The patriarchal and archaic quality of the room vanished. It was neither one thing nor the other. I was in that same state myself. I could visualize and sense what this room looked like – a foreign manor house (not a castle), filled with portraits of ancestors and their relics – but I was incapable of converting its characteristic essence in practical terms.

It is a painful situation when you cannot express yourself and cannot guess the thoughts of another person. But neither Simov nor Kolupayev had anything to suggest. They argued this way and that, but found no firm ground under their feet. They finished the model, shook their heads, and realized it was not right. Nemirovich-Danchenko came in. He had missed our earlier searchings so he could not, of course, grasp very readily all we had been through. First he began to criticize what we had done, repeated his advice, and urged us to make the very mistakes we had eliminated. 'Why did you throw out the fireplace and the staircase?' We answered, 'Because to show them in profile wouldn't leave any comfortable acting areas, and we couldn't show them full front because they take too much from the view of the landscape,' etc., etc. Andreyev was even more irritating. He kept offering naïve and banal proposals. We simply had to inform him that two times two equals four. My nerves gave way. I was harsh and began to say unpleasant things. Apparently this outburst of temperament worked on my imagination. My nerves reached such a pitch that there and then I managed, though with great difficulty, to sketch out the whole room. Of course, all I could do was to indicate the position of the windows, doors, furniture; nor could I catch the spirit of the setting. In the vacant corners I put new furniture, pictures, a clock. Gradually the room was filled with my grotesque and incorrect drawing of objects and a faint suggestion of mood. The others felt this but were unanimous in saying that it was too Russian. I felt the same way, but nevertheless it did fit the needs of the *mise-en-scène*, which was no mean accomplishment. We began to consider how to inject a Norwegian flavour into it. The furniture would be arranged as in my plan but would be replaced by things that were typically Norwegian. There would be panels of worn red velvet or silk. The windows would be foreign in style, the stove and the bay window Norwegian. Simov waxed enthusiastic after he was given detailed explanations of the drawing, and he was all the more pleased with it because it offered a sense of space for air and a view of the outside landscape. He drew a pencil sketch which included all the details.

On my way home I began to get the feel of various scenes in my set and to visualize them. Everything fell beautifully into place, but in the evening, when I read over the long stretches of dialogue which did not suggest any basis for crosses or even of any real movement, I realized that my plan was probably inadequate. So I began to draw and added areas so the furniture could be rearranged. All in all, everything seemed workable for the first act. I began to plot the first scene and immediately stumbled on a vexing obstacle. In Ibsen's text the carpenter (Regina's father) enters the living room without motivation and stands there doing nothing while engaged in a lengthy conversation. But this is the theatre. There must be changes! So I invented this: From the start of the act he is busy fixing the lock on the door leading into the garden. Then a steamer passes. The carpenter begins to hammer. At the noise, Regina hurries in. The scene continues with him doing his job while she tidies up the room. However, to do this it will be necessary to change some of the words in the very beginning and to transpose some phrases. What else can one do? I think that it would be pedantic not to make such modifications.

February 4, 1905.
I arrived late at the theatre, almost two o'clock. Simov and Kolupayev were upstairs working on a model based on yesterday's drawing. Kolupayev was glueing, Simov was making sketches. We went all over it again and criticized it. The originality of the design lies in the shallowness of the downstage acting area (near the footlights). There was too little space for movement, so they decided to shift the furniture more centre. Near the fireplace they decided to put a glazed tile bench with cushions and to angle it parallel with the footlights. The bay window is good and serves to give both a dark and multi-coloured effect since the panes will be various tones of bottle glass. The cornices and the ceiling will be decorated in Norwegian style, with reindeer, primitive figures, etc. The ordinary wooden panels on the walls will be replaced by panels covered with velvet or silk (old materials, beautiful, faded). They may be bordered or plain. I recall that the floors in Norway or Sweden are painted white (we decided to do that too.) A balcony with a door leading out on to it proved to be necessary for the *mise-en-scène*.

In discussing this we discovered an effect. We will put in a trap below the balcony, cover the balcony with a painted tarpaulin and let rain drip down on to it. The water will flow over the tarpaulin into the trap; and the balcony floor, as well as the balustrade, will gleam with the moisture. We decided to omit the steamer. . . .

February 5, 1905.
Judging from Simov's sketch he is using modern Norwegian

art. That's what it looks like. In an old family house, filled with the sins of generations, suddenly we are confronted with *art nouveau!* This is dreadful. I must find some way of aging it. There is something in the back of my head but I can't quite pin it down. . . .

February 6, 1905.

Simov did not appear. Luzhski brought some things in from Madame Take, who lived for a long time in Norway – nothing of interest or adaptable for stage use; also some books. They suggested something about life in Norway and the play's background. But the day was wasted.

In the evening I did some writing and found myself caught up in the early scenes. I sensed the stillness in the house, the wet weather, the time of day. Various details became clear and sharp. I have written as far as Oswald's entrance. That is a great deal.

February 7, 1905.

We sent for those lazybones, Simov and Kolupayev. During the morning they finished the sketch (it's not bad but it's still too much on the *art nouveau* side) and they built the first rough model without any colour at all. We set the stage according to the model. It turned out that they had made a mistake in their measurements. We had to remove the fireplace because it blocked the bay window. The bay window will have to be enlarged. The other windows are so wide they look like gates. The space for the writing table is too small. The staircase is too high and it resembles the one in *Pillars of Society*. Anyhow there was a general resemblance to *Pillars of Society* so we decided to reverse everything (strangely enough we always tend to overload the left side of the stage).

The arrangement of furniture proposed was not good. We had to change it because it left two tables standing right beside each other. This was not the case on my drawing, but I had not made it to scale so this is how it turned out on stage. It originally looked as though, by placing the pieces parallel, there was an effect of style. This must be tried out.

Now I see that the bay is a place where one can stage a scene, and even the terrace can be used; the main acting focus is by the staircase, which runs parallel with the footlights. I made a note of a place that calls for Oswald to have his moments of deep thought: on the bench next to the fireplace – he can stand on it beside a pillar (at the foot of it he looks like a condemned man, bound to a pillory).

In general the long shallow room is turning out to be original, and the four to five characters playing near the footlights are thrown into high relief. It is all very easy to play in. But now we have to add some archaic flavour.

(iii) The Steps; 1913 by Edward Gordon Craig

FIRST MOOD: *Plate* XXXII

I think it is Maeterlinck who pointed out to us that drama is not only that part of life which is concerned with the good and bad feelings of individuals, and that there is much drama in life without the assistance of murder, jealousy, and the other first passions. He then leads us up to a fountain or into a wood, or brings a stream upon us, makes a cock crow, and shows us how dramatic these things are. Of course, Shakespeare showed us all that a few centuries earlier, but there is much good and no harm in having repeated it. Still I think that he might have told us that there are two kinds of drama, and that they are very sharply divided. These two I would call the Drama of Speech and the Drama of Silence, and I think that his trees, his fountains, his streams, and the rest come under the heading of the Drama of Silence – that is to say, dramas where speech becomes paltry and inadequate. Very well, then, if we pursue this thought further, we find that there are many things other than works of Nature which enter into this Drama of Silence, and a very grand note in this Drama is struck by that noblest of all men's work, Architecture. There is something so human and so poignant to me in a great city at a time of the night when there are no people about and no sounds. It is dreadfully sad until you walk till six o'clock in the morning. Then it is very exciting. And among all the dreams that the architect has laid upon the earth, I know of no more lovely things than his flights of steps leading up and leading down, and of this feeling about architecture in my art I have often thought how one could give life (not a voice) to these places, using them to a dramatic end. When this desire came to me I was continually designing dramas wherein the place was architectural and lent itself to my desire. And so I began with a drama called *The Steps*.

This is the first design, and there are three others. In each design, I show the same place, but the people who are cradled in it belong to each of its different moods. In the first it is light and gay, and three children are playing on it as you see the birds do on the back of a large hippopotamus lying asleep in an African river. What the children do I cannot tell you, although I have it written down somewhere. It is simply technical, and until seen it is valueless. But if you can hear in your mind's ear the little stamping sound which rabbits make, and can hear a rustle of tiny silver bells, you will have a glimpse of what I mean, and will be able to picture to yourself the queer quick little movements. Now on to the next one.

SECOND MOOD: *Plate* XXXIII

You see that the steps have not changed, but they are, as it were, going to sleep, and at the very top of a flat and deep terrace we see many girls and boys jumping about like fireflies. And in the foreground, and farthest from them, I have made the earth respond to their movements.

The earth is made to dance.

THIRD MOOD: *Plate* XXXIV

Something a little older has come upon the steps. It is very late evening with them. The movement commences with the passing of a single figure – a man. He begins to trace his way through the maze which is defined upon the floor. He fails to reach the centre. Another figure appears at the top of the steps – a woman. He moves no longer, and she descends the steps slowly to join him. It does not seem to me very clear whether she ever does join him, but when designing it I had hoped that she might. Together they might once more commence to thread the maze. But although the man and woman interest me to some extent, it is the steps on which they move which move me. The figures dominate the steps for a time, but the steps are for all time. I believe that some day I shall get nearer to the secret of these things, and I may tell you that it is very exciting approaching such mysteries. If they were dead, how dull they would be, but they are trembling with a great life, more so than that of man – than that of woman.

E.T.—8

FOURTH MOOD: *Plate* XXXV

The steps this time have to bear more weight. It is full night, and to commence with, I want you to cover with your hand the carved marks on the floor and to shut out from your eyes the curved fountains at the top of the steps. Imagine also the figure which is leaning there, placed over on the other side of the steps – that is to say, in the shadow. He is heavy with some unnecessary sorrow, for sorrow is always unnecessary, and you see him moving hither and thither upon this highway of the world. Soon he passes on to the position in which I have placed him. When he arrives there, his head is sunk upon his breast, and he remains immobile.

Then things commence to stir; at first ever so slowly, and then with increasing rapidity. Up above him you see the crest of a fountain rising like the rising moon when it is heavy in autumn. It rises and rises, now and then in a great throe, but more often regularly. Then a second fountain appears. Together they pour out their natures in silence. When these streams have risen to their full height, the last movement commences. Upon the ground is outlined in warm light the carved shapes of two large windows, and in the centre of one of these is the shadow of a man and a woman. The figure on the steps raises his head. The drama is finished.

(iv) On the Ideas of Adolph Appia by Lee Simonson

THE PLASTIC ELEMENTS

The aesthetic problem of scenic design, as Appia made plain, is a plastic one. The designer's task is to relate forms in space, some of which are static, some of which are mobile. The stage itself is an enclosed space. Organization must be actually three-dimensional. Therefore the canons of pictorial art are valueless. The painted illusion of the third dimension, valid in the painted picture where it can evoke both space and mass, is immediately negated when it is set on a stage where the third dimension is real.

The plastic elements involved in scenic design, as Appia analysed them, are four: perpendicular painted scenery, the horizontal floor, the moving actor, and the lighted space in which they are confined. The aesthetic problem, as he pointed out, is a single one: How are these four elements to be combined so as to produce an indubitable unity? For, like the Duke of Saxe-Meiningen, he was aware that the plastic elements of a production remained irretrievably at odds if left to themselves. Looking at the stages about him he saw that the scene-painter of his day merely snipped his original picture into so many pieces which he stood about the stage, and then expected the actor to find his way among them as best he could. The painted back-drop was the only part of an ensemble of painted scenery that was not a ludicrous compromise. Naturally the scene-painter was interested, being a painter, in presenting as many stretches of unbroken canvas as possible. Their centre of interest was about midway between the top of the stage and stage floor at a point where, according to the line of sight of most of the audience, they attained their maximum pictorial effect. But the actor works on the stage floor at a point where painted decorations are least effective as painting. So long as the emphasis of stage setting is on painted decoration, the inanimate picture is no more than a coloured illustration into which the text, animated by the actor, is brought. The two collide, they never meet nor establish any interaction of the slightest dramatic value, whereas, in Appia's phrase, they should be fused.

'Living feet tread these boards and their every step makes us aware of how meaningless and inadequate our settings are.' The better the scenery is as painting, the worse it is as a stage setting; the more completely it creates an illusion of the third dimension by the pictorial conventions of painting, the more completely an actually three-dimensional actor destroys that illusion by every movement he makes. 'For no movement on the actor's part can be brought into vital relation with objects painted on a piece of canvas.' Painted decorations are not only at odds with the actor but also with the light that illuminates them. 'Light and vertical painted surfaces nullify rather than reinforce each other. . . . There is an irreconcilable conflict between these two scenic elements. For the perpendicular, painted flat in order to be seen, needs to be set so as to catch a maximum amount of light.' The more brilliantly it is lighted, the more apparent the lack of unity between it and the actor becomes. 'If the setting is so placed as to refract some of the light thrown on it its importance as a painted picture is diminished to that extent.'

For Appia there was no possibility of compromise by keeping actors away from perspective back-drops where doors reached only to their elbows, or by warning them not to lean on flimsy canvas cut-outs down stage. He denied painted simulation of the third dimension a place in the theatre with a finality that gave his analysis the air of a revolutionary manifesto. He was the first to banish the scenic painter and his painted architecture from the modern stage. To Appia the actor was *massgebend* – the unit of measurement. Unity could be created only by relating every part of a setting to him. He was three-dimensional, therefore the entire setting would have to be made consistently three-dimensional. The stage setting could have no true aesthetic organization unless it was coherently plastic throughout. Appia's importance as a theorist is due to the consistency and the practicability of the methods he outlined for achieving this result.

One began to set a stage not in mid-air on hanging back-drops, but on the stage floor where the actor moved and worked. It should be broken up into levels, hummocks, slopes, and planes that supported and enhanced his movements, And these were again not to be isolated – a wooden platform draped with canvas here, a block or rock there, planted on a bare board floor, a 'chaise-longue made of grass mats'. The stage floor was to be a completely fused, plastic unit. Appia in this connection thinks in terms of sculpture. In order to make a model of a stage floor as he described it one would have to use clay. He considered the entire space occupied by a stage setting as a sculpturesque unit. The solidity achieved by setting wings at right angles to each other to imitate the corner of a building seemed to him feebly mechanical. He conceived much freer stage compositions where the entire area could be modelled as a balance of asymmetrical, spatial forms, a composition in three dimensions, that merged imperceptibly with the confining planes that bounded the setting as a whole.

Appia expressed in dogmatic form much of what the Duke of Saxe-Meiningen had demonstrated pragmatically. But in promulgating his theory of a stage setting he completed its unification by insisting on the plasticity of light itself, which no one before him had conceived. He demonstrated in detail, both as a theorist and as a draftsman, how stage lighting could be used and controlled so as to establish a completely unified three-dimensional world on the stage. Appia distinguishes carefully between light that is empty, diffuse radiance, a medium in which things become visible, as fish do in a bowl of water, and concentrated light

striking an object in a way that defines its essential form. Diffused
light produces blank visibility, in which we recognize objects
without emotion. But the light that is blocked by an object and
casts shadows has a sculpturesque quality that by the vehemence
of its definition, by the balance of light and shade, can carve an
object before our eyes. It is capable of arousing us emotionally
because it can so emphasize and accent forms as to give them new
force and meaning. In Appia's theories, as well as in his drawings,
the light which in paintings had already been called dramatic
was for the first time brought into the theatre, where its dramatic
values could be utilized. Chiaroscuro, so controlled as to reveal
essential or significant form, with which painters had been pre-
occupied for three centuries, became, as Appia described it, an
expressive medium for the scene-designer. The light that is important in the theatre, Appia declares, is the light that casts
shadows. It alone defines and reveals. The unifying power of
light creates the desired fusion that can make stage floor, scenery,
and actor one.

> Light is the most important plastic medium on the stage. . . . Without
> its unifying power our eyes would be able to perceive what objects
> were but not what they expressed. . . . What can give us this sublime
> unity which is capable of uplifting us? Light! . . . Light and light
> alone, quite apart from its subsidiary importance in illuminating a
> dark stage, has the greatest plastic power, for it is subject to a
> minimum of conventions and so is able to reveal vividly in its most
> expressive form the eternally fluctuating appearance of a phenomenal
> world.

The light and shade of Rembrandt, Piranesi, Daumier, and Meryon
was finally brought into the theatre as an interpretative medium,
not splashed on a back-drop, as romantic scene-painters had used
it, but as an ambient medium actually filling space and possessing
actual volume; it was an impalpable bond which fused the actor,
wherever and however he moved, with everything around him.
The plastic unity of the stage picture was made continuous.

If one looks at reproductions of stage settings before Appia –
and the history of stage setting might almost be divided by B.A. as
history in general is divided by B.C. – they are filled with even
radiance; everything is of equal importance. The stage is like a
photograph of a toy theatre; the actors might be cardboard dolls.
In Appia's drawings for the first time the stage is a microcosm of
the world. It seems to move from 'morn to noon, from noon to

dewy eve', and on through all the watches of the night. And the actors in it seem living beings who move as we do from sunlight or moonlight into shadow. Beneath their feet there is not a floor but the surface of the earth, over their heads not a back-drop but the heavens as we see them, enveloping and remote. There is depth here that seems hewn and distance that recedes infinitely further than the painted lines converging at a mathematical vanishing point. In attacking the conventions of scene-painting Appia created an ultimate convention. For the transparent tricker of painted illusions of form he substituted the illusion of space built up by the transfiguration that light, directed and controlled, can give to the transient structures of the stage-carpenter. The third dimension, incessant preoccupation of the Occidental mind for four centuries, defined by metaphysicians, explored by scientists, simulated by painters, was re-created in terms of the theatre, made actual. The stage more completely than ever before became a world that we could vicariously inhabit; stage settings acquired a new reality. The light in Appia's first drawings, if one compares them to the designs that had preceded his, seems the night and morning of a First Day.

(v) *Form for the Theatre of Cruelty* by Antonin Artaud

Besides this need for the theatre to steep itself in the springs of an eternally passionate and sensuous poetry available to even the most backward and inattentive portions of the public, a poetry realized by a return to the primitive Myths, we shall require of the *mise en scène* and not of the text the task of materializing these old conflicts and above all of giving them *immediacy;* i.e., these themes will be borne directly into the theatre and materialized in movements, expressions, and gestures before trickling away in words.

Thus we shall renounce the theatrical superstition of the text and the dictatorship of the writer.

And thus we rejoin the ancient popular drama, sensed and experienced directly by the mind without the deformations of language and the barrier of speech.

We intend to base the theatre upon spectacle before everything else, and we shall introduce into the spectacle a new notion of space utilized on all possible levels and in all degrees of perspective in depth and height, and within this notion a specific idea of time will be added to that of movement:

In a given time, to the greatest possible number of movements, we will join the greatest possible number of physical images and meanings attached to those movements.

The images and movements employed will not be there solely for the external pleasure of eye or ear, but for that more secret and profitable one of the spirit.

Thus, theatre space will be utilized not only in its dimensions and volume but, so to speak, *in its undersides* (*dans ses dessous*).

The overlapping of images and movements will culminate, through the collusion of objects, silences, shouts, and rhythms, or in a genuine physical language with signs, not words, as its root.

For it must be understood that in this quantity of movements and images arranged for a given length of time, we include both silence and rhythm as well as a certain physical vibration and commotion, composed of objects and gestures really made and really put to use. And it can be said that the spirit of the most ancient hieroglyphs will preside at the creation of this pure theatrical language.

Every popular audience has always loved direct expressions and images; articulate speech, explicit verbal expressions will enter in all the clear and sharply elucidated parts of the action, the parts where life is resting and consciousness intervenes.

But in addition to this logical sense, words will be construed in an incantational, truly magical sense – for their shape and their sensuous emanations, not only for their meaning.

For these exciting appearances of monsters, debauches of heroes and gods, plastic revelations of forces, explosive interjections of a poetry and humour poised to disorganize and pulverize appearances, according to the anarchistic principle of all genuine poetry – these appearances will not exercise their true magic except in an atmosphere of hypnotic suggestion in which the mind is affected by a direct pressure upon the senses.

Whereas, in the digestive theatre of today, the nerves, that is to say a certain physiological sensitivity, are deliberately left aside, abandoned to the individual anarchy of the spectator, the Theatre of Cruelty intends to reassert all the time-tested magical means of capturing the sensibility.

These means, which consist of intensities of colours, lights, or sounds, which utilize vibration, tremors, repetition, whether of a musical rhythm or a spoken phrase, special tones or a general diffusion of light, can obtain their full effect only by the use of *dissonances*.

But instead of limiting these dissonances to the orbit of a single sense, we shall cause them to overlap from one sense to the other, from a colour to a noise, a word to a light, a fluttering gesture to a flat tonality of sound, etc.

So composed and so constructed, the spectacle will be extended, by elimination of the stage, to the entire hall of the theatre and will scale the walls from the ground up on light catwalks, will physically envelop the spectator and immerse him in a constant bath of light, images, movements, and noises. The set will consist of the characters themselves, enlarged to the stature of gigantic manikins, and of landscapes of moving lights playing on objects and masks in perpetual interchange.

And just as there will be no unoccupied point in space, there will be neither respite nor vacancy in the spectator's mind or sensibility. That is, between life and the theatre there will be no distinct division, but instead a continuity. Anyone who has watched a scene of any movie being filmed will understand exactly what we mean.

We want to have at our disposal, for a theatre specatcle, the same material means which, in lights, extras, resources of all kinds, are daily squandered by companies on whom everything that is active and magical in such a deployment is forever lost.

(vi) *Svoboda: the architect of total theatre; 1967*
   by Ronald Bryden

Scenery is scarcely the word for what Svoboda creates. It's all Gordon Craig dreamed of, but hadn't the machinery to achieve, said one producer ecstatically, looking at one of the models in his RIBA exhibition. It represented the set for a *Hamlet* at the Belgian National Theatre in Brussels two years ago: an abstract honeycomb of cells, platforms and stairways, whose sections ground back and forward, as the action indicated, like great gunmetal tanks. They made possible a staging as fluid as the wildest vision of Ellen Terry's visionary son. Sculpting fingers of light could carve out at will a battlement in the Baltic dawn, the echoing hall of Elsinore, a royal closet, the cramped solitude of a mind imprisoned in a maze of public and private morality.

It was also, when you studied the miniature closely, an immensely ingenious joiner's toy, its parts sliding in and out like secret drawers in a Louis Quinze escritoire. That too is one of Svoboda's crafts – the first. He was born 47 years ago in Caslav, a small town 45 miles from Prague, the son of a local carpenter who apprenticed him to his own trade. From the age of 15, he worked as a cabinet-maker himself – he says it taught him the fundamentals of design: to think functionally, and in three dimensions.

Svoboda was just 18 the summer of Munich. During the German occupation, he trained as an architect at Prague's School of Applied Arts. The war ruled out new building; while it lasted, he channelled his talents and feelings about the régime into constructing, with light, paint and what materials he could lay hands on, sets for his own theatre company, a group of young actors who specialized in Strindberg's volcanic studies of domestic tyranny and hatred. After the liberation, they named themselves the Theatre of 5 May, and continued to work together until Svoboda's appointment as scenographer to the Czech National Theatre in 1948.

In the 19 years since then he has designed over 300 productions, an average of more than 15 a year; in Germany, Italy, Hungary, Britain and the US as well as his own country. He comes to each, he says, like an architect to a vacant site: with no preconceptions or single style, but in search of a form which will express the play's particular identity. Certainly his designs vary widely. For a *Tempest* in Prague, he made an abstract pattern of fronded cut-outs which suggested at once plates of coral, exotic foilage and the curling foam of Hokusai's famous Wave. For a *Don Giovanni* in Bremen, he cleared the full depth of the stage for a fantastic, Dali-esque perspective of sombrely mathematical chequers, globes and arches, with the Statue at its remote apex.

For an *Oedipus*, he has filled the whole stage with a vast, classically bare flight of white, ascending steps: for Gogol's *Government Inspector*, with a riotous Russian clutter of onion domes, provincial furniture and spiralling stairways. Often his work is expressionistic – he staged Osborne's *Entertainer* with three unconnected walls and a piano open to a sky filled with criss-crossed tram-cables and a huge, hanging clock. But he's equally capable of naturalism: for Puccini's *Tosca*, he elaborated ponderous interiors of Roman baroque.

Certain techniques recur, however, most of them his own innovations. He likes to use mirrors for trick-effects which are sometimes profounder than tricks. In his Brussels *Hamlet* a giant looking-glass hung at an angle above the set. In it, Hamlet communed with the Ghost – his own image, reflected in the darkness above him. It amounted to an interpretation of both character and play. For the Čapek brothers' *Insect Play*, a Czech National Theatre production brought last year to Peter Daubeny's World Theatre season in London, he angled over the stage two great mirrors broken into octagonal prisms. These looked down on the action from the dispassionate, titan vantage of a man standing over an anthill – but, redoubling the play's ironies about the similarity of human and insect behaviour, the 'insects' wore human dress and the eye staring down at them did so through the 100 decanter-stopper facets of some colossal insect-optic.

Slinging these gigantic looking-glasses in mid-air was made possible by using a light-weight, newly-invented Czech reflecting plastic. Svoboda keeps abreast of new developments in technology and materials – a modern designer, he says, needs to be not just draughtsman but chemist, engineer, electrician. He has built sets of fibre-glass, plastic foam, pure light and gauzes: 'If I decided a play needed a set made of cheese,' he says, twinkling, 'I'd use it.'

But above all he likes to use projections: photography thrown on to screens, cycloramas, the floor of the stage itself. The invention which first brought him international fame was his Laterna Magika Theatre, consisting of actors romping with their own filmed images, which was seen at the Brussels Expo in 1958. Svoboda went on to adapt the technique to conventional drama under the name Polycran – screens placed here and there on the stage for simultaneous projection.

'I want a kinetic scene, where movement becomes law, a stage which can change form and structure in the course of a play, depending on its needs and content,' Svoboda has said. His Polycran technique abolishes not only a fixed stage-space, but also stage time: it can surround an actor with past, present and future, or fragments of all three merged together in a fluid visual mosaic. Something of this appeared in his designs for Ostrovksy's

The Storm at our National Theatre last year, with its shifting projections of moonlight through branches, sunlight on water.

Svoboda's use of projections carries him well beyond the imaginings of such historic theatrical innovators as Adolph Appia, who first proposed the evocation of stage-atmospheres by light alone, or Gordon Craig, who envisaged a theatre of almost pure light and movement. It brings him abreast of the theories of Marshall McLuhan, who distinguishes the modern consciousness from all others in history by its enveloping bombardment of impressions and information from all sides and senses at once, as opposed to the 'linear' intake of the ages of reason and the printed word.

The traditional theatre we know belongs to them. It arranges events in an Indian-file order of one at a time: cause leading to effect, scene to scene, image to image, in logical procession of pictures hung before us in the dark. That method has been usurped, and improved, by cinema and television. To survive, as theatre folk have been saying desparingly for 50 years, the stage needs to isolate some factor other media cannot offer: some sense of immediacy, of reality and impact they cannot achieve.

So far, it has concentrated on the fact that it is 'live', its actors flesh and blood. But so long as they move through the static picture framed by a proscenium, they possess in fact less mobility less immediacy than their fast-moving images on a screen. This has led to the various experiments in 'open' staging and 'theatre-in-the-round' – attempts to take advantage of live actors' presence in three dimensions, creating a theatre with the many-sided reality of sculpture as opposed to photography and painting.

Svoboda's work starts from this notion of sculpture, and builds beyond it. With his moving sets, he continually alters the space within which the actor works, making his actions primary – in the same way that someone studying a statue moves round it, looking at it in new positions and relationships, Svoboda moves his scenery round the player, altering perspectives for the audience while it remains sitting still. But his mirrors and projections do more. They present the audience with more than one image of the play's action simultaneously: with the view of the insects as seen by man, say, at the same time as a view of man as seen by some Insect-God. They can show not merely a character, but his memories, thoughts and fantasies; not only what is happening to him, but what is happening elsewhere.

Svoboda could be called the first architect of a Total Theatre: one which envelopes its audience on more than one plane of perception, bombarding the mind with messages to more than one level. His is a theatre of not only three dimensions, but many: the most complete experience offered by any artistic medium.

Perhaps it's most modern in offering in one total impact a fragmented experience: the kaleidoscope of centrifugal facts, incoherent knowledge, to which the Western mind has been reduced by the collapse of its great traditional systems. One of his profoundest designs was for a 'Faust' in Warsaw: a palatial Renaissance interior projected over broken screens and surfaces, which shattered the image like a jigsaw. The only unity is the audience's perception.

'I'd like to design a new kind of theatre altogether,' he says. 'Something more like a film studio, where the action can go on in several places, with the audience brought right into the middle of it instead of sitting outside.' He is constantly hamstrung by the equipment of the traditional theatres he works in. 'To do what I really want at Covent Garden, they'd have to strip out all their old equipment and install completely new machinery – it's like asking a symphony orchestra to play pop, they'd have to buy completely new instruments. But they're very understanding, very co-operative.'

(vii) Against Falsehood; 1965 from a lecture by John Bury

I became what would now be called assistant electrician to Joan Littlewood's Theatre Workshop. At that time in the 1940s we were on the road, playing in whatever halls we could find. We toured a set of black drapes, to create a nothingness, and an enormous amount of lighting equipment, with three dimmer boards.

It was there that I discovered the importance of light. Lighting is the most flexible scenery there is; you can isolate an actor, place him in a locale, create worlds of changing shape and size. I still think that lighting is the key to making sense in the theatre; the audience interprets the set from what they can see of it. And the illumination of the actor, the way the light falls on his face, can feed the audience's imagination. I remember after the war we did a documentary with Joan about various kinds of work, unemployment and so on. We had a completely bare stage, but the way the light was directed on to our actors – the glint of a furnace, the strong overhead light in a railway station – convinced the audience that they had actually seen these places.

After eight years on the road, we moved to Stratford East, and I had to face a really testing time. We were no longer in a fit-up world, with minimal elements of scenery. We were doing basic plays like Shaw and Molière, and we needed sets. At that time I did not think of myself as a designer; we worked with a succession of bright young designers out of art school. Often they were very good, and they certainly shared a set of intellectual principles with us. But both Joan and I felt that their sets were interposing between the audience and the real nature of our work, making an unnecessary comment on it. We pushed the sets around, turned them upside and back to front, but eventually we decided that I would have to try my hand at the job myself.

I wanted to work so that the set would grow organically out of the rehearsal process. We didn't fix anything before we began, but brought in elements – chairs, a table, doors, a window – as and where they were required by the action that came out of the work. We would start rehearsal with nothing but a heap of junk – odd chairs and windows, the scenery from the last production. When we had reached a workable set-up, I would move in to tidy up. But one thing I never did was to pretty things up. In my use of materials at that time, I was resolutely against falsehood. I wanted to use the real materials, not transmute everything into the fairytale unreality of canvas and scene-paint. We were running a theatre for people who would be put off by what I call decorative frou-frous. We wanted to show them reality on the stage. So we searched out paving-stones from the Council to cover the floor, we borrowed used stained tarpaulins from lorries in railway yards and nailed them to frames for our walls, we made walls out of brick, wood and plaster instead of painting them on canvas.

I can still remember, when I was trying to borrow an iron radiator to put on the stage, an old stage-carpenter saying to me. 'Laddy, you can't put real things like that on the stage, they always look wrong.' Well, in his theatre of painted canvas they may have looked wrong, but I was searching for a theatre in which anything painted on canvas would seem unreal. I had my own stage, my own workshop, my own set of overalls. If we wanted a set, we would collect the material, put it on the stage, push it around, pull it apart, nail it together again. It became an inhabitant of the theatre just as much the actors. That way we made objects that grew out of the stage.

Well, success began to bring its own problems. In order to make enough money to keep the theatre going, we had to transfer shows to the West End, sets had to be built to schedule, actors were separated from the nucleus of the company. At one time we had three shows in the West End and one on tour, as well as keeping Stratford East going. Joan and the rest of us decided that the thing had served its purpose, that our next steps would have to be elsewhere.

After a couple of months I came to Stratford-upon-Avon, first as guest designer for various productions, then as associate, and now as head of design. It was a new world, very different: huge stage, the need for planning three months ahead, before the director could possibly commit himself. How was one to preserve the flexibility we had achieved at Stratford East? How was one to find the precise texture of each play when the organic growth of a set was made difficult by having to be laid down so far in advance?

Because of the difference of scale, because Stratford-upon-Avon is a repertory stage, where the sets are changed almost nightly, unlike Stratford East, where they take possession of the stage for a determined period and are then jettisoned, I had to reconsider my views on materials. When you ask actors or stage-hands to move scenery, it mustn't weigh a ton. I had to make real textures once more, but this time out of artificial materials. Fortunately, at this time the plastics industry was expanding, and all sorts of synthetic materials, such as expanded polystyrene and the polyurethenes, were coming on the market. This led to an entirely new function for the paint shops, creating surfaces rather than painting them. Surfaces which were the right weight, density and reflective index, in addition to the right colour. This was very exciting, and was the beginning of the route which led to the 'world of steel' for the Histories last year. The distance I had travelled can be measured in this: if I had been asked for a world of steel in Theatre Workshop days, I would have begged and borrowed steel sheets. Instead we used sheets of copperleaf stained and treated with chemicals. But I was still light-years away from the omnipresent stage-painter, who would have said,

'Steel, laddy? Right – a bit of white paint, a bit of black, a bit of silver – there's steel for you!'

In my first few sets for Shakespeare plays, I continued in the direction we had staked out in our Shakespeare productions at Stratford East. Fluidity of scene was the keynote; make the action flow swiftly. So for *Measure for Measure, Macbeth, Julius Caesar*, I created an open platform which was an over-all statement, and allowed the director to play the scenes without the interruption of a single blackout. Within this there were a number of mobile elements – chairs, tables, and so on – which could be carried in by the actors in the rhythm of the situation. Incidentally, we've become very aware of the importance of scene-changing in the dramatic rhythm. The actors have to bring on their things in the right rhythm, and the stage-hands must be rehearsed like actors. This rhythm-of-the-scene thing is very important; I've often noticed that if anyone has to move or work in the wings while a scene's being played, they can cut backstage noise almost to nothing if they're aware of and work with the rhythm of what's happening on stage.

By the time I came to work with Peter Hall on the Histories, I was already feeling that the open platform basis was constricting. It was too free, too bare; if you brought on a set of courtiers, they had to be grouped carefully, no one could sit down. So the basis of the *Wars of the Roses* set was two moving walls, which enabled us to change the area of the stage, to summon up (though not naturalistically) interiors, then open out to battlefields, hills, mountains, expanding or focussing as we wished. There was a definite gain in concentration, increased by our search for an image-object for every situation – a cannon, a council-table, a throne, a bishop's chair, the right hand-prop.

The same thing went for costumes. I wanted to take the fancy-dress out of costumes. But attempts to produce a 'timeless' costume were failures – I think you nearly always end up with variants on the spacemen or superman-with-a-helmet image. What we try to do now is to remain true to the period in silhouette, but by use of tailoring techniques, choice of materials, modern parallels, to reduce the historical identity down to essentials, and to create a costume which is truly functional in telling us as much as possible what we want to know about the wearer. Again, in costume, it is essential that approximation and indication is avoided and the image must be precise and organic – in fact, they must be clothes, not costumes. An example of the attitude one is trying to combat is the girl I once interviewed for wardrobe work who said she could cut me Gothic style, Renaissance style, Restoration style, but when I asked her if she could cut a suit for a modern play, said no. Which makes you wonder how real her versions of Renaissance costume were . . .

Now there is one big thing I would like to do. I want to create for this company an atelier of designers, all working together continuously to forge a true Royal Shakespeare style of design. I think its possible this way to make something that is richer and deeper than the vision of one man. Designing should be able to work like the production of a play – the interplay between a director and the actors enriches his vision of the play, prevents it from remaining cerebral. In the same way there can be a team of designers who work on the same production, each contributing their special knowledge and gifts to the elaboration of a conception they all share. Equally, we must create a new race of craftsmen, who will bring their own independent contribution to the process, not simply do it the way a particular designer likes it done, as has so often happened in the theatre.

In this way, a company like the Berliner Ensemble, by creating a team and firmly searching for a distinctive style, has created over ten years a coherent and unified scenic language. Our way would be different of course, but we could do as much. It happens in other large-scale designing activities, like architecture; so why not in the theatre?

V. PRODUCTION

(i) Directing the Classics by John Gielgud

SEVEN OR EIGHT of Shakespeare's plays are very familiar to me –
too familiar perhaps. I find it difficult to read them freshly without
confusing my impression of the characters with the performances
of certain actors in productions which I have already seen; in fact,
to approach the play as I would a brand new manuscript.

It is not difficult to discover, with the help of the scholars and
commentaries, what the actual words mean, where cuts may be
sanctioned, how the act waits may best be placed. But one cannot
digest too many outside opinions, and it is always dangerous in
the theatre to substitute scholarship and critical opinion, however
brilliant, for contemporary instinct and fresh vital imagination.

I find it hard to work in detail before beginning to work with
the cast of a play I am to direct, and I have never been altogether
convinced that completely meticulous preparations beforehand
can ever be entirely satisfactory. Until the day when all the participants meet together to begin the work, theory and planning, even
on paper, can be no more than a daydream. Yet the impression
created in one's imagination, after reading the play through
several times, must be the foundation of one's work as a director.
Unfortunately this impression is likely to be extremely nebulous,
yet I believe one should try to fix it in one's mind as a basic start.
I mean that the play must be continually developed from what one
conceives, in reading it, to be the sound and texture of the words
the movement and development of the action, and the kind of
physical and pictorial atmosphere that seems to be demanded by
the author. . . .

It is no use planning the shape and balance of a production if
the director does not consult the leading players to some considerable extent. By failing to do so, he may easily lose the invaluable confidence and help that he might otherwise gain from their
co-operation. Their opposition or conflicting personal views may
not only blow his own schemes sky high, but may also affect the
loyalty of the other actors.

And yet one does not wish to discuss one's ideas beforehand
with too many people, or to have too many outside opinions
confusing or conflicting with one's own. At the same time it is of

enormous advantage to work for a manager or impresario whose opinion one respects, and who is capable of giving practical advice in moments of rehearsal crisis. Also it is a relief (at any rate to me) to have the whole of the financial side of theatrical business taken care of by someone who is an expert on such matters. . . .

The actor who is also a director is necessarily in rather a special kind of position, working in his double capacity. Provided he is at one with the author, he has the advantage of being able to develop his own strong feelings about the play without question or argument, since his authority will be undisputed in every department of the preparations. Then, too, he may understand his colleagues better, their moods and vanities, because he is himself an actor. He may allow them greater liberty to improvise, and is well equipped to deal with their moments of obstinacy or carelessness, their flashes of inspiration or despair. On the other hand, he may become too easily impatient with their technical deficiencies as compared with his own actor's skill, and be tempted to try to make them imitate him slavishly, forcing inflections on them, or showing them up by caricaturing their efforts. If they still fail to satisfy him, he may be tempted to cut the text, or try to cover the weaknesses of certain players with showy distractions of movement or business which he may invent, thus altering the balance of scenes so as to draw the audience's attention away from certain moments in the play which can never be achieved successfully, he thinks, with the material at his disposal. Time is short, the play is cast and in rehearsal. It is a great temptation to bully the players of the smaller parts who dare not answer back, and to flatter the leading actors by giving them their heads.

The ideal director of Shakespeare needs to have remarkable gifts besides the fundamental qualities of industry and patience. He should, of course, have sensitivity, originality without freakishness, a fastidious ear and eye, some respect for, and knowledge of, tradition, a feeling for music and pictures, colour and design; yet in none of these, I believe, should he be too opinionated in his views and tastes. For a theatrical production, at every stage of its preparation, is always changing, unpredictable in its moods and crises. Every person concerned in it has a different attitude, a different problem. Players of tried skill sometimes have to be toned down in order to balance and harmonize with those of lesser accomplishment, while the less experienced may need encouragement in order to gain greater confidence and style. There must always be room to adopt an unforeseen stroke of inventiveness, some spontaneous effect which may occur at a good rehearsal and bring a scene suddenly and unexpectedly to life. Yet the basic scaffolding must be firm, the speech modulated, clear, and varied, the phrasing elegant and clear, unaffected, constantly varying in pace and pitch. The movements should be simple (or apparently so), and calculated to put each speaker in the best possible position, so that the eyes of the audience are drawn inevitably towards him at the right moment. The positioning and grouping, in stillness or movement, in distance-relationship, should continually help the audiences to concentrate on the all-important words.

What the director cannot contribute, but the players can, is the life of the play; that is, the reality of the situation and its effect (or failure of effect) upon the audience. And so, it seems to me, the actors must always be considered first and last.

For a director is not in the same position as an orchestral conductor – though he may seem to be so at rehearsals, and the more inspiring his influence during this critical period the better. But when the play comes at last to be performed, and everything depends on the contact between the actors and the audience, the director is no longer presiding over the stage. His work is over now, and if the actors fail him (to say nothing of the electricians and stage management) he will have worked in vain. So the performers must not be so dependent on him that they are lost without him. His control over everything – scenery, lighting, music, acting, grouping, speaking – may have been brilliant or inept, but the final responsibility rests with the players once the curtain has risen and the audience is in their seats.

Actors need hints on carriage, diction, manner – and especially motive, though it is the character 'for their purpose' that usually interests them most, the character they have privately conceived. They may sometimes, at rehearsal, convince the director that he must change the whole balance and arrangement of a scene. A player may now feel he will appear to better advantage if he stands still while the others move, even though, in studying the scene beforehand, it had seemed essential to the director that the others should be still and he should be the one to move. Every scene and character may be remoulded continually in rehearsal to suit the actors, provided the basic mood and shape of the main conception is not destroyed or blurred by doing so. Endless varieties of groupings and movements are possible. To change continually in rehearsal is not, to my mind, necessarily a fault on the part of a director, though actors often resent it, and it is generally considered to be one of my besetting sins. Of course it tries the nerves of the actors if changes are continually demanded of them till the very last rehearsal, but I feel it is never too late to improve and alter – and especially to simplify – even when a play has been running for many weeks.

There has already been a complete revolution in the acting and directing of Shakespeare over the last fifty years. At the turn of the century, William Poel's experiments and the books and designs of Gordon Craig led the way to Granville-Barker's Shakespeare seasons at the Savoy, just before the 1914 war, when he built a modified apron on to the existing proscenium, with runner curtains alternating with simple, stylized, semi-permanent settings, decoratively designed by Albert Rutherstor and Norman Wilkinson. Later, the permanent set 'with varia-tions' began to come into more general use, in Shakespearian productions by J. B. Fagan and Bridges-Adams, achieving greater speed and economy, and elaborate academic picture scenery gradually became a thing of the past.

In my own productions at the New and Queen's Theatres, in the nineteen-thirties, I hedged uneasily between various styles of presentation, and only once, in *Romeo and Juliet* in 1935, did I achieve, with the help of Motley who designed the production, something of a successful balance, at once picturesque, speedy and varied, in the use of the stage space. My second *Hamlet* production in 1939 (designed also by Motley for outdoor per-formances at Elsinore but seen in London previously at the Lyceum before it ceased to be a theatre) was, though Elizabethan in intention, a compromise in playing space, with intermediate scenes played on a long narrow apron in front of billowing traverse curtains, and cramped like a booth at a fair. We should have had the courage to build an upper stage and also a real apron of the right Shakespearian proportions.

Robert Atkins (who had begun with Tree) should be given great credit for his many admirable productions at the Old Vic in the twenties (in several of which I walked on as a super) especially as he achieved his remarkable results with an absolute minimum of time and money. Harcourt Williams, an equally dedicated artist (trained in his career as an actor by Benson, Ellen Terry and Barker), under whose direction I worked so happily in 1929 and 1930, followed Atkins at the Vic working on similar lines, with little money, admirable taste, and selective discrimination. Both men served the theatre with real integrity of purpose, modestly giving place to their successors, Tyrone Guthrie, Anthony Quayle, Michael Benthall, Glen Byam Shaw and Peter Brook, all of whom, working over the last twenty or thirty years both at the Vic and Stratford-on-Avon, have brought their respective talents to bear in different ways on developing style, speed and originality in their many brilliant Shakespearian productions. Today the permanent set with variations, the house curtain only dropped once or twice during the performance, and the playing of an almost full text – innovations unheard of at the beginning of the century – are now taken for granted by audiences.

Despite many fundamental improvements in the general scheme of technical presentation, however, I do not think any really basic solution to the playing of Shakespeare has yet been found during my forty years as an actor and thirty as a director. Of course the players and actors of each new generation need to rediscover Shakespeare in terms of their own particular time. Hence the freakish tendencies between the two wars – the modern dress productions under Barry Jackson in the twenties (not wholly unsuccessful, and useful in breaking many of the old traditions), and Komisarjevsky's experiments at Stratford-on-Avon, which were the more remarkable, since he achieved them with not more than a couple of weeks' rehearsal, and covered the weaknesses of such a shameful emergency by devising brilliant accompaniments – music, décor and pantomime – to keep them spinning along, even though the plays themselves had not been properly rehearsed. This kind of experimental novelty rightly attempted to encourage contemporary audiences to take a new interest in the plays. But the dignity and lucidity of true poetic style in diction, the balance and rhythm in declamation or soliloquy, the sword play and dancing, the deft juggling with words, pace and mood, whether in verse or prose, the infinite skill and variety needed to bring the genius of the plays to life, all these important ingredients are seldon given sufficient time and care. A company is collected at random and trained to a necessary minimum of efficiency in four hectic weeks. Such conditions are simply not good enough to serve a great play worthily. In a concert hall no audience is expected to tolerate an orchestral performance of a classical work played by inexperienced executants. Yet how seldom has one ever been able to see a Shakespeare play with more than two or three of the parts played really brilliantly, or without several fatally weak performances among the supporting cast.

Now let us suppose the play is chosen, the actors cast, the main lines of production planned with the designers, the music and stage effects in hand. The company is gathered for the first reading of the play, and the director must now decide how he will begin the work in order to communicate something of what he feels himself, and hopes to bring to life, with their help, in the ensuing weeks. I myself believe it is unwise to deliver a long lecture at this early stage of the proceedings. The models and costumes have been brought by the designer, and the actors look at the drawings for the scenery perfunctorily – they will have their backs to it anyway, and entrances and exits are their only immediate preoccupation. But they probably examine the costume designs more carefully, and one sees the leading players making an immediate mental note of the dresses which they cannot (or will not) wear.

The reading begins, and the younger members of the cast try to listen obediently to the scenes that do not concern them, while the principal players either mumble apologetically or declaim uncertainly, suspecting the unspoken criticism of their colleagues. Irving was accustomed to read the play aloud, taking every part, and this, says Ellen Terry, was a great and inspiring experience for the company. Shaw was also a superb reader of his plays, but I know of no actor, author, or director today (not even Noel Coward) who would attempt to inflict such an ordeal upon his company. The readings of a Shakespeare play should, of course, in theory, be as important and constructive as the action rehearsals, but personally I have never found them very satisfactory. It is hard to hold the attention of a large company when the urgency of staging a play is in question, and the leading players long to make their first experiments alone with the director. They are too self-conscious to read and stop and argue theoretically, though lately, in the so-called *avant-garde* theatres, discussions among the players and long harangues by the director appear to have become the fashion.

Personally I prefer to have only one or two readings, and then slowly to begin to place the scenes. There will be time later on to sit down and study the pace and sound of individual passages in greater detail with one or two actors separately, after the main lines of the production are beginning to take shape. Every director has to choose the method that seems to him to give the best and quickest results, and his actors most confidence, for there is always the race with time to be considered. What then is the most efficient way to guide a company of players, supposing that the director is satisfied (as he seldom is) with the main pattern of the action that he has devised beforehand?

First the question of speech. He must criticize affectation, inaudibility, lack of feeling for musical shape, wrong inflections, a tendency to excessive declamation on the one hand or too great naturalism on the other. Next the cadence of speech, for in Shakespeare rhythm and sound can often be as important as they are in singing. A stylized projection of manner and voice must not be used inflexibly. An actor who begins a speech in heroic style must be able to swiftly change (as Shakespeare's words so often do) to a sudden appearance of simplicity. There must be constant variety of pace and tone, stillness in repose, liveliness in attack. In comedy, especially, the physical distance between actors is very important, and the director should experiment continually to make the best possible use of it. The audience needs time to appreciate points between the exchanges in the text, while the ball, just as in a game of tennis, is bandied expertly from one character to another and back again. Comedy 'points' can so often only be achieved by the give-and-take of both actors in a duologue – one offers the saucer, the other puts his cup on it.

Instinct is perhaps one of the most unpredictable and exciting qualities of really good acting, and I think it is often a mistake when actors try to approach their work too intellectually. I have known indifferent actors who can talk quite brilliantly on the craft of acting, and fine actors whom I have heard talk great nonsense about it too.

Of course no director can hope to drive his actors beyond a certain degree of accomplishment. But once the audience is present as a kind of sounding-board, he may begin to correct the balance of his production once again, and may even find it possible to develop the actors' performances further, though there is always the danger that they will prefer to elaborate rather than to simplify. Laughter and applause breed constant danger. The actors tend to forget the essential background mood of a scene through their interest developing little points of detail. To insist on a false effect of pace may only result in producing an artificial vivacity – the thought must always precede the word. On the other hand, too much naturalistic pausing (to appear to be looking for the word or phrase) can easily be overdone, and produces an effect of dragging and portentousness. Long runs develop a fatal tendency to mechanical repetition. It is in the first few weeks of a run that actors are at the most sensitive in reaction when they themselves are still fresh from the director's hand, and the audiences responsively at their best. Later, when the quality of the audiences begins to deteriorate, the performances on the stage will begin to slacken too, and the director will have to work hard to restore the necessary balance.

Changes in a cast are frequently necessary during a very long run, and though replacements can seldom hope to fit into the pattern which is already achieved to the complete satisfaction of everyone concerned, the necessity of rehearsing the play again nearly always brings fresh possibilities to light. In reviving an old production, or rehearsing a play already done in London for a new production elsewhere, on the Continent, say, or in America, I do not like to use my old prompt books in order to repeat moves and business with mechanical accuracy. If the same scenery is to be used again, there is naturally a certain amount of positioning which will be the same in a second version; but to say at rehearsals, 'This is when we get a big laugh by doing so and so' is an extremely dangerous way to go to work, and kills the whole impetus of a new company. It is sometimes hard to revive one's own enthusiasm for a production, however successful originally, that has become too familiar through many months of playing. In my last revival of *Much Ado About Nothing,* in New York, I felt my own spark was no longer lively enough to spur the company to the very best possible result – and the perfection of the ensemble in *Love for Love,* in London, seemed to me to put the company, which I afterwards took to New York in the same play, at a disadvantage, although, taken individually, one or two of the performances seemed to me actually better in America.

It seems to be easier to improve one's work in directing a contemporary play. In *Five Finger Exercise,* though the company, with only one exception, was the same as in London, the New York production gained considerably by fresh rehearsals and the background of a different set. Working again on the play, after a year's run in England, the actors were difficult to manage at first and reluctant to make the effort to revise their performances. The play opened to rather a lukewarm reception at Wilmington, and the company began to lose confidence and became alarmed. But the author, who was fortunately with us, suddenly saw a way of adding a few extremely valuable lines to the end of the first scene, and rewrote entirely the first ten minutes of the play, which I restaged completely while we were trying it out for a week in Washington, and this, I believe, contributed greatly to the excellent reception we received afterwards in New York, This shows that one is never really finished with work in the theatre, and how valuable it is to persevere and experiment continually.

(ii) *Brecht as Director* by Carl Weber

I asked at the office if I could watch a rehearsal, and they told me that anyone who had a legitimate interest could watch rehearsals unless Brecht, as happened rarely, thought an actor was extremely nervous – even then he would work with that actor separately, but the rest of the rehearsals would be kept open. He wanted actors to get used to spectators, to get laughs, to be in contact with the people down there as early in the process as possible, to work *with* an audience. At that time they were rehearsing the *Urfaust*, which Goethe wrote when he was about 25, decades before he did the final version of *Faust*. Brecht preferred the *Urfaust* for several reasons. It is written in *Knittelvers*, a verse which is un-rhythmic or of changeable rhythm, and rhymes either not at all or very forcefully. It was used in the farces and mystery plays of the late Middle Ages and early Renaissance; also, it is the language of German Punch and Judy shows. *Faust* itself, however great, is the play of an old man, with a detached view of society and of the individual – the *Urfaust* is a *Sturm und Drang* work with a young, aggressive approach to the world. In its treatment of the love story, it is remarkably close to the way Brecht wrote in *Baal* and *Drums in the Night*.

I walked into the rehearsal and it was obvious that they were taking a break. Brecht was sitting in a chair smoking a cigar, the director of the production, Egon Monk, and two or three assistants were sitting with him, some of the actors were on stage and some were standing around Brecht, joking, making funny movements and laughing about them. Then one actor went up on the stage and tried about 30 ways of falling from a table. They talked a little about the *Urfaust*-scene 'In Auerbachs Keller' (Mephisto brings Faust into an inn where drunken students enjoy themselves with dirty jokes and silly songs). Another actor tried the table, the results were compared, with a lot of laughing and a lot more horse-play. This went on and on, and someone ate a sandwich, and I thought, my god this is a long break. So I sat naïvely and waited, and just before Monk said, 'Well, now we are finished, let's go home,' I realized that this *was* rehearsal. And it was typical of the loose way Brecht often worked, of his experimental approach and of the teamwork the Ensemble was used to. Whatever ideas he brought to rehearsal he tried out, threw away, tried something else; sometimes 40 versions of one scene were tried, once in a while only two. Even when a production had opened, and been reviewed, he re-worked parts of it, re-rehearsed it, changed the blocking. The actors also took an experimental attitude. They would suggest a way of doing something, and if they started to explain it, Brecht would say that he wanted no discussions in rehearsal – it would have to be tried. Of course, his whole view of the world was that it was changeable and the people in it were changing; every solution was only a starting point for a new, better, different solution.

All this was – of course – not just for love of experiment. Brecht was mainly concerned with the play as the telling of a story to an audience, clearly, beautifully, and entertainingly. If he found that in an almost completed production one certain part was opaque or boring, he cut it. I have never seen anyone cut a script as mercilessly as Brecht cut his own. Brecht had another important ability: if he had worked at a scene, and then dropped it for a week, he could come back and look at it as if he never seen it before. I remember a scene from the third act of *Caucasian Chalk Circle*, when Grusha, with her adopted child and her brother Lawrentij, arrives at the house of the dying peasant whom she is forced to marry. The scene hadn't been done for about three weeks (the play was rehearsed for eight months); he came back to it, and we all thought it was going rather well when suddenly Brecht yelled, 'Stop!' He asked what the actor playing Lawrentij, who was walking across the room, was doing. Well, we answered, there's a good reason; he has to be over there for his next line, you blocked it this way. Brecht denied this angrily, saying there was no reason for such a move. 'But his next line asks for it.' 'What line?' he barked. The actor said the line. 'But that's impossible, I couldn't have written that!' We had to show him in the book that he had indeed written it, and he was furious – at us. But he rewrote the scene. He had looked at it as if it were by someone else, from a play he'd never heard of before, which he was judging as a spectator, and it failed.

The initial preparation of a play usually took about half a year, while it was discussed, and adapted (if it was a translation). The set was developed on paper and as a model during that period, as were the costumes. Then, when Brecht went into rehearsal, it could take three to four months to block the play. This blocking involved the working out of a considerable number of details. To Brecht, blocking was the backbone of the production; ideally, he thought, the blocking should be able to tell the main story of the play – and its contradictions – by itself, so that a person watching through a glass wall, unable to hear what was being said would be able to understand the main elements and conflicts of the story. To work out blocking this clear takes an enormous amount of time; he would try out every thinkable possibility – and if a scene didn't seem to work in dress rehearsal, the first thing reworked would be the blocking.

After the basic blocking was finished, we started to work on the acting detail; by this time the actors knew their lines completely, and could play around with them freely. The most meticulous attention was paid to the smallest gesture. Sometimes it took an hour to work out whether an actor should pick up a tool one way or another. Particular attention was devoted to all details of physical labour. A man's work forms his habits, his attitudes, his physical behaviour down to the smallest movement, a fact usually neglected by the stage. Brecht spent hours in rehearsal exploring how Galileo would handle a telescope and an apple, how the kitchenmaid Grusha would pick up a waterbottle or a baby, how the young soldier Eilif would drink at his General's table, etc. Often paintings or other pictorial documents of the play's period were brought into rehearsal for the study of movements and gestures. Brecht's favourite painters were Breughel and Bosch: their paintings told 'stories' (not in the sense of the veristic nineteenth-century school, of course), their people were stamped by their lives and occupations, their vices and beliefs. The influence of pictures he had seen often could be felt in Brecht's work; certain moments of the blocking, as well as character-images, were derived from paintings or photos.

Each moment had to be examined: for the characters' situation, for the story's situation, for the actions going on around the character. When all these details had been brought to a certain point, not of completion, but of diminished possibilities, Brecht would have the first run-through. This might be six months after the actors started work on the play, six months of working on blocking, single beats, and small units of scenes. The first run-through was usually a disaster – it was impossible for the actors to pull things together so fast. But this was just what Brecht was waiting for; in the second and third run-throughs, a rhythm began to appear, and all the mistakes made so far emerged clearly. So then Brecht broke the whole thing down again into short beats and small units, and reworked every part that had been unsuccessful. After the second break-down of the play, the final period of rehearsal usually came. This included run-throughs – but interrupted by frequent reworking of scenes and details. A week or more was given to the technical rehearsals. Lighting a show sometimes took five days alone, and extras were used to walking through all the motions, so the actors wouldn't waste their time and energy. During dress rehearsals, details were constantly changed or developed further, including the blocking and quite often even the text. I remember first nights, when actors would find a little note from Brecht on their dressing-room tables, wishing them good luck and asking them to say a new line in scene X instead of one Brecht had decided to cut, because audience reactions in dress-rehearsals had indicated that the former line didn't work the way Brecht intended it.

After the last dress rehearsal Brecht always did an exercise, which he called the 'marking' or 'indicating' rehearsal: the actors not in costumes, but on the set, had to walk quickly though all the actions of the show, quoting the text very rapidly, without any effort of acting, but keeping the rhythm, the pauses, etc., intact. The effect – if you were sitting far back in the house – was very much like an early silent movie: you saw people moving and gesturing very quickly, but you couldn't hear the words or get any kind of emotions, except the most obvious ones. This proved to be an extremely helpful device; it made the actors relax, helped them to memorize every physical detail and gave them a keen sense for the show's rhythmic pattern.

Finally first night came, which in fact was a preview with audience, after which rehearsals were used to change the production according to audience reactions. After five to eight previews, the official 'opening' with press and invited guests took place. Brecht introduced these previews to Germany, probably drawing on his American and English experiences. In the beginning, the German critics strongly rejected this procedure; now other theatres have followed Brecht's example. After the opening, work on the production didn't stop. The director – or one of his assistants – watched every performance, and whenever changes or a reworking were felt necessary, rehearsals were scheduled.

This sounds like a monumentally laborious process, and to some extent it was. But it took place in an atmosphere of humour, ease with experimentation, relaxation. Actors (and directors) new at the Ensemble were usually very tense, and tried to get results right away – as they must when they have only a few weeks rehearsal time. Brecht would tell them, 'Fast results are always to be regarded with suspicion. The first solution is usually not a good solution. Not enough thinking goes into it. Instinct is a very dubious guide, especially for directors.'

Brecht regarded designs as of the highest importance and had worked out his methods of handling it with his friend Caspar Neher. When Neher designed a play for him, he started with little sketches depicting the important story situations – sometimes he arrived at a kind of comic strip of the entire play. He began with people, sketching the characters in relation to a given situation, and thus visualizing the blocking. When he and Brecht were satisfied with the sketches, they started to develop a set. For Brecht, for Neher when he worked with Brecht, for Otto and von Appen, who worked with Brecht in the fifties, the set was primarily a space where actors tell a certain story to the audience. The first step was to give the actor the space and architectural elements he needed; the next was to work out the set so it by itself would tell the audience enough about the play's story and conflicts, its period, social relations, etc.; the last step was to make it beautiful.

Whatever is called the 'style' of Brechtian productions was always something arrived at during the last phase of production. Brecht never began with a preconceived stylistic idea, even something

so 'basic' as whether the production should be 'period,' 'naturalistic,' or whatever silly labels theatre convention usually pins on
plays. He began with a long exploration of the intricate social
relationships of the characters and the behaviour resulting from
them. Their psychology was not left out, but was developed from
the social relations. The designer watched, working out his ideas
as Brecht rehearsed. Twice I saw about 75 per cent of a completed
set – and the finished costumes that went with it – thrown away
after the first dress rehearsal, because although it was beautiful
it did not tell the audience what Brecht and von Appen wanted.
An enormous amount of money was poured into these experiments, but certainly not wasted. One of Brecht's favourite
proverbs – 'The proof of the pudding is in the eating' – was
always applied to his theatre work.

From the time Brecht began directing in Munich in the twenties,
until the end, he liked to have people around him when he directed.
He asked everyone he trusted to come to rehearsal and constantly
asked their opinions; he controlled his work through their
reactions. In the fifties, his productions were always team-work,
and he constantly used all the people connected with a production
– assistants, designer, musicians (Eisler was at many rehearsals).
Brecht asked the Ensemble's technicians to attend dress rehearsals,
and afterwards sought their opinions. I remember the last
rehearsals of *Katzgraben* (a play by the contemporary East German
novelist and playwright Erwin Strittmatter, which Brecht produced in 1953), to which Brecht had invited a group of children
between 10 and 14. He spent two hours with them after rehearsal
to find out what they understood and what not, trying to pin
down the reasons. The discussion's result was a reworking of
many scenes to achieve more clarity, a higher quality of 'telling
the story'. Brecht believed strongly in the unspoiled and un-
prejudiced observation of children. They possessed the naïve and
poetic quality of thought he felt so important for the theatre.

In the Ensemble, Brecht decided that the young directors
should co-direct – two or even three of them as directors of the
same standing. This worked well. The directors would arrive at
a basic concept on which they could agree before going into
rehearsal. But in actual rehearsal, beautiful things would come
out of the tension between different minds working on the same
problems – better solutions than any one of the directors could
have arrived at on his own. In fact, many productions before and

most productions after his death were directed this way. For instance: *Playboy of the Western World* by Synge (Palitzsch/Wekwerth), *The Day of the Great Scholar Wu* (Palitzsch/Weber), *Optimistic Tragedy* by Wishnewski (Palitzsch/Wekwerth), *The Private Life of the Master Race* by Brecht (Bellag/Palitzsch/Weber), *Arturo Ui* by Brecht (Palitzsch/Wekwerth), *Coriolanus* by Brecht/Shakespeare (Tenschert/Wekwerth), *Little Mahagonny* by Brecht (Karge/Langhoff).

Brecht never cared how his actors worked. He didn't tell them to go home and do this or that, or to go behind the set and concentrate. He didn't give a damn about the mechanics they used, he just cared about results. Brecht respected actors and was extremely patient with them; he often used their suggestions. During breaks, he would listen sometimes to rather obvious nonsense from the actors, wanting them not to feel uncomfortable with him, wanting to gain their confidence in all matters. He himself could probably have become a great actor. He could be a marvellous clown; sometimes the actors would provoke him to demonstrate something, for the sheer joy of watching him. He did not prod the actors to ape what he had demonstrated, but rather would exaggerate enough so that while they saw exactly what he wanted, they were never tempted to copy him.

It is interesting to compare the way in which I saw Brecht direct actors with what's reported by Leon Feuchtwanger's wife (who was there) about his first directing. When Brecht was 24, and his play *Drums in the Night* was being rehearsed in Munich, the director found to his surprise that the young author was coming to rehearsals, interrupting him, yelling at the actors, and demonstrating how they should do things. Pretty soon Brecht had almost taken over the entire production, and the director – a mature man – was practically his assistant. As usual in the German theatre of that time, the rehearsal period was short, somewhat under three weeks, but the by last week the actors, some of whom were quite prominent, were trying very hard to do what Brecht wanted them to. Basically, he was attempting to wean them from the pompous, over-ambitious typical German manner of the time, to bring them back to a realistic treatment of the lines. Mrs Feuchtwanger's report is of great interest: that very young man, who came to attend rehearsals of his first play, kept yelling at the actors that what they offered was shit. When I met him in his fifties, mellowed perhaps, but not the least weakened in his determination, he was still busy cleaning the stage (and all art) of the 'sweet lies' which keep man from recognizing the world as it is.

Brecht tried to present in his theatre a real view of the world, no goldplated images of false heroes, no 'revealing' photos of rabbits, busy nibbling cabbage and humping their mates, of whatever sex. Doubt in man-made gods, doubt in man-made rules, doubt in whatever man is told to accept was proclaimed on his stage. And a profound insight into man's weakness and longing to conform, an insight, by the way, which was not without understanding, and even compassion.

Brecht used his theatre as a laboratory, to experiment with plays and players. Human behaviour, human attitudes, human weakness – everything was explored and investigated, to be exposed finally to a public which often enough refused to recognize its image in this very clear, but sometimes perhaps too well-framed, mirror. The realistic treatment of the lines, which Brecht demanded from his first hour in the theatre to the last, was more than a theatre-man's protest against the theatre's degraded conventions. For him, the stage was a model of the world – the world we all have to live in.

(iii) Directing at the Royal Court, London; 1961
by George Devine

I don't believe that it matters how you achieve what you achieve so long as what finally appears on the stage is theatrically valid. You can take any moral or aesthetic attitudes you like, provided that something exciting and true is created. If you have a director who says that every actor has to stand on his head for half an hour every morning before he starts to rehearse, and the director and his actors actually get something out of that, then – fair enough – that works for the moment. But there are basically two kinds of direction. There's the kind that imposes a strong personal stamp on the play, the stamp of brilliant people like Joan Littlewood and Tony Guthrie and Peter Brook. I think that in one way we suffer from the lack of that stamp at the Royal Court. If I did all the productions and said 'Right, THIS is the way we produce plays', then we might do better at the box office. But I don't believe that this kind of direction is very fertile for the dramatist, and what we're trying to do here is to practise the other kind – which attempts to get the best out of each particular element in a production and make them work together in realizing the play. This place is a sort of school, after all, with different talents and points of view – as different as Tony Richardson, Bill Gaskill, John Dexter and Lindsay Anderson. But they do share a certain attitude towards the author.

No, I wouldn't say that the director is the author's servant. That's too strong. I don't think that an author really knows what he's written, in theatrical terms, when it comes to interpretation on the stage. It all seems so obvious to him that he can't understand why the actors shouldn't see it at once. It's usually there in the lines, of course, but somebody has to discover that and interpret it to a group of people, while being completely faithful to what the author basically felt. That somebody is the director. He has to induce all the people concerned to make their own individual personal contributions inside the framework, while he is responsible primarily to the source material. He has to make the actors feel, finally, that it's their show, because from the first night onwards he isn't there. He's got to let them take it away. There was a period about five years ago when I was working at Stratford and the Vic and other places when I found that the reliance of actors on the director was much too great, for my money. They expected you to tell them absolutely everything about the characters they were playing. But that, I think, is work the actor must do for himself. Nowadays I always say to actors here: 'I'm not going to do your job for you. I will help you in every way I possibly can. I will guide you, select for you, tell you what I think the play is about and what the relationships are between the characters, because I have an overall view. But it's up to you to discover what is inside the character.' When you do that the actor makes a much bigger contribution than if you marshal him, and I think the young actor prefers it – especially as in general he's much more serious than the young actor of thirty years ago, when I started in the theatre. He talks far more about the theatre in general and the world outside it, for one thing. In my day young actors talked about Money or Billing. And he has a more serious attitude to his work. He's less willing to sell himself as an article worth so many pounds a week, to be shoved around by a clever director who will Do Something with him, in any kind of play.

Just to be a director by itself, producing one play here and one play there, isn't enough. You should try to create conditions of work, perhaps even by starting your own company or running your own theatre. We're the only people in the theatre whose temperaments fit us for that kind of job. You can't expect an author or an actor to do it, as a rule. I feel that part of my job of creating conditions is to train directors here. I have two or three at a time, working three months as assistants to me, then spending a month in the office and a month in the workshops. They have to learn stage management, and they have to know all about business. I think a director ought to have been an actor, too, if possible, because then he'll have a better idea of what the actors' problems are. Some people who want to be directors think of him as a sort of superior being who has wonderful Ideas. But anybody can have ideas: the point is what you do with them, how you turn them into theatre fact. This is where the fight comes in. I also encourage these assistants to learn about the other arts. None of us – dramatists or directors – know enough. I urge them to keep in touch with the other movements, and not just to live inside the theatre. We can't afford to be so absorbed in our own little world of the stage. We've got to participate, we've got to read, we've got to know what's going on.

(iv) *Theatre Laboratory 13 Rzedow* by Eugenio Barba

In 1959, in a small, provincial Polish town, Opole, a young director, accompanied by a young critic, opened a small theatre which from the very start had a specific character: a laboratory in which Jerzy Grotowski and Ludwik Flaszen experimented with actors and audiences. They were trying to build a new aesthetic for the theatre and thus to purify the art.

Grotowski wished to create a modern secular ritual, knowing that primitive rituals are the first form of drama. Through their total participation, primitive men were liberated from accumulated unconscious material. The rituals were repetitions of archetypal acts, a collective confession which sealed the solidarity of the tribe. Often ritual was the only way to break a taboo. The shamans were the masters of these sacred ceremonies, in which every tribesman had a part to play. Some of the elements of primitive ritual are: fascination, suggestion, psychic stimulation, magic words and signs, and acrobatics which compel the body to go beyond its natural, biological limitations.

It would have been difficult, of course, to revive these ceremonies in our day. New means had to be found to force the spectator into an active collaboration. Grotowski preserves the essence of primitive theatre by making the audience participate, but he leaves out the religious elements and substitutes secular 'stimuli' for them. Grotowski uses archetypal images and actions to unleash his attack on the audience. He breaks through the defences of the spectator's mind and forces him to react to what is going on in the theatre.

The archetypes must be found in the play's text. And, in this context, archetype means symbol, myth, image, leitmotiv – something deeply rooted in a civilization's culture. It is a metaphor and model of the human condition. For example, Prometheus and the Sacrificial Lamb correspond to the archetype of the individual sacrificed for the community. Faustus, Tvardovski, and Einstein (in the imagination of the masses) correspond to the archetype of the shaman who has surrendered to the devil and in exchange has received a special knowledge of the universe. The essential task is to give life to an archetype through the staging of a play. It is what the poet Bronieski called 'the expression by the voice and the body of the very substance of man's destiny'.

Several examples from Grotowski's work will illustrate this.

The Ancestors by Mickiewicz has been treated as a ritual drama. The audience is a collective group participating in the action. Spectators and actors are scattered through the whole room. The actors speak to everyone who is there. They treat the audience as fellow actors and even invite them to become active participants. The last scene of the play tells the story of Gustav-Konrad who, from a Czarist jail, rebels against the established order. He is the rebel with whom Poland, torn and conquered, identifies. Ordinarily this scene is presented as a metaphysical revolt and played with great pathos. In the Theatre Laboratory it demonstrates the naïveté of the individual who believes himself to be a saviour. The long soliloquy has been changed into the Stations of the Cross. Gustav-Konrad moves among the spectators. On his back he carries a broom, as Christ carried his cross. His grief is genuine and his belief in his mission sincere. But his naïve reactions are shown to be those of a child who is not aware of his limitations. Here the director used a specific dialectic: entertainment versus ritual, Christ versus Don Quixote.

The meaning of the production becomes clear in this final scene, where the individual revolt aimed at effecting a radical change is shown as hopeless.

Kordian, by Slovacki, is another example of Grotowski's methods. It is a Polish classic, as well known to Poles as *Peer Gynt* is to Norwegians. It takes place in the divided Poland of the nineteenth century. A young aristocrat, Kordian, wants to sacrifice himself for his country and free it from Russian rule. An attempt against the Czar's life fails and, after being committed to a lunatic asylum, Kordian is judged sane and condemned to death. Grotowski considers the scene in the hospital the key to the play. Hence, the entire play is set in the hospital. All of Kordian's experiences, the people he meets, the plots he organizes, the women he loves, are presented as hallucinations. An evil doctor who turns into the Pope, then the Czar, and finally an old sailor, brings about the hallucinatory crises. In the original text, Kordian recites a solemn soliloquy on the top of Mont Blanc. There he offers his blood to Poland and Europe. In Grotowski's production, the doctor takes a blood sample: dialectic of derision and apotheosis. The sufferings of Kordian are real, but the reasons for his suffering are imaginary. His sacrifice is noble, but naïve.

'It is not the first time that our Laboratory presented a heroic personality obsessed with the idea of saving mankind,' said Flaszen. 'The director analyzed the meaning of an individual act in an era where collective action and organization are the guarantees of success. Today, the man who tries to save the world alone is either a child or a madman, and I am not sure that in our world he could even claim the charm of Don Quixote.'

Or, as Grotowski said:

No rule is sacred, not even the rule that a single archetype must be represented. Ordinarily there are several archetypes in a text. They branch out and intermingle. One is chosen as the pivot of a play. But there are other possibilities. One could, for example, present a set of archetypes all of which would have the same value in the play. It is by means of the archetype that the dialectic of derision and apotheosis attacks a system of taboos, conventions, and accepted values. In this way, each production has a 'multiface mirror' effect. All the facets of the archetype are successively destroyed; new taboos rise from the destruction and are, in turn, destroyed.

Five years of work and experimentation have brought success to the theatre. The point is no longer to present convincing characters, but to use the text as a catalyst setting off a violent reaction in the spectator. 'Not to show the world as separated from the spectator, but, within the limits of the theatre, to create with him a new world.' The main problem of the Laboratory was to find new means of expression. 'Many people are surprised that our productions have nothing in common with literary theatre,' Grotowski said.

Faithful recitation of the text and illustration of the author's ideas are the goals of the traditional theatre. We, on the contrary, believe in the value of a theatre that some have called 'autonomous'. For us the text is only one of the play's elements, though not the least important. The 'peripetia' of the plays (as we do them) do not correspond to the text, They are expressed through purely theatrical means. The director takes liberties with the text. He cuts, he transposes. But he never indulges in personal interpolation. He lovingly preserves the charm of the words and watches carefully to see that they are spoken. The text is artificial and composed, but it is the author's text.

This free treatment of the text is the first decisive step in liberating the theatre from literary servitude. The director uses the playwright's text as the painter uses landscape motifs and as the poet uses semantic material accumulated by his civilization. As a text undergoes transpositions and scoring, it acquires new interpretive possibilities. It becomes the experimental ground on which the creative director works. Of course, the reborn text has only limited powers if it is not supported by a completely new acting technique.

Grotowski begins with the assumption that 'everything which is art is artificial'. Pushing this to its extreme expression, he has come up with the following:

No technique is sacred. Any means of expression is permitted, provided that:

1. It is functional, justified by the logic of the production. Walking on one's feet demands the same justification as walking on one's hands. The logic of life cannot be substituted for the logic of art.
2. It has been deliberately chosen. It can no longer be changed, except in certain scenes where limited improvisation is permitted.
3. It is 'built', composed. Theatrical techniques form a structure whose parts cannot be altered.

We are especially interested in an aspect of acting which has seldom been studied: the association of the gesture and intonation with a definite image. For example, the actor stops in the middle of a race and takes the stance of a cavalry soldier charging, as in the old popular drawings, This method of acting evokes by association images deeply rooted in the collective imagination.

According to Grotowski, there are three kinds of actors. First, there is the 'elementary actor', as in the academic theatre. Then there is the 'artificial actor' – one who composes and builds a structure of vocal and physical stage effects. Thirdly, there is the 'archetypal actor' – that is, an artificial actor who can enlarge on the images taken from the collective unconscious. Grotowski trains this third type of actor. In developing his actors, Grotowski instills in them certain principles which are characteristic of the Theatre Laboratory:

The deficiences of the actor are used, not hidden. An actor's handicaps are as important as his qualities. An old actor can play Romeo if he emphasizes his limitations. That is, if he situates his part within a definite composition. The part then becomes that of Romeo in his old age reminiscing with Juliet.

Costumes and props are the actors' partners or they are 'artificial extensions of the actor'. The actor gives life to the prop by treating it as a living thing. It is friendly or hostile to him. The 'partner' may be a costume – in that case there is a contrast between the two: the actor is young and handsome and the costume is ugly: or the situation is poetic and the costume is vulgar and coarse. When used as extensions of the actor, costumes and props accentuate the gestures by inhibiting them. For example, a sleeveless costume prevents the actor from using his arms. In any case, the accessories must not be used as ornaments. Their only function is to increase the actor's power of expression. In *Kordian*, for example, the hospital beds are used as acrobatic parallel bars.

Each character is depicted most purely by vocal or physical effects. The actor gives concrete expression to his desires, passions, thoughts, etc., by a physical action (gymnastics, acrobatics, or pantomime) or a vocal action (incantation, production of associated sounds, etc.). To make the effect properly suggestive, it must be done in a trance (concentrating all the physical energies). To achieve communication, it must be a sign which awakens associations buried in the audience's unconscious. The sign must be a revelation which starts a train of reactions and brings to consciousness latent feelings linked to individual or collective experiences. These experiences will be related to the culture, history, and folklore of the country.

There must be direct contact between the actors and audience. There is no stage. The actor speaks directly to the spectator, touches him, is around him all the times, startles him by frequent surprise effects. There is individual contact between one actor and the whole audience and there is collective contact between a team of actors and the audience. There are several forms of collective contact. In Byron's *Cain* the spectators are descendants of Cain. They are present but remote and difficult to approach. In Kalidasa's *Sakountala*, they are just a crowd of monks and courtiers. In Mickiewicz' *The Ancestors,* they are made to participate in the crop and harvest ritual. An actor becomes the Chorus Leader and the audience the Chorus. In *Kordian* the spectators are patients in the asylum; as such they are the doctor's enemies. In Wyspianski's *Akropolis* they are completely ignored, because they represent the living while the actors are ghosts. The actors speak while gliding between the spectators, but there can be no contact.

Theatrical magic consists in doing publicly that which is considered impossible. For example, the actor transforms himself into another man in full view of everyone. Or else he becomes an animal or an object. Acrobatics liberate the actor from the laws of gravity.

Makeup is unnecessary. Makeup does not accentuate the physical characteristics of the actors. The actor can change the expression on his face through control of facial muscles. Lighting, sweat, and breathing transform his muscles into a mask.

The spectator's unconscious is deliberately attacked. The actor does not give a visual representation of the archetype – this would be familiar and banal. Through his techniques he evokes and attacks a collective image. In the improvisation in *The Ancestors,* Gustav-Konrad does not look like Christ and he does not carry a cross. But with his ridiculous broom and quixotic outbursts he collides with the popular representation of Christ: hence the shock value. A faithful reconstruction of either Gustav-Konrad or Christ would have been familiar and boring.

The artificiality which Grotowski strives for must stem from reality, from the organic necessity of the movement or the intentions. Deformation must have a value as form, or else everything becomes a frivolous puzzle or, even worse, pathology. Artificiality is tied to life by an unbreakable umbilical cord. A few examples will help to show what is meant:

Every gesture must be composed. A short series of motions is a micro-pantomime which must illuminate the character. There can be no complication for its own sake. The actor must be able to shift the spectator's attention from the visual to the auditory, from the auditory to the visual, from one part of the body to the other, etc. This is the skill of magicians.

There must be theatrical contrast. This can be between any two elements: music and the actor, the actor and the text, actor and costume, two or more parts of the body (the hands say yes, the legs say no), etc.

Parts are exchanged during performance. Romeo becomes Juliet and Juliet becomes Romeo.

The actor metamorphoses. An actress is a secretary, then a mistress, then the boss, then a telephone, typewriter, table, sofa, etc. This was done in Mayakovski's *Mystère-Bouffe.*

Characters are built on several levels. A doctor is in fact the devil who becomes the Pope, then the Czar, and then an old sailor (*Kordian*).

Styles change rapidly. The same scene is played by the same actor in artificial, naturalistic, pantomimic, improvisational and other styles.

Physiological manifestations are used. In the improvisation of *The Ancestors,* for example, Gustav-Konrad is exhausted and drips with sweat. He does not try to hide it. His gestures suggest that it is the blood that Christ sweated.

The word is more than a means of intellectual communication. Its pure sound is used to bring spontaneous associations to the spectator's mind (incantation).

Each day the actors work their way through a series of exercises:

1. Diction, vocal work, artificial pronunciation (incantation). They shift from one timbre to another, chant, whisper. These exercises are always accompanied by breathing exercises. The secret of good diction is breathing. The experiments at the Laboratory investigated the part played by the brain in the formation of sound; the importance of the throat muscles for an appropriate opening of the larynx; how to determine the proper pauses for a specific role; harmony between breathing and the rhythm of a sentence; breathing as a dramatic effect (where it is not a physiological necessity); complete breathing from the abdomen *and* chest (usually only the abdomen is considered necessary); simultaneous use of the cranial and thoracic sounding boards; loss of voice as a result of psychological problems or faulty breathing.

2. Plastic motion following the Delsarte method and others. Simultaneous activity of different parts of the body, each at a different rhythm (the arms move fast, the legs slowly, the actors speak at different speeds); muscle control; instant relaxation of the muscles not engaged in motion (Hatha-Yoga is used).

3. Study of mime, both artificial and naturalistic.

This training results in a decidedly anti-naturalistic style in which rhythm and dynamism are as strictly fixed as in a musical score. The actor must be highly skilled and rigorously trained to control a technique which governs each gesture, each breath, each voice tone, and which uses acrobatics and gymnastics. The actor must provoke and fascinate the audience. To do so he must play his score correctly – but in a trance of concentration – while deliberately attempting to subjugate the spectator. As a shaman, he must create a magic action and prod the spectator into participation. He must force the audience to drop its social mask and face a world in which old values are destroyed without offering in their place any metaphysical solutions.

A struggle therefore ensues between performer and spectator. The one tries to fascinate the other and overcome all defences; the other fights against the spell of gestures and words, grasping at old logic and seeking shelter in a social shell. According to Grotowski, the director shapes the two groups, actors and spectators. They both must become aware of being part of the ritual-spectacle. It is this very awareness that distinguishes theatre from the film. The future of the theatre depends upon this close contact between spectator and actor, which makes possible an act of collective introspection. Of course, putting the audience on stage (there is no 'stage', but the action takes place in the space where the audience sits) presents problems. A new theatre architecture is needed. From the moment when Grotowski eliminated the stage, he was involved in architectural problems. A young architect, Jerzy Gurawski, has joined the company to help with these investigations.

The Theatre Laboratory rejects the eclecticism which has cancerously eaten away at the modern theatre. It is foolish to try to 'modernize' the theatre by using electronic music, abstract settings, and clownish makeup. These are only superficial copies of what an audience can see at a concert, art exhibit, or circus. These elements are not essential to the theatre, which needs only the physical and vocal expressions of the actors. Theatricality could be defined as a deformation and/or reformation of life with its own autonomous aesthetic. Movies and television have taken over the social function of the theatre and the only way for the theatre to survive is for it to exploit its unique characteristic: the direct contact between actor and audience. The actor, each night, faces the live critical audience; he recites his part *at* a public eager to note his slightest mistake. Every night he must find new ways to fascinate and control the audience; and every night it is a different audience challenging him. The Theatre Laboratory is looking for new forms of theatrical magic, for new alphabets to be used by the actor-shaman. Much is written, but little is done because directors and actors must make money. What madman would dare finance an experiment so eccentric, so shocking by its aggressiveness, and demanding so much skill from its actors? The Polish government has understood the necessity and has proven its goodwill by supporting Grotowski's experiments. Will others follow suit in other countries?